The Bible Is Human

The Bible Is Human

A STUDY IN SECULAR HISTORY

By Louis Wallis

IN LITTERIS LIBERTAS

1754·1893

COLUMBIA UNIVERSITY PRESS, NEW YORK

MCMXLII

To

MARY FELS, *humanitarian*,

THIS BOOK IS DEDICATED BY

GRACE AND LOUIS WALLIS

PREFACE

THE TITLE is based on the view that religion arises within the commonplace terms of life; the religious problem itself being found, therefore, in the contents of the moral experience as an evolving process. But on the other hand, ecclesiastical orthodoxy avoids experience by positing a Power totally external to man, which irrupts into the stream of history, leaving a deposit of doctrine, and then retreating into its proper sphere—a transcendent realm beyond the orbit of human life. The simplest form of orthodoxy is best observed among tribes whose religious rituals, evolving within terms of secular experience, are afterward said to have been established in the dim past by the tribal god who lives perhaps on some distant mountain.

Orthodoxy is always *post eventum;* and while the belated nature of dogma gives no inconvenience at first, it is one cause of religious difficulty in a scientific age. Thus, Judaism and Christianity grew out of certain experiences among the ancient Hebrew people, which were described in writings under such titles as "The Book of the Wars of Yahweh," "The Book of Yashar," "The Book of the Acts of Solomon," and so forth. By taking selected passages out of these ancient writings, inscribing them on rolls of papyrus, and interpolating *post eventum* comments between the excerpts, the Bible was gradually brought into existence through the work of compilers and editors who were not contemporary with the events described and whose interpolations represent stages in the development of Jewish and Christian orthodoxy.

Having originated thus, and having been adopted as Holy Scripture by official authorities, the Bible has practically monopolized the interpretation of Hebrew history up to our own day. But the interpolations vary from the excerpts taken out of "source books,"

showing that the compilers and editors of the Bible have desecularized the history of Israel by transforming it into a religious drama.
In other words, Hebrew history has been converted into what is
called "Bible history," which has always impressed the popular
imagination as a tale of supernatural marvels and miraculous events
contrary to the rules of cause and effect recognized by scientific
method.

The foregoing considerations explain more fully the title given
to the present volume, which aims, in brief, to reverse the method
of Biblical compilation and bring into view the secular history
which produced the monotheism common to the Jewish and Christian religions. Such an undertaking would, of course, be impossible
without the previous work of Biblical criticism, by which the fundamental sources have been carefully distinguished from the comments and interpolations of the compilers.

But the mere separation of the literary elements composing the
Bible does not in itself restore the history. For the task of Biblical
criticism has been, first of all, to challenge the literary structure of
the writings which compose the Bible and consequently at the same
time to formulate a new theory of the sources. Such was the work
of the critical school which came to a climax in *Geschichte Israels*
("History of Israel"), by the German professor Wellhausen. But
the volume was misnamed "History"; and its title was retracted by
the author in later editions. Other scholars, however—German,
British, French, and American—were not deterred from producing
books under such titles as "History of the Hebrew People," "History of Israel," "Old Testament History," and so forth. These works
have been serviceable in promoting the claims of criticism as a
method of approach to the Bible; but they deal mainly with source-
theory and with disjointed materials of history, instead of present-
ing intelligible explanations of the process which brought the religion of Israel into existence and which, after all, is the only reason
for taking any special interest in Hebrew history.

This book is the concluding number of a trilogy begun many
years ago—the first being *Sociological Study of the Bible* (1912),

the aim of which was to propose a method of handling the Biblical
material so as to give effect to the underlying sociological and economic forces in Hebrew history. That the German critics had not
given a scientific interpretation of the history and that a minority
of trained historical scholars in that country were already aware of
the fact is indicated by the reaction of Professor E. Troeltsch, of
Berlin University, who, in the course of a lengthy and careful review of the above-mentioned volume said, "This is the path which
theological research must follow if the history of religious ethics is
to be understood. This is one of the most suggestive and instructive
books that have come into my hands in many a day." [1]

The application of the proposed method resulted in modifying
the source-theory of the reigning critical school so that it is possible
to distinguish more clearly between the "J" (Yahwistic, Judaic)
document and the "E" (Elohistic, Ephraimite) source. The former
had been currently regarded as earlier than the latter, whereas the
fact now clearly emerged that the Ephraimite documents preceded
the J element; the two sources being contrasted not only in the order
of time, but by hitherto unobserved linguistic distinctions. The second volume in the series, *God and the Social Process* (1935), accordingly, dealt with Hebrew religious evolution on the basis of the
new source-theory. The manuscript of the book was examined by
Dr. Stanley A. Cook, Regius Professor of Hebrew in the University
of Cambridge, England, who wrote as follows:

You point out, in a way I at least had not clearly realised, the significance of the Joseph-core of tradition [that is, the Ephraimite element].
This question you handle in a quite original manner . . . and I think
your argument requires very careful attention. We are approaching a
stage where our conceptions of the Bible, and of the history in and behind it, will have to be completely remodeled. We need a secular history of Israel; and it is obvious that our theology needs adjustment to
the facts. I have enjoyed perusing your original and highly stimulating
study.

The facts and problems of the subject are not, of course, handled
exhaustively by the present volume, *The Bible Is Human*. Its pur-

[1] *Theologische Literaturzeitung*, July 19, 1913.

pose is to interest the scholarly public and the lay public in acquiring a more accurate sense of the evolutionary process back of the Bible and of the religion which, manifested in Judaism and Christianity, is moving on today as a vital stream of progressive thought.

That a new period is dawning in the apprehension of Hebrew history is indicated by the attitude of certain members of the Anglican Church Commission on Doctrine. These members find themselves unable to hold that miraculous events actually occurred; and they feel that in the present state of historical knowledge and scientific method it is no longer possible to make evidential use of Biblical narratives in relation to alleged miracles. In similar wise, referring to the dogma of the Virgin Birth, Dr. C. C. Morrison, editor of *The Christian Century*, says, "It is easier for me to believe that the exquisitely beautiful story of the Annunciation grew up in the devout imagination of the Church than to believe that it is a literal account of an objective physiological fact." [2] Speaking of the Bible as a literary production, Dr. Morrison says, "It does not occur to me that its words were dictated, or authorised, or guaranteed in any way essentially different from the manner in which any other ancient writing on a highly important subject was set down"; and he adds, "What I have said does not divorce God from the Bible,—indeed it brings him more intimately into it." [3]

Professor Herbert L. Willett, of the University of Chicago, writes:

Most nations have wonder stories to lend dignity and divine sanction to their origins. The Hebrew traditions regarding their contacts with other nations were on the moral level of the age from which they came, and reflect the nationalism and race prejudice of a primitive culture.[4]

Neither Judaism nor Christianity was established upon a foundation of logical argument. Both became realities in human life on the basis of experience and function; whereupon Jewish and Christian theology took form as attempts to rationalize what had already taken place. But in both cases the resulting dogmatic formulas

[2] *Christian Century*, Mar. 30, 1938, p. 393.   [3] *Ibid.*
[4] *The Christian Century*, Sept. 29, 1937.

usurped the religious field with such devastating power that religion itself was compromised. This is the situation with which the present book seeks to deal.

L. W.

July 1, 1942

ACKNOWLEDGMENTS

THE WRITER is grateful to all who have examined, or commented upon, or criticized, the manuscript of this book. It is hoped that no name has been omitted from the following list. The late Professor Shailer Mathews, the University of Chicago; Professor Mordecai Kaplan, the Jewish Theological Seminary of America, New York City; Bishop Francis J. McConnell, New York City; Professor Samuel A. B. Mercer, Toronto University, Toronto, Canada; Professor Edward A. Ross, Wisconsin University; Professor Ovid R. Sellers, the Presbyterian Theological Seminary, Chicago; Professor Herbert L. Willett, the University of Chicago; Reverend Ralph Sockman, Christ Church, Methodist, New York City; Professor Julius Bewer, Union Theological Seminary, New York City; Professor James Moffatt, Union Theological Seminary; Professor Leroy Waterman, University of Michigan; Professor George Dahl, Yale University; Professor W. L. Sperry, Harvard University; Professor W. A. Irwin, the University of Chicago; Professor Albert E. Haydon, the University of Chicago; Professor Edwin E. Aubrey, the University of Chicago; Professor H. G. May, Oberlin School of Theology. Special thanks are due to Dr. Irwin and Dr. Sellers, whose many comments and suggestions have improved the text in many places.

CONTENTS

CONTENTS

———

CONVENTIONALIZED SCHEME OF HEBREW

HISTORY   37

The Bible Is Human

"SLOWLY miracles have ceased to serve me in the evolution of my belief, in the moral campaign of my spirit."—George A. Gordon, late minister of the Old South Church, Boston, in *Religion and Miracle*, Preface.

"I HAVE NO expectation that any man will read history aright who thinks that what was done in a remote age, by men whose names have resounded far, has any deeper sense than what he is doing today."—R. W. Emerson, *Essay on History*.

"MANY MEN have believed too implicitly with Plato that 'ideas make the world.' Such men have told the story of *history* as though it were a ghost-dance on a floor of clouds. They have tried to explain how spirits with indiscernible bodies have brought about the visible results. They would not admit that the facts of human association have been the work of flesh-and-blood men with their feet on the ground."—Albion W. Small, The University of Chicago, in *The American Journal of Sociology*, V, 518.

I. INTRODUCTION

THE TREMENDOUS importance of God for today, as revealed in the secular history of Israel, is the fundamental theme of this book. What is the meaning and value of the idea which we designate by the word "God"? Does its meaning today have the same force which it had in the far distant epoch when the term was coming into the vocabulary of ancient Israel? It meant something very definite in the mind of Jeremiah the prophet, for example, when he denounced King Jehoiakim, son of the good King Josiah, saying, "Did not thy father do justice and righteousness? He judged the cause of the poor and needy. Was not this to know me? saith Yahweh" (Jer. 22:15, 16). When estimated by the measuring rod of Jeremiah, our modern idea of God lacks the definiteness, concreteness, and humanity that it has in the foregoing passage. Or again, in the light of Jeremiah's words, consider the following sentences from the prophets Amos and Micah: "Let justice roll down like waters, and righteousness like an overflowing stream" (Amos 5:24). "What doth Yahweh thy god require of thee but to do justice, and to love mercy, and to walk humbly with thy god?" (Mic. 6:8).[1]

It is evident that something has come between this very simple idea of God and the indefinite, confused theological notions of most people at the present day; because the prevailing idea of God in the world around us tends to be something very dogmatic and misty, as compared with the voices that have just given their testimony. Official orthodox theology has made God uninteresting and has had a share in alienating a large part of the modern world from religion. Orthodoxy, without any doubt, was far better than the pagan theologies which it dispossessed; and it supplied the only prac-

[1] See note on name Yahweh in Appendix.

tical forms under which the religion of the Bible could issue forth from Palestine into the classic and modern civilizations. But these facts do not prove that orthodoxy should live forever. That the official Christian and Jewish theologies are *post eventum* attempts to explain what happened in the course of Bible history is not generally understood. And while they seem to be contemporary with the times about which the Old and New Testaments tell, they are not in fact coeval with the actual events which the compilers of the Bible seek to describe. Interpreting God as extrinsic to human history, they view religion as a deposit of supernatural doctrine, thrust miraculously into the stream of human experience from a transcendent realm beyond the orbit of mundane affairs.

Prophets interpret God as intrinsic to history

In the view of Amos, Yahweh brings the Philistines from Kaphtor, and the Arameans from Kir, and the Israelites from Egypt— on the ground of secular migrations common to all races (Amos 9:7). Accordingly the Mesopotamian powers advancing into Palestine are described as instruments of Divine wrath against Israel for doing injustice and worshiping Baal. Thus, Isaiah declares that the Assyrian army is to do the will of God upon sinful Israel: "O Assyrian! The rod of mine anger,—the staff in whose hand is mine indignation" (Isa. 10:5). In the same way, Jeremiah proclaims, "Thus saith Yahweh, I will give all Judah into the hand of the king of Babylon; and he shall carry them captive to Babylon" (Jer. 20:4).

Prophetic theology does not depend for its rationale upon the so-called "miraculous" or "supernatural." It finds God in the commonplaces of secular experience. And while it does not, of course, formulate its case in modern scientific terminology, its dealings are with what is now recognized as "the cause-and-effect" succession of daily events, and it contemplates both God and man as factors energizing the onward flow of history. If the question be raised, "How can the will of God be interpreted within the terms of secular experience?" the reply is twofold: (1) This view makes no more difficulty than the assumption that the human will is a factor in the same phenomena; and (2) it raises no greater problem than does the orthodox theology which undertakes to explain human history by trafficking in wonders and dealing in the supernatural.

Frustration of Josiah's policy leads to messianic hope

That justice would be imperiled if established merely in Israel was realized when Josiah's policy was frustrated by the interference of Babylon, which destroyed Jerusalem and carried the remnant of Israel into captivity. The long-continued anguish of exile inspired the second Isaiah's vision of a purified Israel, "the servant of Yahweh," by whom the gospel of justice was to be carried throughout the world:

Behold my servant, whom I sustain, my chosen in whom my soul delighteth. I have put my spirit upon him. He will bring forth justice to the Gentiles. He will bring forth justice in truth. He will not fail nor be discouraged till he have set justice in the earth; and the far countries shall wait for his instruction [Isa. 42:1–4].

Thus, the doctrine first clearly uttered by the prophets in Palestine as a national gospel for Israel entered a new stage because of the pressure of captivity and became the vision of a world made safe for justice.

Israel wedded to social injustice; Baal worship

It is well known that the Bible describes the Hebrew people during their term of residence in Palestine as wedded to social injustice and Baal worship. The two things as we shall see, were identical. Baalism symbolized injustice and sex immorality; while on the other hand the worship of Yahweh stood for justice and a purer way of life. That a great struggle of some kind occurred over the worship of Baal is known vaguely to most persons who have attended Sunday school, church, or synagogue, or who possess a Bible. The inveterate worship of Baal was denounced by the prophets, who foretold national downfall and captivity if the practice were not abandoned.

Judean remnant of Israel terrorized into monotheism

The Babylonian invasion of Judah, the frightful destruction of Jerusalem, the exile of thousands marching in chains across a hot desert—these distressing events proved to be landmarks not only in the experience of Israel but also in the history of the world. For the calamities which befell the Hebrews vindicated the prophets and effected a mass-conversion of the Jews to monotheism. In other words, the Jewish people (the remnant of Israel) were shocked out of Baal-worship and terrorized into the cult of One God, not on the abstract merits of monotheism, but simply by the appalling pressure of secular history.

Mass conversion to monotheism raises new problem

This new epoch of religious evolution, in which monotheism was becoming a fact, brought with it a new problem. The leaders and thinkers among Babylonian Jews were confronted by the necessity to explain or to philosophize the events and forces which had led up to victory of the One-God cult. The written scrolls which the first generation of exiles had brought with them across the desert were full of the fury and thunder of the great struggle between Yahweh and Baal. But how should that conflict be understood and explained? How did it begin? And whence came the thunder of religious warfare that rolled across the centuries while Israel dwelt in the land of Palestine? The great conflict was already past, having receded into the silence of the ages. How should it be handled for the instruction and edification of posterity? These questions were not visionary and theoretical. They were practical and real because the Jew in exile, if he were to remain a Jew and not be swallowed by the *goyim* ("gentiles"), must be made to learn systematically from the experience of Israel in the past. And yet the problem was full of difficulties. There were no investigators competent to make use of source material, as scholars do now, so that the history of Israel could be interpreted according to scientific methods. And even if such men had been available, their services would have been useless;

because academic lectures were not what was needed by that age. What the Jews in captivity, and in the centuries to come, really needed was material of a hortatory, sermonic nature.

Hebrew Bible evolves, viewing history as nonsecular

For the use of Jews in and after the Babylonian exile the Hebrew Bible, or Old Testament, was gradually compiled from written sources older than the Bible itself; and all through the older material the compilers, or editors, interpolated brief comments and sometimes longer passages intended to point out the moral of Hebrew history in the land of Canaan, or Palestine. Thus the Bible of the synagogue slowly evolved; and since it was not a scientific work we shall be prepared to understand that its interpretation of Israel's life in Palestine treated the events primarily as religious phenomena and had the effect of desecularizing Hebrew history.

It is at first very difficult for modern readers and students of the Bible to grasp the essentially simple fact that in the days before the exile the strict and exclusive Yahweh party was a minority without official status; whereas the same situation, viewed in retrospect from the standpoint of Babylonian captivity, became an acute problem, which had to be definitely handled if a basis were to be discovered upon which the new religious life of the Hebrew remnant might come to rest. It is profoundly instructive to observe the course followed by Jewish religious leaders in this trying period of their history.

Bible treats monotheism as imparted miraculously

Unable to give a scientific interpretation of the Baal-Yahweh struggle in Palestine, the compilers of Hebrew Scripture elaborated upon a non-Jewish tradition already current in Canaan before the exile of Judah. The original, or at least the earlier, form of this tradition is contained in a writing, or source, which took its rise outside Judah, in a part of the country known as "Ephraim," which we shall call the "Ephraimite" document (E). According to E the monotheistic religion was given at a single stroke on a flaming mountain called "Horeb," located somewhere in the desert of Arabia. The Ephraimite prophet Elijah is said to have visited Horeb in the course of his campaign against Baal, while the book of Deuteronomy stems from the Ephraimite source and uses the name Horeb also. But over and above the Ephraimite and Deuteronomic sources the Jewish writers built a much more extensive document, the "Priestly writing" (P), which contains minute ordinances of sacrifice, constituting the bulk of the Pentateuch and identified with Mount Sinai.

Hebrew history exploited by obscuring Yahweh-Baal struggle

The history of Israel in Palestine, then, is interpreted as devoid of all evolutionary meaning and is viewed as a dull, neutral epoch, in which a struggle takes place between defenders and opponents of a religion from beyond the orbit of human experience, imparted in the desert before Israel had even appeared on the stage of history in Canaan.

In other words, the Jewish compilers of the Hebrew Bible exploit Hebrew history by stripping it of all developmental significance, thrusting the history itself into obscurity behind the overshadowing prestige of alleged miraculous events occurring at some undated period in the dim past.

The rule of experience is that the prevailing ideas and practices in every department of life are evolved and built up gradually through concrete stages. Thus, language and the arts come into existence according to psychological conditions inherent in the human mind. But in the case of Israel's religion the orthodox view goes contrary to all experience by alleging a sudden abstract revelation to have taken place without any reference to environmental conditions or the laws governing the operations of the human mind. The theory behind the compilation of the Old Testament is that God, the Master Psychologist, instead of leading Israel slowly onward through concrete experiences, took the opposite course and precipitately imposed an abstract monotheism upon desert tribes whose ancestors had been cattlemen and slaves in the land of Goshen on the frontier of Egypt.

Compilers admit that abstract revelation failed

The orthodox theory, indeed, represents God as making what corresponds to a demand upon kindergarten children that they learn lessons of high school grade. And the compilers of the Hebrew Bible could not escape the admission into Scripture of incontrovertible evidence that the alleged revelation failed in its effect. Thus, the book of Nehemiah, written after the exile, says,

Neither have our kings, our princes, our priests, nor our fathers, kept thy law, nor hearkened unto thy commandments and thy testimonies wherewith thou didst testify against them. For they have not served thee in their kingdom, and in thy great goodness that thou gavest them, and in the large and fat land which thou gavest before them; neither turned they from their wicked works. . . . Our fathers dealt proudly, and hardened their neck, and hearkened not to thy commandments [Neh. 9:16, 34f.].

To the same effect is the testimony of Jeremiah:

Thus saith Yahweh. . . . They are not humbled even unto this day; neither have they feared, nor walked in my law, nor in my statutes, that I set before you and before your fathers [Jer. 44:7, 10].

Likewise the compiler of Kings declares:

For so it was that the children of Israel had sinned against Yahweh their god, which had brought them up out of the land of Egypt. . . . And they rejected his statutes, and his covenant that he made with their fathers. . . . Therefore Yahweh was very angry with Israel . . . and rejected all the seed of Israel, and delivered them into the hand of spoilers [II Kings 17:7, 15, 18, 20].

If a revelation such as the orthodox theory alleges were indeed given to Israel in the wilderness, there is no wonder that the nation failed to follow it from the beginning, since the manner of imparting it was contrary to all the laws of psychology and inconsistent with the circumstances under which it is said to have been given.

We shall see in due time how the orthodox theory was mistaken and how, by reversing the method of the Biblical compilers, the real nature of Hebrew history in Canaan comes out into relief as a purely secular process, containing within itself the potentialities of that monotheistic faith which formed the starting point, not of Israel's history in Palestine, but of Judaism after the Babylonian captivity. The orthodox theory was useful at the time when it arose and for many centuries thereafter among Jews and Christians. But the fact remains that by depotentializing Hebrew history, the Jewish compilers of the Bible exploited Israel's life in the land of Canaan, emptying it of all creative significance in the interests of a dogma which projected the focus of Hebrew history into the Arabian desert and the realm of the supernatural.

Hebrew history subjected to Christian manipulation

The first Christians were Jews; and the only Bible they had was the Old Testament. The Jewish membership, however, was more and more offset by the addition of non-Jews outside Palestine, so that the Hebrew element was finally swamped and Christianity became a religion of gentiles. Centering in the person and memory of a Palestinian, and accepting the Hebrew Bible as Holy Scripture, the new movement raised the problem of its relation to Hebrew history, which was thus again subjected to manipulation and exploitation, but from a different point of view and for a different purpose. A long period of uncertainty elapsed, however, before any definite doctrines about Hebrew history were generally received as official tenets in the churches; and this period coincided with the gradual formation of a literature which finally became the New Testament.

Connection with Hebrew history denied by some Christians

Many Christian writings of a private, unofficial nature were in circulation. These documents, toilsomely written and then copied, were the property of individuals and sometimes of groups. Because they were private property, their owners felt free to add marginal comments based on their own feelings and beliefs and on tradition. This new material was incorporated in the text when additional copies were made.

Some followers of Jesus believed that the deity of the Hebrew

Bible, although of great power, was an inferior god, who created the world, but whose influence was overshadowed by a superior God proclaimed through the life and preaching of Jesus. This version of Christianity took form under the name "Marcionism"; and significantly the earliest New Testament appeared as a handbook of this belief about a century after the crucifixion. It consisted of eleven little writings, or "books," which had been previously floating about as independent private letters. Ten of the letters bore the name of Paul; while the eleventh had been passing from hand to hand under the name of Luke. They were brought together in one collection by a certain Marcion, who was the son of a Christian bishop in Asia Minor; and they were edited by him so as to be serviceable to his idea of religion. This man, who was a person of great energy, started what would today be called a Christian denomination, and his churches continued to exist for hundreds of years. He and his disciples, without realizing it, of course, were struggling with the problem now recognized as "the development of religion." They had no accurate knowledge of Hebrew history, and their dogma concerning the Old Testament deity as an inferior god was a blind, crude, unscientific way of saying that an evolution of religion had occurred among the Hebrews in Palestine. While the Marcionite Scriptures were never adopted into general, or "catholic," use, this fact must be placed alongside the equally important consideration that for a long time nobody else had any more success than Marcion in creating a universally accepted New Testament.

Hebrew history exploited as fountainhead of mechanical predictions

But when the New Testament finally emerged in its official form, it included a great deal of material whose purpose was to find in Hebrew history a series of mechanically "inspired" predictions pointing to Jesus. This feature of the New Testament originated in the struggle which had been going on to explain the relation between Israel and the Christian churches; and it was expressed in the reiterated formula "that it might be fulfilled which was spoken by," and so forth. New Testament pragmatism, accordingly, is responsible for dislocating the Hebrew prophets from their actual character as champions of justice and metamorphosing them into mechanically inspired foretellers, thus giving prophecy the character of mere unintelligent prediction. By such manipulation of Hebrew material the authors of the New Testament unwittingly did as much, in their own way, to obscure the real history of Israel as had been done already by the post-exilic Jews who compiled and edited the Hebrew Bible.

An instructive example of such manipulation is found in the treatment of Isaiah 7:14f. by the book of Matthew. The Isaiah passage, written more than seven hundred years before Christ, relates to the fast-approaching invasion of Israel by the Assyrians and predicts that before the event a young woman (*almah*) shall bear a son. It is important to observe that the Hebrew term *almah* signifies a young woman, either married or single, without any reference to her sexual experience. Consequently the Jewish English Bible translates "young woman." [2] When the Hebrew text itself mentions a virgin, *per se*, it uses another term, *bethulah*, as in speaking of Rebekah: "The damsel was very fair to look upon,—a virgin (*bethulah*); neither had any man known her" (Gen. 24:16).

The Isaiah passage is used by the book of Matthew in the interests of Christian dogma, as a prediction of the birth of Jesus, being translated as follows by the King James version: "That it might be fulfilled which was spoken of the Lord by the prophet, saying, '*Behold a virgin shall be with child, and shall bring forth a son*'" (Matt. 1:22, 23). The treatment of the Hebrew text for this dogmatic purpose demands notice for two reasons. (1) A passage referring specifically to the general period in which it was written, not to a time seven hundred years in the future, is lifted bodily from its historical context and used for a different purpose. (2) In the Hebrew text of the Isaiah passage the Hebrew definite article *ha* is prefixed to *almah*, so that the Jewish English version, already referred to, not only translates "young woman," but "the young woman." Nevertheless the

[2] Philadelphia, 1917, p. 487.

King James version (1611) insists upon translating with the indefinite article, that is, "a virgin"; while the American Revised version, in its Old Testament section, translates the Isaiah passage itself "a virgin," but puts the definite article "the" in the margin as an alternative rendering. Thereafter, in the New Testament section, the same Revised version translates Matt. 1:23 as "the virgin."

The second point, indeed, shows with special force how theologians and scholars in the past have wandered far from the realities of human life. The presence of the definite article in the Hebrew text of the Isaiah passage has given rise to a vast amount of learned conjecture and argumentation. For example: Does the article in this particular passage have an "individualizing" effect, making it refer to some particular woman, such as the mother of Jesus? Or does it merely have an indefinite, general meaning? Discussions revolving around such matters have thrown a cloud of dogma over the actual history of Israel and have retarded scientific study of the Old Testament.

Hebrew history exploited in translated Bibles

The exploitation of Hebrew history in behalf of dogma was carried to a climax by translators who introduced italicized running heads of their own at the tops of pages and at the beginnings of chapters. This matter had no place in the Hebrew Bible itself; but it was artfully spread through the Old Testament section of translated Bibles for the purpose of impressing upon the "laity" certain ideas alien to the Hebrew text. Good examples are found in the King James version, as well as in the Catholic translation published in Belgium and issued in America with the approval of Bishop John Hughes, of New York. These modern Bibles carry a large amount of purely interpolated matter.

Thus, in the King James Bible the following dogmatic statements occur at the beginning of the "Song of Solomon": "The church's love unto Christ. She confesseth her deformity. The church and Christ congratulate one another." An example even more pronounced occurs at the beginning of Isaiah 49: "Christ, being sent to

the Jews, complaineth of them"; and again, at the opening of Isaiah
52: "Christ persuadeth the church to believe his free redemption";
and at Isaiah 53: "The prophet, complaining of incredulity, excuseth
the scandal of the cross."

This interpolated matter is carried in Christian Bibles (both
Protestant and Catholic) for the purpose of theological propaganda;
and it has remained in these translations for centuries; the result being that it has acquired sanctity and prestige by the mere passage of
time.

Modern revised version rejects dogmatic running heads

About 1870 a company of scientific scholars, British and American, began to work on a new translation of the Bible. The British
edition was brought out in 1885; the American in 1901. The Revised Bible summarily throws out all the dogmatic, interpolated
matter carried by previous translations, and instead the new volume
has running heads which give a literal and honest report of what actually stands in the text.

The rejection of interpolated headlines, however, is only one of
the differences between the King James translation and the modern
Revised version. For instance, the older Bible contained the following passage in First John: "There are three that bear record in
heaven, the Father, the Word, and the Holy Ghost" (I John 5:7).
This was confidently quoted by orthodox theologians as the inspired word of God, furnishing an assured basis for the doctrine of
the Trinity. But the Revised version deliberately omits the verse, the
reason being that it is not found in any of the earlier manuscripts
and occurs in the latest manuscript only as an interpolation.

The new Bible was immediately denounced by the orthodox element in the churches; and even today it has not overtaken the popu-
larity of the older version of 1611. Those who object to the Revised
Bible fail to notice that the King James translation, on its title page,
declares itself to be "translated out of the original tongues, and with
the former translations diligently compared and revised."

Problem of Bible history and modern Revised version

The issue between the newer and the older versions goes deeper than appears on the surface. The King James translation, by its pragmatic headlines and its inaccurate, biased renderings of the text, throws a heavy smoke screen over Bible history and holds back the progress of scientific scholarship in seeking to reach the intelligent public. But on the other hand, the Revised version is a tacit challenge to orthodox dogma, and it quietly bears witness to the fact that a new era has commenced in the interpretation of Bible history. The work of revision, indeed, was done by scholars who in varying measure were sympathetic with so-called "higher criticism"; and while these men had not, in their day, reached clear and final views on the nature and facts of Bible history, they believed in the ultimate reign of scientific methods. This is the fundamental reason why the Revised Bible has been opposed by so large a part of the Christian public.

Bible history obscured by orthodox dogma

If the post-exilic Jewish view is correct that Hebrew history in the land of Canaan was merely a struggle over a miraculous revelation imposed upon Israel in the desert; if the writers of the New Testament gospel are not correct in treating Hebrew history as a storehouse of predictions concerning the birth and life of Jesus; and finally, if the Christian translators of the Bible were erroneous in viewing Hebrew history as a mere forecast, or anticipation, of the Church; what, then, is the secret of that far-away struggle between the worshipers of Yahweh and the followers of Baal? What is the real meaning of the monotheistic faith which the Babylonian exile carried to victory, and which according to the New Testament was the spiritual training school of Jesus? These questions have not been answered by orthodox theology; nor have they been dealt with to the satisfaction of progressive religious minds by the higher criticism, which, until recently was under the influence of German scholars devoid of both democracy and social vision. It is the contention of this book that the real nature of Bible history has been obscured by the dogmas of synagogue and church alike, as well as by the newer conventionalism of critical scholarship; and that the secular experience of Israel in the land of Canaan furnishes the foreground not only for democracy but for the social gospel also.

———

"The living God is as present in the critical construction of the history as in that to which tradition has wedded us."—*W. Robertson Smith*

II. THE SCIENTIFIC APPROACH

THAT THE HISTORY of all nations ought to be investigated with equal objectivity is a principle admitted in the abstract by every scientific scholar. It follows, then, that Hebrew history is entitled to be approached in the same spirit of candor with which we consider the facts of Greek, Roman, French, English, or any other history. The subject should, therefore, have impartial standing in the curricula of all schools professing to give adequate introductions to the field of general culture. Students in search of a well-rounded education should be encouraged to elect the scientific study of Hebrew history with the same freedom that they elect courses in the history of other nations.

Hebrew history denied academic and scientific standing

There are good reasons, however, why in actual practice Hebrew history is denied academic standing on a par with history in general. This peculiar situation is due to the simple fact that the subject is bound up with our inherited ideas about God and morality. The conventional religious ideologies of both Christendom and Judaism have required that Hebrew history, or Bible history, should be envisaged and explained according to certain predetermined systems of dogma, whether such dogma is consistent with scientific method or not. This predetermination of Hebrew history was welded into the practices and beliefs of the synagogue; and it has been one of the outstanding features in the "Church-and-State" regime during most of the Christian era. In other words, throughout the larger part of Jewish and Christian experience the State has virtually decreed how Hebrew history shall be understood and explained. Thus, conventional religious ideologies had such an early start and such tremendous momentum, while enjoying the artificial prop of government sanction, that even after the "disestablishment" of creeds and the legal "toleration" of nonconformity, the older dogmatic views about Hebrew history still retain their sway and power throughout large areas of every modern community.

Dogma, indeed, has laid its hand so heavily upon the Hebrew past that whenever the commonly received scheme, or plan, of Hebrew history has been called in question by scientific scholarship, an outcry has been raised that the interests of religion will be imperiled; that belief in God will be unsettled; that the salvation of souls will be endangered; and that the entire moral order of society will be menaced. Such fears were entertained universally a short time ago; and they persist in lesser degree today, the consequence being that Hebrew history has been, and is now, surrounded in one way or another by various "taboos," both crude and subtle, which have operated effectively in hampering the onward march of scientific Biblical scholarship and in denying to Hebrew history the full freedom of the educational field.

Hebrew Bible not single, consistent book

The Old Testament, like the New, is in reality not a single or separate volume by itself; it is a collection of books, written from different standpoints. Moreover, the individual books are in most cases built up out of preëxisting documents, or sources, which upon examination prove to be more or less in conflict. These pre-Biblical writings were at first privately-owned manuscripts written on rolls of papyrus and were not united in a single collection. Their owners had the right to make additions and annotations on the margins or between the lines; or they might employ some scribe to do the work. Such manuscripts eventually found their way into the hands of new owners through sale, gift, or inheritance. Whereupon the new possessor could hire a scribe to make a fresh, clean manuscript on a blank roll of papyrus, copying the marginal or interlined matter directly into the running text.

The attitude of antiquity toward writings of this kind was very different from that of modern people with reference to books of accredited authorship; and under such conditions a manuscript could go through what seems to us a very peculiar history. The owner, as just remarked, might not only wish to make additions of an explanatory nature but also might belong to a school of thought unlike that of the original author and might find himself disagreeing with its contents. He was then free to write matter into the margin which was at variance with the main text; or he could put the conflicting statements on a separate sheet and attach this new sheet to the old roll; after which all the matter, whether consistent or not, might be copied off in a single, running text on a new piece of papyrus.

It was through such processes that the books of the Hebrew Bible passed while on their way toward sanctity and "canonization." And when these writings were at length officially adopted by the authorities of the Jewish church after the Babylonian exile, they soon acquired the prestige of antiquity, being left without further editing or changing even when their contents did not always harmonize completely. If the various books disagreed in their testimony, or if a given book spoke in two voices which gave contrary witness, the matter was not for a layman to decide; because when the period of canonization had at length arrived, the interpretation of the literature was lodged in the hands of professional scribes and priests. These authorities, if unable satisfactorily to explain discrepancies, took the position that all such problems would be finally solved by the prophet Elijah in the future messianic age.

Relation of Jewish writers to Hebrew Bible

The bulk of the Hebrew nation consisted of the so-called ten (or eleven) tribes of Ephraim in the center of Canaan, or Palestine; and when the leading elements in these tribes were deported by Assyria, nothing further was heard about them; so that the national tradition was thereafter carried on by the single tribe, or community, of *Judah* (that is, the Jews) at the southern end of the Holy Land.

This little remnant of Israel therefore became the only organized channel through which Hebrew history and religion were impressed upon future ages, both Jewish and Christian.

As the only surviving fragment of the Hebrew people, the Jews thus naturally acquired a peculiar importance which did not attach to the tribe of Judah in earlier ages of the national history. Being now the sole representatives of Israel, the Jews tended to look back upon the entire past from a distinctly Judaic standpoint; and their scribes, who compiled the Hebrew Bible out of earlier documents, gave the text a Jewish tone or coloring wherever possible.

Thus the importance of the Jewish community became so great that their scribes may well be excused for projecting the later significance of Judah back upon the earlier Hebrew history in Palestine, and still further back into the dim, legendary patriarchal age before the Hebrew nation existed. This outstanding fact of *post eventum* Jewish editorial manipulation must be clearly realized, and then held steadily in mind, if we are to understand the Old Testament as a collection of material dealing with what is popularly called "Bible history."

III. PRE-HEBREW CANAAN

THE LAND of Canaan had already gone through a long history before the nation called "Israel" took form in that country. The earlier period was not only "pre-Hebrew" in the more immediate sense but was also "prehistoric," stretching back and back over thousands and thousands of years before the land was even called Canaan. Yet all this far-away human and sub-human life had a direct, historical connection with everything which took place in the times covered by the books of Judges, Samuel, and Kings—the epoch between the emergence of Israel from the Arabian wilderness and the day, six hundred years later, when Judah, the remnant of the nation, was carried into the Babylonian captivity.

Hebrew history, then—or what is loosely called "Bible history" —strikes its roots into distant pre-Hebrew ages. The history of Israel in Bible times cannot be logically understood and explained apart from circumstances and events in pre-Hebrew Canaan, as well as in the Arabian wilderness. Bible history itself, as a matter of fact, can only be viewed as a continuation of earlier history.

Hebrew history a "melting pot"

The historic nation called Israel evolved from two points of origin —the Arabian wilderness, from which the early clans of Israel emerged, and pre-Hebrew Canaan itself. Statements in certain parts of the Bible have produced a general, or popular, impression that when the Israelites came out of the wilderness into the country that was to be their future home they completely exterminated the earlier inhabitants and took possession of an empty land; that pre-Hebrew history thereupon came to an end; and that the history of Israel in Canaan thus made a clear-cut beginning in territory divided by lot among exactly twelve tribes.

But in sharp contrast with this traditional, or "orthodox," idea of Bible history, certain parts of the Old Testament point out that Israel did not begin its Canaanite experience in an empty land; that the Canaanites themselves were not by any means completely exterminated; that a very large part of the pre-Hebrew inhabitants of Canaan remained in the country after the Israelite invasion; and finally that the earlier population fused and intermarried with the invaders to produce the actual, historic Hebrew people of Bible times: "And the children of Israel dwelt among the Canaanites. . . . And they took their daughters to be their wives, and gave their daughters to their sons" (Judg. 3:5, 6). In other words, the nation called "Israel" arose in precisely the same way that all other nations have evolved—namely, as a coalescence between two or more parent races. The Greek, Roman, French, German, English, American, and other peoples came into existence in this way; and so did all other historic nations. There are no "linebred," or "pure," nations anywhere in the world; and Israel was no exception to this universal rule.[1]

Early Stone, or Palaeolithic, Age in Canaan

The land of Canaan, like many other parts of the earth, has prehistoric deposits in layers, or strata—the earliest being the deepest

[1] On Palestinian archaeology, the following works will be found useful: M. Burrows, *What Mean These Stones? the Significance of Archaeology for Biblical Studies* (New Haven, 1941); N. Glueck, *The Other Side of the Jordan* (New Haven, 1940); G. A. Barton, *Archaeology of the Bible* (Philadelphia, 1937); W. F. Albright, *Archaeology of Palestine and the Bible* (New York, 1932); J. W. Jack, *The Ras Shamra Tablets* (London, 1935); W. M. F. Petrie, *Ancient Gaza* (London, 1931); A. H. Rowe, *Beth-Shan, Topography and History* (Philadelphia, 1930); Turville-Petre, *Researches in Prehistoric Galilee* (London, 1937); G. A. Barton, *Semitic and Hamitic Origins* (Philadelphia, 1934). Consult also: A. E. Cowley, *The Hittites* (Oxford, 1926); L. Delaporte, *Mesopotamia* (New York, 1925); D. D. Luckenbill, *Ancient Records of Assyria and Babylonia* (Chicago, 1926-27); J. H. Breasted, *Ancient Records of Egypt* (Chicago, 1906-7). On prehistoric man in general: Goldenweiser, *Anthropology; an Introduction to Primitive Culture* (New York, 1937); G. G. MacCurdy, *The Coming of Man* (New York, 1935); H. H. Wilder, *Man's Place among the Anthropoids* (Oxford, 1934); A. L. Kroeber, *Anthropology* (New York, 1934); G. A. Dorsey, *Man's Own Show: Civilization* (New York, 1931); R. H. Lowie, *Introduction to Cultural Anthropology* (New York, 1934); A. G. Keller, *Man's Rough Road* (New York, 1932); G. F. Renard, *Life and Work in Prehistoric Times* (London, 1929).

and most primitive, consisting of rough stone tools used by a race which inhabited caves in small family groups. There was no knowledge of agriculture, domestic animals, or the use of fire in that early age of primitive savagery. The cave habitat was used for shelter and for safety against wild animals. The food supply in the rough stone age was both restricted and precarious. The uncertain subsistence and the lack of tools for developing natural resources were the conditions which made it impossible for palaeolithic men to associate in large groups. They were like Ishmael, whose hand was against every man, while every man's hand was against him (Gen. 16:12).

Deep significance of prehistoric human life

Let us reflect a moment upon the meaning of this primitive, prehistoric life of man, which existed not only in Canaan but also in many other localities widely distributed over the earth. It was in the world for uncounted ages prior to the beginnings of written history. In fact, the so-called "historical" period is only a brief moment in the total experience of the human race. That the prehistoric epoch was immense in its long-drawn-out evolution is the unanimous testimony of archaeological scholars whose explorations have been going on for almost a century. That the chronology of prehistoric man runs into hundreds of thousands of years is a conclusion as firmly established as the facts of astronomy or physics. No claim has ever been made by archaeologists that the prehistoric age was equal in duration at all points on the earth; because in many cases the cave man evidently migrated into a given region from some other locality in a so-called "recent" epoch.

So far as our concern with pre-Hebrew Canaan goes, the precise chronology is not important. What we have to contemplate is the solemn fact of human life struggling slowly upward through the mental darkness of uncounted millennia in the very land where eventually Judaism and Christianity were to arise. The desolate existence of the cave man revolved around food and physical safety. Possessing only tools of roughly shaped stone and wood, he ventured forth by day to seek edible vegetation and slay some weaker animal, which he devoured uncooked. The close of day brought a season of terror, when, hiding with his woman and progeny in a cave whose mouth was barred by stones, he heard the howls of wild beasts ranging the night in search of prey. The majestic spectacle of the heavens meant nothing to him. Sun, moon, and stars crossed the sky in monotonous alternation of day and night; but the mind of the cave man was a bewildered center of crude ideas and feelings focused on subsistence and personal safety.

Emphasis here falls upon the fact that this upward-struggling human life was inexorably compelled to go on for countless eons as a condition preliminary to the birth of historic civilization. The general fact remains to be adjusted with religious faith and the formulas of theological doctrine. If Bible history has transcendent, spiritual meaning, that meaning has import for us today only when it includes pre-Hebrew Canaan, as well as all "prehistoric" history throughout the world and the biological evolution antecedent thereto, and the processes which even before the appearance of living things gave shape and motion to the universe.

Bible interested in "prehistory"

That the Bible was written by persons who had an interest in prehistoric times is evident from the opening chapters of Genesis. Two narratives, taken from the "Priestly" and the "Judaic" documents, deal with physical, biological, and human stages in the drama of creation. They are preoccupied, however, not with the philosophical or theological phase of the problem, but with its moral aspect: scarcely has the universe been created and set in motion before something goes wrong.

And Yahweh saw that the wickedness of man was great in the earth, and that every imagination of the thoughts of his heart was only evil continually; and it repented Yahweh that he had made man on the earth; and it grieved him at his heart. And Yahweh said, I will destroy man whom I have created from the face of the earth; both man, and beast, and the creeping thing, and the fowls of the air; for it repenteth me that I have made them. But Noah found grace in the eyes of Yahweh [Gen. 6:5–8].

It must be borne in mind that these documents of Genesis are only in form prehistory, that they are, in fact, the output of writers who lived after the great Hebrew prophets had accomplished their unique work of ethical criticism. The sentences which begin the passage which is quoted on page 24 reflect the ideas of prophets such as Hosea:

Hear the word of Yahweh. . . . There is no truth, nor goodness, nor knowledge of God in the land. There is nought but swearing and breaking faith, and killing, and stealing, and committing adultery; they break out, and blood toucheth blood [Hos. 4:1-2].

Thus saith Yahweh. . . . Run ye to and fro through the streets of Jerusalem, and see now, and know, and seek ye in the broad places thereof, if ye can find a man, if there be any that doeth *mishpat* [justice], that seeketh faithfulness; and I will pardon her. . . . But they have refused to receive correction; they have made their faces harder than a rock; they have refused to return [Jer. 5:1-3].

But the point of view assumed in Genesis (while unassailable and legitimate in itself) merely transfers prophetic imagery into the dawn of time and contemplates the distant past as a theater for the tragedy which in literal truth took place during Hebrew experience in Canaan. This method of handling the past as a means of moral instruction for the present was indeed followed uniformly by the compilers and editors of the Old Testament, who did their work in the spirit of the prophets. But, as all investigators of the Bible now recognize, the method is unscientific and illogical in application to Hebrew history; it therefore has the same defect when carried back into the infancy of the human race.

That is to say, the Stone Age and the cave man cannot be brought within the formulas of Genesis, even by way of symbolism. For science reveals a universe in process of creation—not a universe which (including man) was made complete and perfect at a single stroke; not one which could be pronounced ethically "good" at the start. The shortcomings of the cave man were not in the same category with the moral perversion of the imaginary Adam pictured by the legends in the first book of the Hebrew Bible.

Age of Metals arrives in pre-Hebrew Canaan

In the strata lying above palaeolithic deposits, implements and objects begin to appear which are made of metal, such as copper. In this period pre-Hebrew Canaan, as well as other parts of the earth, rose gradually out of the Rough Stone Age. A new epoch began— still prehistoric, but far advanced over the preceding era and marked by several important discoveries of revolutionary effect: the foundations of agriculture were laid by saving seeds and planting them in the ground; a few of the animal species were tamed for domestic use; methods were learned for making fire; bows and arrows were manufactured, both for hunting wild game and for waging war upon mankind; and other weapons and implements were fabricated, such as the ax, the spear, and the sword.

This new material progress, by stabilizing and increasing the food supply, made possible the evolution of larger and larger social groups, which left cave life behind as a thing of the past, while the population multiplied at central points, where clusters of huts were built, completely surrounded by defensive stockades of wood and later of stone. In other words, villages and towns began to appear in pre-Hebrew Canaan. These developments, again, brought progress in articulate speech, the rise of dialects and languages, and the invention of calculating and writing.

We are now in a position to understand that one of the most important features of progress in pre-Hebrew Canaan (as well as elsewhere) was the accumulation of an economic surplus which banished the brutal hand-to-mouth existence of the Stone Age. The prehistoric man, in fact, began to be a "capitalist" by possessing tools, and weapons, and seeds, and domestic animals, and houses, and facilities for storage. Economic surplus appears to be a very simple thing; but it complicated the entire process of social evolution.

Warfare passes from extermination to domination

Since progress in the material arts endowed human labor with power to create an economic surplus, the victors in prehistoric warfare, instead of exterminating the foe as hitherto, began to spare life and enslave a portion of the enemy. And thus, throughout a great part of the prehistoric world, not only in Canaan but also elsewhere, the larger and more powerful groups absorbed the smaller, giving rise to communities having a comparatively thin upper stratum of aristocratic free families and a large lower class of slaves. Finally, in place of small groups and clans there began to arise communities of national and imperial dignity, settled in favored regions such as the valleys of the Nile and of Mesopotamia, and the curtain rolled up on the stage of written history.

Most of the advantages brought by the new age of material progress were shared by pre-Hebrew Canaan. But at the same time geographical and geological conditions of the country held it back as compared with the great oriental empires. The Canaanites, for instance, never developed into a single nation under one local government. But instead, a large number of separate "city-states" came into existence around fortified capitals. Many of these pre-Hebrew centers actually survived from the dim past and became factors in Bible history. For instance, there was a strong walled city, with more than a thousand population, in central Canaan, by the name of Shechem which remained from a dim antiquity long before the Israelite invasion. This place continued to stand throughout a large part of the epoch described in the book of Judges; but it was at length destroyed and its inhabitants exterminated by the Israelites under interesting circumstances, which will come before us when we survey the history. In contrast with the fate of Shechem, there was another pre-Israelite, non-Hebrew city, known as Jebus, or Yebus, which had still stronger walls. This place was never destroyed by the Israelite invaders, but was taken over, with its foreign inhabitants, and became the capital of the united Hebrew kingdom in the time of David, being then better known as Jerusalem; while its people intermarried with Israel according to the general formula in Judg. 3:5–6, quoted above. Some other walled cities which originated in the faraway prehistoric time and became assimilated with Israel were Taanach, Megiddo, Gibeon, Bethshemesh, Hazor, and others.

Pre-Hebrew Canaan battleground of contending empires

Being a strip of territory between the Mediterranean sea and the desert of Arabia, Canaan was a kind of land bridge, or highway, over which the commerce of oriental nations and empires flowed back and forth. Great economic advantage therefore accrued to any power that was able to rule the country or to control the trade routes running through it. And so, during the centuries immediately preceding the rise of Israel as a Canaanite state, a number of outsiders made their influence felt in that region. Thus the early Babylonian empire, of the Euphrates valley, was in such close commercial relations with Canaan that its language had considerable effect upon the speech and writing of the Canaanite upper classes. But in the fifteenth century, B. C., the Egyptian empire seized the land and appointed governors for Jebus (Jerusalem), Tyre, Ashkelon, Gezer, and Hazor. The new regime did not last long, however; and within another century Egypt was compelled to withdraw, when the country was taken over by the Hittite kingdom of Asia Minor. This power controlled Canaan for only a short period; but a remnant of the Hittite ruling class continued far into Bible times (I Sam. 26:6; II Sam. 11:13; Exod. 3:17). In fact, the Hebrew nation was able to take form and evolve in Canaan simply because for several centuries the great empires were preoccupied elsewhere and the country stood temporarily free from outside interference.

Regime of baalism in pre-Hebrew Canaan

When the empires retreated from Canaan, the land again fell under the control of independent walled cities. There was no national government. Each little state was ruled by a kinglet, whose capital was a fortified city, such as Jebus, Megiddo, Taanach, and so forth. The social system was aristocratic. The upper class consisted of men who were both slaveowners and landholders, like the corresponding element in Egypt, Assyria, Babylonia, and other oriental nations.

The men at the head of the Canaanite regime were known individually by the term *baal* (pl. *baalim*). The word signifies "owner," "master," or "proprietor," such as "baal of a house," or "baal of an ox," or "baal of land," or "baal of a woman." A slave's master was called his baal; and likewise a woman's husband was her baal. In the city of Jebus a Hittite named Uriah, is called the baal of his wife (II Sam. 11:26). He was also the owner of house and land (*ibid.*, vs. 8). He is referred to by this term in the Hebrew text of the Bible, not because *baal* was originally a Hebrew designation for such a person (for it was not), but because Uriah the Hittite was a *non-Hebrew* citizen, or burgess, of the Canaanite city Jebus. A still better example is the walled city Shechem, in the hill country of Ephraim, which continued in the midst of Israel as a pre-Hebrew center for a long time, until the Israelites destroyed it completely. The proprietary class of Shechem is called by the term *baal* sixteen times in the Hebrew text (Judg. 9); but this is hidden in most modern translations as "men."

It is very important to obtain a clear idea about the regime prevailing in the land of Canaan during pre-Hebrew times, because, although the *baal* system was partly destroyed by the Israelite invasion, it was not wholly shattered, and eventually it reasserted itself within the social fabric of the Hebrew nation so that it became one of the primary factors impelling the primitive cult of Yahweh upward in the direction of monotheism.

A *baal*, then, was originally a human being—a man of the aristocratic, upper class, who owned slaves, animals, goods, and last but not least, houses and lands. Moreover, *baalism* contemplated every aspect of the regime not simply as a matter of static proprietorship but also from the standpoint of commercialism. In other words, not only were human beings, animals, goods, houses, and land considered the property of the *baal* class but also all such property could legally be bought and sold. The peculiar force of this emphasis will be clear when the situation comes more sharply into view.

Term "baal" applied to pre-Hebrew gods of Canaan

Originally and continuously human in meaning, this term was carried up to the gods of pre-Hebrew Canaan as divine symbols of the social regime over which they were imagined as presiding. The gods of Canaan may, indeed, be logically regarded as deified human baalim, established in the realm beyond death, but representing every phase and function of existence in which the visible, earthly baalim participated.

The Baal-cults accordingly functioned in the life of pre-Hebrew Canaan in two general ways.

1) *Social-economic:* they stood for the prevailing aristocratic regime and validated its legal customs of property and contract by means of covenants and oaths in the name of Baal. Thus, for one to "swear by Baal" or to offer sacrifice at an altar of Baal signified that one consented to the existing social-economic regime.

2) *Biological:* as figurative divine lords and masters of Canaan the Baals were supposed to send rain and to fertilize the soil. That is to say, they were gods of good crops. Each Baal had a sacred place, or *kedesh,* with a priesthood; one of the important and popular features of the cult being the "holy woman," or *kedeshah,* who was attached to the *kedesh,* or holy place, as a ritual prostitute. The practice of ritual prostitution was general, not only in Canaan but also throughout the ancient Semitic world. It symbolized the fertility-power of Baal. These women plied their calling either at a shrine, or on the streets, or on the highways of the open country. An illustration occurs in the legends of Genesis which tell about the mythical patriarch *Y'hudah* (Judah). In order to see the facts in their proper setting it is necessary to understand that this prehistoric worthy was in the habit of wandering away from his relatives in the house of Israel and of making friends among the *goyim,* or gentile people, in the Canaanite walled city of Adullam. At this place he married the daughter of a Canaanite, by whom he had two sons (Gen. 38:1–5). His Canaanite wife died; and then, one day, as Y'hudah was walking by the wayside in the country, he was seduced by a woman whom he supposed to be a ritual harlot because her face was veiled:

And he turned unto her by the way . . . And she said, What wilt thou give me, that thou mayest come in unto me? And he said, I will send thee a kid of the goats from the flock. . . . And Y'hudah sent the kid of the goats by the hand of his friend the Adullamite . . . but he found her not. Then he asked the men of her place, saying, Where is the *kedeshah* that was . . . by the wayside? And they said, There hath been no *kedeshah* here. And he returned to Y'hudah and said . . . the men of the place said, There hath been no *kedeshah* here [Gen. 38:16, 17, 20–22].

The foregoing material calls for a number of observations. (1) It puts into legendary form the historical fact set forth in a general way by the passage already quoted from the book of Judges with reference to intermarriage between Israelites and Canaanites. Every student of the history must learn this outstanding feature of the situation, as contrasted with the popular, orthodox myth of a complete Israelite conquest of Canaan, with utter extermination of the previous inhabitants. (2) Even though the woman by the wayside was not a ritual harlot, she was disguised as one and is represented as acting the part well enough to deceive the legendary patriarch. (3) Such passages are not used in popular Bible study, and they are not understood by those who read the Bible chapter by chapter at wholesale. (4) The present investigation makes large use of these obscure, but highly significant, parts of the Bible, because when rightly understood they bring into view a wholly new world of ancient life which helps to explain Bible history in a scientific, objective way. (5) The foregoing passage (Gen. 38), as translated by the King James version, is not rendered so clearly and frankly as it is by the American Revised Bible, which gives a marginal explanation of *kedeshah* having scientific value.

Israelite settlers regard land as inalienable

In contrast with pre-Hebrew, or Canaanite, baalistic methods, the Israelite settlers from the desert of Arabia looked upon the resources of nature from a different standpoint. A wandering clan in the wilderness always thinks of the territory over which it roams— with its oases and wells—as given by the deity of the tribe to the entire group in common. This notion is referred to, not by way of endorsement, but merely as a fact of primitive, nomadic psychology.

The principle reappeared in the life of the Israelite clans when they entered Canaan, where it became a popularly-held canon of justice (*mishpat*), according to which every piece of land held by Israel was viewed as the inalienable possession of the family that owned the soil.

Whereas the Canaanites treated land as an item of sale or exchange, validated by oaths in the name of Baal, the Israelites held that their god, Yahweh, stood for the opposite principle of nonsalability. This primitive idea finds expression in various documents of the Bible, cited here as data in a process of history, not because they offer any concrete ethical guidance in the midst of today's problems.

And Yahweh spake. . . . The land shall not be sold in perpetuity; for the land is mine. . . . And if a man sell a dwelling house in a walled city, then he may redeem it [i. e., buy it back] within a whole year after it is sold. . . . But the houses of the villages which have no wall round about them shall be counted as the fields of the country: they may be redeemed [Levit. 25:23, 29–31].

Every one of the children of Israel shall keep himself to the inheritance of the tribe of his fathers . . . that the children of Israel may enjoy every man the inheritance of his fathers [Numb. 36:7, 8].

On this principle, when king Ahab offered to buy Naboth's land for the worth of it in money, or to exchange a better piece of land for it, the Israelite peasant refused on religious grounds: Yahweh forbid it me! (I Kings 21:1–3).

Economic nature of baalism known to writers of Hebrew Bible

The writers of the Bible were fully aware that the pre-Hebrew masters of Canaan followed legal usages contrary to the ideas of the Israelite clans from the Arabian wilderness. They knew that in contrast with Naboth, who refused to sell his ancestral soil, the pre-Hebrew Araunah, of the city of Jebus, readily sold his land to King David for fifty shekels of silver (II Sam. 24:20–24). They knew the legend which made the pre-Hebrew Hittites of Hebron sell the field of Ephron to Abraham for four hundred shekels of silver (Gen. 23:14–18). They knew about the pre-Hebrew men of Shechem (called *baals*, or *baalim*, sixteen times in the Hebrew text) whose prehistoric walled city remained standing with its foreign population far into Bible times (Judg. 9). They knew of the legend which made these *baalim* sell a parcel of land to Jacob for "one hundred pieces of money"; and how "the prince of the land" said to Jacob and his sons, "Make ye marriages with us, and give your daughters unto us, and take our daughters unto you. And ye shall dwell with us; and the land shall be before you; dwell and trade ye therein, and get you possessions therein"; and they knew how the same prince communed privately with the *baalim* of the city, saying, "These men are peaceable with us; therefore let them dwell in the land, and trade therein. . . . Shall not their cattle and their substance and every beast of their's be our's" (Gen. 33:18, 19; 34:8–10, 21, 23).

Two regimes conflict in Bible history

In other words, if the sons of Jacob consent to intermarry with the people of Shechem, they will be enslaved under the Canaanite property-holding class, or *baalim*, whose leader is not merely a city magistrate, but "the prince of the land" (Gen. 34:2). The baalistic regime of landholding puts the rural classes—farmers and shepherds —into the power of the walled cities. The Israelite country population obtained release from the aristocrats of Shechem only by destroying the city and its inhabitants (Judg. 9:46–49). The fall of Shechem, in fact, completed the Israelite conquest of central Canaan. And here, in the central highlands, a rural proprietary took form during the Judges and Samuel period, each man being called, not *baal*, but by a more archaic term, *adon* (pl., *adonim*). These landholders were devotees of Yahweh as a deity of justice (*mishpat*), based upon the regime of inalienable property in the soil.

And thus comes into view the basic antithesis of Hebrew history, turning around the problem of man's relationship to the earth on which and from which man must live. A very deep and fundamental question! Two opposite legalities, principles, customs, and ideals come into conflict. The one looks backward into an imaginary golden age when "Judah and Israel dwelt safely, every man under his vine and under his fig tree" (I Kings 4:25). The other drives inexorably toward a future void of hope, wherein the Hebrew prophets cry "Woe unto them that join house to house, that lay field to field, till there be no room, and ye be made to dwell alone in the midst of the earth!" (Isaiah 5:8). The primitive usage of "inalienability" will not work in a settled civilization. But in practice the opposite principle of liquidity develops into monopoly by a small class, not alone in Israel but also in Greece, Rome, France, Russia, Germany, England, and America—wherever men congregate in settled communities.

Both terms of the great Hebrew antithesis, then, were impossible. Moreover, between the two impossibilities no possible compromise loomed. Yet the clash of the two standards produced the great struggle which, thundering across the ages, eliminated Baal and carried Yahweh toward monotheism.

IV. THE JOSEPHITE ENCLAVE

THE PREVAILING idea of "Jacob" makes him a peaceful patriarch, who wanders in Mesopotamia, Canaan, and Egypt at
the head of a small family group, numbering seventy souls
at most, like a band of gypsies. But there is another tradition among
the early legends of Israel, as recorded in the book of Genesis, which
makes Jacob a fierce and relentless military chieftain, commanding
hardy followers equipped with bows, arrows, and swords, who take
the highlands of central Canaan away from the previous inhabitants,
the Amorites. This territory, later known as "the hill country of
Ephraim," is conquered by "Jacob," on behalf of his son "Joseph,"
whose two sons, Ephraim and Manasseh, become identified with
central Canaan during the epoch of the Judges. Thus, in the little-
known military legend the patriarch Jacob, speaking to Joseph, says,
"I have given thee one portion above thy brethren, which I took out
of the hand of the Amorite with my sword and with my bow" (Gen.
48:21–22).

What we are dealing with is a projection of Hebrew history in
Canaan, throwing the events back into the dim past as a legend
which carries a basis of truth, but cannot be accepted as a literal report of a definite person named Jacob. Moreover, it should also be
noticed that the tradition which makes Jacob a military chief, commanding an army powerful enough to invade and conquer the highlands of Ephraim, is incompatible with the more familiar story
which regards him as a mere individual at the head of wandering
gypsies who eventually settle in "the land of Egypt."

The military tradition finds actual, objective point of reference in
the early period covered by the book of Judges, when a horde,
which was then or later known as "Joseph," emerged from the desert
and came westward across the river Jordan, swarming up into the

hills of central Canaan: "And the house of Joseph, they also went up against Beth-el. And . . . they smote the city with the edge of the sword. . . . And the hand of the house of Joseph prevailed" (Judg. 1:22, 25, 35)—*circa* 1250 B. C.

Inconsistency in legends of Jacob

In contrast with the foregoing Ephraimite legend, the Judaic legend says "Jacob was a quiet man dwelling in tents" (Gen. 25:27); "and he went down into Egypt, and sojourned there, few in number" (Deut. 26:5). From this point, the conventional tradition is drawn out along lines more or less familiar to everybody. Jacob's twelve sons are the ancestors of twelve tribes in Egypt, where they remain four hundred years without leaving any word or trace which appears in Egyptian history or even in the conventional tradition itself. They are set free from Pharaoh by direct, supernatural intervention of Deity, acting through stupendous miracles. The nation is then conducted into the desert, where the religion of One God is impressed upon Israel by a further display of signs and wonders at a flaming mountain called "Horeb" in the Ephraimite document, and "Sinai" in the Judaic sources. A system of minute and complex priestly ritual is given; a tabernacle is built and carried about in the wilderness for many years. In these transactions the tribe of Judah has a prominence unknown throughout Hebrew history in Canaan, but entirely compatible with the religious function of Judah after the Babylonian Exile (when, in fact, the priestly narrative was compiled). Finally the Hebrew people, organized as a grand army, descend in full force upon Canaan, exterminate the Amorites, root and branch, and then divide the empty land by lot among the twelve tribes. Thus the primitive age of marvels comes to an end in the book of Joshua, which is an appendix to the tradition unfolded by the "Pentateuch."

But when we turn to the narratives embodied in the books of Judges, Samuel, and Kings, the contrast with the picture thus drawn is very sharp. There has been no sweeping conquest, but only an invasion by a few clans which have penetrated the hill country of

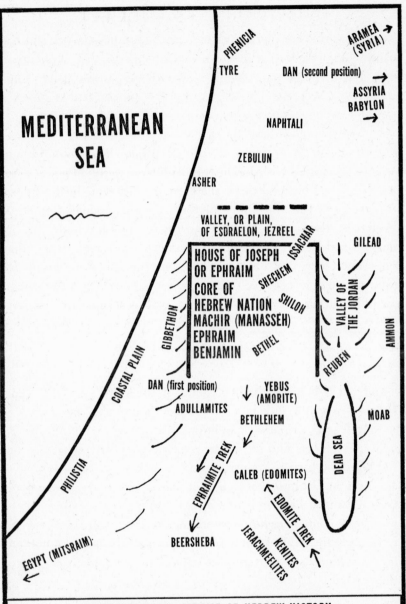

CONVENTIONALIZED SCHEME OF HEBREW HISTORY

FROM SOCIOLOGICAL AND ECONOMIC STANDPOINTS, YEBUS (JERUSALEM) WAS OUT OF CENTER AS HEADQUARTERS OF NATIONAL ORGANIZATION.—THE TRUE CENTER WAS IN EPHRAIM.—THE RULE OF THE HOUSE OF DAVID WAS ONLY AN INTERLUDE WHICH TEMPORARILY DEFLECTED THE MOVEMENT OF HEBREW HISTORY BEYOND ITS NATURAL ORBIT.

central Canaan, leaving the earlier inhabitants (Amorites and Canaanites) in possession of many strong walled cities and adjacent villages. The immense and splendid system of the priestly tabernacle is nowhere to be seen. The organization of twelve tribes grouped around a national center of authority does not appear. There is, in fact, no nation, and there are no twelve tribes in sight. Nor is any tribe of Judah in evidence. Even the place which later became specially identified with Judah (the Amorite city of Jebus, or Jerusalem), has not been taken by the Hebrew invaders, but remains in possession of "the inhabitants of the land" all through the period covered by the book of Judges and the first book of Samuel. The conventional picture of Jacob as a quiet individual with twelve sons, going down to Egypt, and so forth, has usurped the attention of subsequent ages so effectively that it has buried in oblivion the simpler legend picturing a patriarch who took central Canaan "with sword and bow."

Militant legend of Jacob in harmony with Judges, Samuel, Kings

And yet it is precisely the legend of the victorious clan leader (little known though it be) that carries us into the very center of the simple and primitive conditions prevailing in the age of the Judges. For it sets him in exclusive relationship with what is called "the house of Joseph," consisting of the clans, or tribes, known as Manasseh and Ephraim, which, as a matter of history, did actually take the central highlands of Canaan, leaving the previous inhabitants of the country secure in more than twenty walled cities which lay beyond the central hills. The history thus begins to come into view as a purely secular process, going forward like that of any other people.

Israelite legends patterned upon Hebrew history

We have now reached a point where it will become even clearer that the legends of Genesis do not emerge from the mysterious depths of prehistoric times, but that in reality they are "folk tales" patterned upon the evolution of Hebrew history in Canaan itself. The communities, or tribes, known as Manasseh and Ephraim were mentioned above as holding the central highlands. Gideon says, "My family is the poorest in Manasseh" (Judg. 6:15); and in his capacity as chieftain he sends out a war call to the colors: "So all the men of Ephraim were gathered together" (Judg. 7:24). These tribes are said to constitute "the house of Joseph," which takes possession of the hill country (Judg. 1:22). Turning then, to the legends of Genesis we find that Manasseh and Ephraim are accounted the two sons of Joseph, whereof Manasseh is the elder (Gen. 48:1, 14). Accordingly, in the Judges period the older and more important tribe is Manasseh; while the tribe of Ephraim was formed later and was at first of less importance. But in course of time the younger tribe, Ephraim, rose to such power and prestige that the name of Manasseh disappeared from the map, and the whole region of the central highlands became known as "the hill country of Ephraim."

Following the pattern of this evolution in central Canaan, the legends of Genesis tell about the lads Manasseh and Ephraim being taken by their father Joseph into the presence of the patriarch Jacob to receive his blessing. It was the custom that a first-born son should be blessed more abundantly than his brothers; and therefore Joseph expected his elder son Manasseh to receive greater consideration than Ephraim at the hands of Jacob. The story follows:

And one told Jacob and said, Behold thy son Joseph cometh unto thee. . . . And Israel [that is, Jacob] beheld Joseph's sons and said, Who are these? And Joseph said unto his father, These are my sons, whom God hath given me in this place. . . . And Joseph took them both, Ephraim [the younger] in his right hand toward Israel's left hand, and Manasseh in his left hand toward Israel's right hand. . . . But Israel stretched out his right hand, and laid it upon Ephraim's head, who was the younger, and his left hand upon Manasseh's head. . . . [thus crossing his arms]. And when Joseph saw that his father laid his right hand upon the head of Ephraim, it displeased him; and he held up his father's hand, to remove it from Ephraim's head unto Manasseh's head. . . . And Joseph said unto his father, Not so, my father: for this is the first-born; put thy right hand upon his head. But his father refused and said, I know it,

my son, I know it. . . . But truly his younger brother shall be greater
than he. . . . And he set Ephraim before Manasseh [Gen. 48:2, 8–20].

By interpreting the legends of Genesis in this way, as natural out-
growths of Hebrew history in Canaan, we shall find that the Pentateuch (and especially Genesis) plays an important part in recovering
the secular history.

New Hebrew community, or "tribe," called "Benjamin," 1200 B. C.

The groups known as Manasseh and Ephraim, after settling in
the central highlands, increased and multiplied, overflowing toward
the south, where in course of time a new and smaller community,
or "tribe," came into existence. That the term "south," in this case,
does not refer to the section of Palestine which eventually became
known as Judah should be clearly understood. It indicates the southernmost part of the central highlands to the north of Jebus (or
Jerusalem) which even then was an unconquered Amorite city. The
term for "south" in Hebrew is *yemen;* while the word for "son" is
ben. Thus the newly formed tribe came to be known as *Ben-yemen*,
or Benjamin—"Son of the South." That is to say, it originated, or
was "born," here in the southeast corner of the Ephraimite hill country. It was a "native" of Canaan; whereas, Manasseh and Ephraim
had come in from the desert as foreign born.

Accordingly the legend-building faculty, which works in all peoples, evolved a story about the birth of Benjamin at precisely this
point. The tale was that Jacob's favorite wife, Rachel, in giving birth
to Benjamin, died and was buried here. The tomb of Rachel, in the
land of Benjamin, comes to view many years later with reference
to Saul the Benjaminite. This man was anointed king by Samuel the
seer, who said to him: "When thou art departed from me this day,
then thou shalt find two men by Rachel's sepulchre in the border of
Benjamin at Zelzah" (I Sam. 10:2). The Benjaminite prophet Jeremiah also speaks in a symbolic way about Rachel, in her tomb
near Samuel's village of Ramah, as weeping for the lost tribes of

Ephraim, which had already vanished before the time of this later prophet: "The words of Jeremiah . . . of the . . . land of Benjamin. . . . A voice is heard in Ramah, lamentation and bitter weeping, Rachel, weeping for her children. She refuseth to be comforted for her children, because they are not" (Jer. 1:1; 31:15).

Special notice must be taken of the material covering this point: "And they journeyed from Beth-el. . . . And Rachel travailed, and she had hard labor. . . . And it came to pass, as her soul was in departing (for she died) that she called his name Ben-oni; but his father called him Benjamin. And Rachel died, and was buried in the way to Ephrath—the same is Bethlehem" (Gen. 35:16–19).

In the words "the same is Bethlehem" we see inserted by the Jewish compiler, what is called a "gloss," which was probably written at first on the margin of the manuscript, and then placed in the main text by later scribes when making fresh copies of the Genesis-narrative. The same gloss is also found in Gen. 48:7. The Jewish editor seeks thus to transfer the tomb of Rachel from its traditional Ephraimite location, several miles north of Jerusalem, to the Judahite village of Bethlehem, several miles south of Jerusalem. It was hoped that in this way the prestige of Rachel's tomb would be monopolized by the Jews instead of by the rival Ephraimite section of the country, between which and Judah there was always hatred.

Jacob-Rachel clans

We have now reached a point where the central, outstanding Hebrew community, depicted in the book of Judges, begins to take definite form. The Manassites and Ephraimites find a common ancestor in Joseph; while their younger brother is Benjamin, originating by overflow into the south central highlands. Thus arose the necessity for discovering a common traditional ancestor to account for association between the Josephites and Benjaminites; which brought into view "Jacob," whose favorite wife "Rachel" was the mother only of Joseph and Benjamin (Gen. 29:17; 30:22–24; 35:16–18).

Here, then, we find the original, primitive Hebrew people, the house of Joseph, developing as an "enclave" in the central highlands, or hill country of Ephraim; while even yet, many of the earlier Amorite "inhabitants of the land" remain in possession of more than twenty strong walled cities, including Jebus, or Jerusalem, outside the Josephite enclave area.

How the rest of the Hebrew nation took form and how the remaining "sons" and "wives" of Jacob are accounted for by legend will appear in due time. The Rachel group (known collectively as Ephraim, or house of Joseph) claims attention at the beginning of the history as the starting-point of Hebrew evolution.

Greek mythic ancestor "Hellen" similar to "Jacob"

The common father of Israel emerges into view under circumstances comparable to those which gave rise to the Greek ancestor "Hellen." The tribal chiefs of the local Greek communities were said to have descended from this forefather. The historic and mythological evolution of Greece is reflected in the literature known as the Iliad, which, like the Bible, was written by various compilers and editors who lived in successive generations. The Iliad was at first a local series of poems based upon local events. But additions were made betokening broader horizons, and the final interpolation is the catalogue of ships, intended to show that the warriors who made the attack on Troy came in vessels from all parts of Greece, not from one locality. The tendency to generalize the poems was identical with the impulse to find a common ancestor for all the Greeks.[1]

Jacob as "Man-of-Rachel" ("Ish-rachel," or "Is'ra'el")

Jacob is pictured as being preëminently the man, or husband, of Rachel. In Hebrew the word for man is *ish*. Hence the suggestion put forward by Steuernagel that the name "Israel" may have come by elision from *Ish*-Rachel. That Rachel was "beautiful and well-favored," that Jacob loved her, and that he offered to serve Laban, her father, seven years in order to win her as his wife are statements

[1] Cf. Bury, *History of Greece* (London, 1940), Vol. I, chap. i.

contained in the Ephraimite form of the Jacob legends (Gen. 29:16–19). The seven years of work "seemed unto him a few days, for the love he had to her" (Gen. 29:20).

But the marriage of Jacob and Rachel was clouded by a fearful tragedy. A wedding feast was held at the end of the seven-year period; and when Jacob retired to the marital tent in the evening, he was in a state of conviviality unfavorable to the exercise of accurate perception. Under these circumstances, Leah, the elder sister of Rachel, was brought into the tent by her father Laban, who deliberately victimized his new son-in-law by forcing upon him, unawares, a woman whom he did not want and whom he had not chosen.

The legend of the two sisters who became the two wives of Jacob will be examined more fully at a later point in our study. It is referred to here as emphasizing the attachment of Jacob for Rachel only and will be adverted to again when the corresponding historical events come into view.

Our preliminary criticism of the Old Testament sources gives us at the start a new orientation upon the secular process which underlies the Bible. The Jewish compilers and redactors succeeded in distorting the history to such an extent that only by close and searching examination of the documents can the perspective be restored in its earlier form.

Rachel clans replace previous Canaanite upper class, 1250–1175 B. C.

Every ancient oriental nation, as observed in Chapter III, consisted of two main classes—an upper stratum, which owned the soil, and a lower stratum of slaves, which the socially superior element held as property and who performed most of the heavy manual work. A "conquest" was not the destruction of all the inhabitants of a given territory—free and slave alike. It was an exchange of masters, in which the previous upper class was either slaughtered or degraded into the slave stratum over which the new masters ruled.

A good example of the Josephite slaveholder is the military chief

Gideon, of the tribe of Manasseh, who selects from among his slaves ten men to do a certain piece of work (Judg. 6:27). The English translations render the Hebrew by the term "servants," concealing the situation from the modern lay reader. But the text itself reads, "Gideon took ten men from his *abadim* [slaves]"—the singular being *ebed*, of which we shall hear frequently. Gideon complains that he is poor: "My family is poor in Manasseh; and I am the least in my father's house" (Judg. 6:15). This means merely that Gideon, who had more than ten slaves, was one of the less wealthy members of the Hebrew aristocracy. Another instance, occurring in the Benjaminite section, is that of Ziba, who had twenty slaves, or *abadim* (II Sam. 9:10). The economic force of this passage also is lost in the translation, which again uses the innocent-appearing term "servants."

The Josephite aristocracy based its domination of the Canaanite slave class on the fortune of war, as already pointed out. Their mastery over the central highland region was pivoted on the city of Bethel, one of the fortified headquarters of the pre-Hebrew *baalim*, or proprietary class, in that part of the country:

And the house of Joseph . . . went up against Beth-el . . . and they smote the city with the edge of the sword. . . . And it came to pass . . . that they put the Canaanites to tribute, and did not utterly drive them out. . . . And the hand of the house of Joseph prevailed, so that they became tributaries [Judg. 1:22, 25, 28, 35].

Bible history, as commonly interpreted, fails to recognize the limited nature of the conquest, as being Ephraimite and as being accomplished by the "house of Joseph"; while at the same time, the two-class, master-and-slave regime is ignored as beneath notice. Likewise, there is no emphasis placed upon the highly important fact that the enslavement of the Canaanites is definitely endorsed and excused by the legends of Genesis, where "Ham," the father of Canaan, beholds the nakedness of the drunken patriarch "Noah," and passes the curse of bondage to his descendants: "And Noah awoke from his wine, and knew what his younger son had done unto him. And he said, Cursed be Canaan! A slave of slaves [*ebed abadim*] shall he be" (Gen. 9:24–25; see also entire passage vss. 18–27).

That the legends recorded in Genesis originated, not in some dim, indeterminate "patriarchal" epoch, but in secular Hebrew history in the land of Canaan will become increasingly clear as we study the fundamental circumstances and events of that history, out of which they arose.

Josephite population increases and needs more territory, 1150 B. C.

The increase of population which gave rise to the "tribe" of Benjamin went steadily on until the need for more territory became pressing. An instructive notice relating to this problem is contained in a brief document fitted into the seventeenth chapter of Joshua, beginning with verse eleven, as follows: "And the children of Joseph said, The hill country is not enough for us; and all the Canaanites that dwell in the land of the valley have chariots of iron, both they who are in Beth-shean and her towns, and they who are of the valley of Jezreel" (Josh. 17:16).

Josephite policy

The Rachel, or Josephite, clans were identified with a wilderness deity whose cult was in strong contrast with the cults of the local, Canaanite Baal-gods. These gods, as we have seen, were the symbols of a regime which made land an item of mortgage and sale, tending to concentrate the resources of a country in the grasp of a few proprietors (see chap. iii). But on the other hand, the ideology associated with the name "Yahweh" was hostile to the sale of one's patrimonial estate. The fundamental idea in Yahwism was the social and economic integrity of an upper class possessing both land and slaves, whereby the small aristocrat should maintain his legal status equally with the wealthier members of the elite.

In connection with the Josephites' desire for more space it is evident that ambition pointed northward, because reference is made to "the Canaanites who dwell in the valley." This refers to the great lowland which cuts across Canaan from the Mediterranean sea to the Jordan river and lies north of the original Joseph territory. Hence, the mention of "the valley of Jezreel," which was the eastern and most accessible part of the lowland. But at the same time the great obstacle against expansion of the Josephites into this fertile territory was the military power of the older population: "All the Canaanites that dwell in the land of the valley have chariots of iron" (Josh. 17:16).

House of Joseph prepares for war

When the Israelite invaders from the desert had fought their way into the central highlands, the older, settled inhabitants of the walled cities outside the little hill district of Ephraim had not been able to send their chariots up into the rough, hill country to oppose the original inrush of the Hebrews. After the intruders had settled themselves, their presence was perforce accepted by the Canaanites, who naturally hoped that no more trouble would be felt from that quarter.

But now disquieting rumors began to fly about over Canaan. It was noised abroad that some kind of campaign was being secretly organized under the inspiration of a busy mother in Israel known as Deborah (the "Bee"), and a leader called Barak ("Lightning")— this name being appropriate, because he moved quickly and unexpectedly over the land.

The focal point of opposition to the house of Joseph was "the kings of Canaan"—the baalim, whose headquarters were in the still unconquered, walled cities, among which were Beth-shan (supra) and "Taanach by the waters of Megiddo" (Judg. 5:19).

A highly valuable source of information about this critical epoch is "The Song of Deborah." It is a poem—an Ephraimite poem— and is perhaps the oldest piece of writing in the Hebrew Bible (Judg. 5). The central force in the campaign was the house of Joseph, represented by three "tribal" names, among which we at once recognize Ephraim and Benjamin (Judg. 5:14). In addition to these well-known Josephite names we naturally scan the same passage for Manasseh; instead we encounter a term which has at first a rather strange effect, "Machir." This name, however, is found in the Ephraimite material at the end of Genesis, where Machir is the "son of Manasseh" (Gen. 50:23). Whether a clan thus designated was all that remained of Manasseh in the time of Deborah or "Machir" was an earlier form of "Manasseh" we cannot say. But we do know that in this poem Ephraim is mentioned first, and is evidently on the way toward that predominance which impressed its name on the entire central highland region.

The foregoing three names (Ephraim, Benjamin, Machir) represent the head and front of Israel's opposition to the Canaanite kings. Only three other names appear in association with them as participators in one of the most important, but little understood, battles in world history.

Descending from the Ephraimite hills into the valley of Jezreel, we find ourselves at once in a Canaanite, or Amorite, region called Issachar, where the peasantry are all in bondage to a non-Israelite aristocracy. The policy of the house of Joseph, as events revealed, was to liberate these farmers from the grip of their baalistic masters and establish them as a dependency, or ally, which could be counted a subtribe of Israel under the paternity of Jacob. Accordingly a check-up of the legends brings the fact of Issachar's economic servitude into bold relief: "Issachar is a strong ass crouching down between two burdens: And he saw that rest was good, and the land that it was pleasant; and bowed his shoulder to bear, and became a slave under taskwork" (Gen. 49:14, 15). After their ultimate release the Issacharites became the butt of a story which made them the descendants of Jacob, not through the loved wife Rachel, but through the hated sister Leah, who was deceitfully forced into the arms of Jacob on his wedding night. Moreover, instead of being willingly the father of Issachar, Jacob was hired to beget him by a present, called "mandrakes" in the translation, which in the Hebrew text is *dudaim*, or "love-apples"—a fruit stimulating to the sexual passions and still used in Syria.

The organizer Barak seems to have been a man of Issachar, working under Josephite auspices; and in addition to his own local community, he was able to enlist peasants from still farther away, beyond the great valley northward, in the hills of Galilee. One of these groups came into the coalition under the provincial name of Naphtali (Judg. 5:18); and in time the legends declared that it sprang from the slave girl Bilhah, who belonged to Rachel (Gen. 30:7, 8). The other group was Zebulun (Judg. 5:14, 18). Later there were legends that the people of this locality had descended from Leah, the rival of Jacob's favorite (Gen. 30:19, 20).

The completed military organization, therefore, embraced only six groups, under the tribal names Ephraim, Benjamin, Machir, Issachar, Naphtali, and Zebulun. That the last three of these were the only adherents which the Josephites were able to find is a commentary on the real position of "Israel" in Canaan at this time.

Four other communities, or groups, which might have coöperated, but which refused, are also mentioned in the Song of Deborah. Their names and locations prove to be matters of considerable importance in the unfolding of Bible history, and they call for careful attention.

On the southwest of Ephraim, stretching down the slopes to the Mediterranean shore, was a community known as Dan. This is rather surprising at first, because when we reach the better-known era of history, Dan is identified with the far north, beyond Zebulun and Naphtali. "From Dan to Beersheba" became a standard expression meaning "All Israel from north to south." But in the early period referred to by the Song of Deborah we see Dan on the southwest of the main Josephite mass. The inhabitants of this locality may have represented an earlier migration from Ephraim, which had become greatly mingled in blood with non-Israelites. The legends finally made them descend from the slave girl Bilhah, who belonged to Rachel (Gen. 30:5, 6). This means merely that the Danites were not of the pure Jacob blood; and, in accordance with this lowly position, the Deborah poem complains about their lack of coöperation, saying, "And why did Dan remain in ships?" (Judg. 5:17). When we have once found the key to the secular history, the various parts of the Old Testament emerge into a new and harmonious perspective.

The Deborah poem also speaks of another noncoöperating community, called Asher, which lay northwest of the Josephite alliance. Like Dan, the Asherites were located on the Mediterranean, but much farther north. "Asher continued on the seashore, and abode in his breaches" (Judg. 5:17). The reason for noncoöperation on the part of the Asherites is made clear by the source in the opening chapter of Judges. The names of seven Canaanite cities are given as being in that neighborhood: "Neither did Asher drive out the inhabitants of Acco, nor the inhabitants of Zidon, nor of Ahlab, nor of Achzib, nor of Helbah, nor of Aphik, nor of Rehob. But the Asherites dwelt among the Canaanites, the inhabitants of the land; for they did not drive them out" (Judg. 1:31, 32). Together with evidence of other unconquered cities in Canaan (such as Jebus, or Jerusalem, Beth-shan, Taanach, and so forth) this passage helps to give a wholly different idea of conditions after the Israelite invasion. Long before the Hebrew people of Bible times were known, "Asher" appears in the inscriptions of Seti I and Ramses II as a place in Canaan. The Asherites eventually found a place in Hebrew legend as descended from a slave girl, Zilpah, who belonged to Leah (Gen. 30:12, 13).

The Deborah poem also mentions another noncoöperating group, Reuben, down in the valley of the Jordan, far away in pasture lands on the other side of that river, southeast of the house of Joseph: "For the divisions of Reuben there were great searchings of heart. Why abodest thou among the sheepfolds, to hear the bleatings of the flocks? For the divisions of Reuben there were great searchings of heart" (Judg. 5:15, 16). The community of this name was a tiny fragment left behind in the east Jordan country when the Josephites went swarming up into the central highlands of Canaan. Later the tradition arose that the Reubenites, being the oldest settlement, were the children of Jacob's eldest son. Being in disfavor among the Josephites, Reuben was held to be, not a full brother born of Rachel, but a son of the hated sister Leah (Gen. 29:32). A discreditable story was told that he had seduced the slave girl Bilhah (Gen.

35:22). He is accordingly denounced in the so-called "Blessing of Jacob," where it is said, "Thou shalt not excel, because thou wentest up to thy father's bed. Then defiledst thou it: he went up to my couch" (Gen. 49:3, 4). "His birth-right was given unto the sons of Joseph" (I Chron. 5:1). That the Reubenites, however, should refuse to join the enterprise headed by Deborah and Barak was not strange in the least; for the territory of "Reuben" lay far down below the highlands of Ephraim, as well as across the Jordan; and there would have been much difficulty in persuading the men of this distant region to send an armed force up into the hills, leaving their families and homes exposed to the assaults of marauders from the nearby desert.

Of equal interest is the reference of the poem to still another community which refused to become active in alliance with the house of Joseph, namely, Gilead, which lay across the river Jordan to the northeast of the central highlands. All that we read, however, is, "Gilead abode beyond Jordan" (Judg. 5:17). The people of that region may have had as good reasons as Reuben for hesitation: they were far distant from the central hills; while their families and property were open to attack by desert clans always hovering on the frontier.

Gilead was equal in importance and population to many other communities of that epoch whose names finally crystallized into legend as individual Hebrew patriarchs. Why, then, did not Gilead become one of the "tribes" of Israel, together with Reuben, Asher, Dan, and the others? That an actual person of this name existed is asserted in the book of Judges, where we read:

Now Jephthah the Gileadite was a mighty man of valour; and he was the son of an harlot. And Gilead begat Jephthah. And Gilead's wife bare him sons; and his wife's sons grew up, and they thrust out Jephthah, and said unto him, Thou shalt not inherit in our father's house, for thou art the son of a strange woman [Judg. 11:1–2].

In commenting upon this passage, Professor Thatcher, of Oxford, says, "Gilead was properly the name of the land." But in that case, all the local names that we are dealing with, at the basis of Hebrew history in Canaan are "properly" the names of localities and groups of people, not the names of individuals. It is regularly the custom of Biblical writers, however, to personalize regions in this way. The pre-Hebrew population of Canaan, for instance, is viewed as descended from an individual patriarch of that name: "And Canaan begat Sidon his firstborn, and Heth, and the Jebusite, and the Amorite . . . and afterward were the families of the Canaanites spread abroad" (Gen. 10:15–18).

The Gileadites not only refused to coöperate with the house of Joseph at this time but also, as we shall see later, continued in their attitude of hostility. And this is probably the reason why the Josephite legend-building power did not number Gilead among the "sons" of Jacob. It is instructive to observe, on the contrary, that the Judaic writers, who disliked the Josephites and produced the "Priestly" document in Genesis-Joshua, were very particular to make the Gileadites descend from Joseph. Thus where the Ephraimite document in Genesis traces Joseph's family through Manasseh to Machir, the Jewish Priestly document goes on and makes Machir the father of Gilead (cf. Gen. 50:23; Numb. 26:29; I Chron. 2:21; 7:17).

Still another question of great importance comes up. Why does the Song of Deborah make no reference to Judah? Many writers have maintained that since Jebus, or Jerusalem, was a Canaanite city in the days of Deborah, this place was a barrier against the northward passage of Judahites, who are imagined as being south of Jerusalem and unable to coöperate with the Josephite alliance. In this case, the Deborah Song makes allowance for the situation and omits reference to Judah. Why, then, does not the Song for the same reason omit reference to Asher, which, as we have seen, was entangled with seven Canaanite cities? Or, again, why was Dan mentioned instead of being considerately left out, since it was also restrained by unconquered Canaanite cities which lay in its vicinity? The Deborah Song may be presumed to have omitted mention of Judah for the simple reason that no community or tribe of Judah existed in the early period which we are studying. There is, in fact, no evidence that any such ethnological aggregate was anywhere to be found in the time of Deborah.

Two other "tribal" names are also absent from the Song—Simeon and Levi. These omissions are partly explained by checking up on the "Blessing of Jacob" in Genesis, where we read,

Simeon and Levi are brethren! Instruments of cruelty are in their habitations. O my soul, come not thou into their secret. Unto their assembly, mine honor, be not thou united; for in their anger, they slew men; and in their selfwill they digged down a wall. Cursed be their anger, for it was fierce; and their wrath, for it was cruel. I will divide them in Jacob, and scatter them in Israel [Gen. 49:5–7].

These words imply a tradition of rapine and slaughter which at some time in the dim past caused the destruction of "Simeon" and "Levi" as organized groups. That these brothers perfidiously killed all the men of Shechem at a period when Jacob and his sons were individual nomads in Canaan, before any "tribes" of Israel had come into existence, is narrated by a legendary tale (Gen. 34). After that the brothers go down to Egypt, where their descendants become the tribes of Simeon and Levi. If they were "tribes" and not individuals in Gen. 34, the situation contemplated by the story contradicts the orthodox Egyptian legend as definitely as the story commented upon above, according to which Jacob as military chief took a district in central Canaan out of the hands of the Amorite "with his sword and his bow" (Gen. 48:22). On the other hand, the Shechem story treats Jacob, not as a military chief, but as a peaceful individual who, instead of taking land by conquest, buys it from the Shechemites "for one hundred pieces of money" (Gen. 33:18–19). The most plausible conjecture, on the whole, may be that shortly prior to the Josephite conquest an adventurous and unsuccessful attack upon Shechem was made by two groups called Simeon and Levi, as a result of which these clans were permanently broken up. For the walled city Shechem, as we have seen, was not conquered at the time of the Josephite invasion, but survived into the Judges period as a foreign place, like Jebus and Beth-shan, full of Canaanite, or Amorite, burgesses, or *baalim* (Judg. 9). The circumstance which makes the difficulty here is the fact that neither "Levi" nor "Simeon" played any part, as communities or groups, in recorded Hebrew history in Canaan; consequently no definite legend is patterned upon these names. Simeon is a ghostly figure; and the Levites, as we shall see in due time, were a professional order at a later period.

One more tribal name about which the Deborah poem has nothing to say is Gad. But here, again, Hebrew history in Canaan affords no trace of a community or clan going by such a term; while the literature contains no definite legend, but makes only a perfunctory reference to an assumed son of Jacob as having this name (Gen. 30:11). Tradition may have assumed a tribe under the name Gad in order to approximate the orthodox number of twelve "sons," or tribes, which were thought later to have constituted the family of Jacob as an individual patriarch. If "Gilead" had made the grade as a patriarch, Gad could easily have been omitted. There had to be twelve sons of Jacob, in any case, just as there were twelve sons of Nahor (Gen. 22:20–24), twelve sons of Ishmael (Gen. 17:20), twelve sons of Esau (Gen. 36:15–19), twelve months in the year, and twelve signs of the zodiac.

Source material relating to the time of Deborah has now been scrutinized closely enough to show that the situation prevailing in Canaan during the period covered by the book of Judges was very different from what is usually taught in orthodox Jewish and Christian Bible history. The center of the picture is filled by the house of Joseph, made up of three groups (Ephraim, Benjamin, and Machir), which constitute the core of the future Hebrew nation; these communities being stratified into classes—an upper layer of freemen holding conquered soil in the hill country by inalienable tenure, and a lower layer of non-Hebrew slaves (*abadim*) originally Canaanite. Beyond the frontiers of Joseph is a native population ruled by unconquered Canaanite walled cities, or fortresses, worshiping gods by the name of Baal, and inhabited by human *baalim* whose purpose is to dominate and exploit the suburban peasants and shepherds who live in small country villages. There is no tribe of Judah. The various localities are known by names taken up later into Hebrew legend as tribes which descended either from slave girls or from an unloved wife imposed upon Jacob by deceit.

In the midst of such an environment, the attempt of Deborah and Barak to organize a revolt against the Canaanite *status quo* could not have appeared very promising. Barak and his aides were compelled to travel about quietly, avoiding the main highway and keeping to by-paths, transporting shields and spears and other implements of war by night so that they could excape observation by spies of the Canaanite masters.

Canaanite upper class defends "old order," 1150 B. C.

Such widespread preparations, however, could not continue indefinitely without becoming known to the aristocracy in the walled cities, and they now made ready to defend the ancient baalistic social system. The intruders from the desert were a terrible portent in the eyes of the Canaanites: they had conquered the central highlands; they wanted the great valley of Esdraelon, just north of the Josephite frontier; they made common cause with peasants of Issachar, enslaved under *baalim* who held a mortgage on that region; moreover, the intruders worshiped a deity (Yahweh) symbolizing the principle that when land had once come into the possession of an Israelite family, the land should never be sold or alienated. This meant that land ought not to be made an item of investment, but that the use and ownership of it should go along together. And this, again, was a challenge to the sacred rights of private property. It was revolution and must be met with all the force at the command of ancient culture.

Battle of Esdraelon, 1150 B. C.

Among the most important battles of world history, the action which took place between the Josephite coalition and the Canaanites in the valley, or plain, of Esdraelon has been ignored and misunderstood. It has been thrust into obscurity and overshadowed by the imaginary miraculous "conquest" of Canaan which orthodox mythology declares to have occurred long before in the time of Joshua, who is pictured as commanding the victorious army of a united Israel, consisting of twelve tribes:

So Joshua smote all the country of the hills, and of the south, and of the vale, and of the springs, and all their kings: he left none remaining, but utterly destroyed all that breathed, as Yahweh, god of Israel, commanded [Josh. 10:40].

If the Canaanites had been thus completely exterminated, why did they have to be fought all over again by the troops of Deborah and Barak? Hence the battle of Esdraelon has been looked at askance by orthodox leaders and theologians who have built up the ideologies of Christianity and Judaism. So the book of Judges, with its heretical background, has been outshone by the fictitious prestige of Joshua.

The army of Canaan, led by Sisera, was called to the colors at Harosheth-hagoyim, or Harosheth of the Gentiles, in the western end of the great valley. Imagine masses of infantry, preceded by nine hundred chariots of iron, whose yelling drivers whip dashing steeds, and there will rise before the mind's eye some faint picture of the Canaanite host as it rushed toward the field of battle.

The soldiers of Israelite Barak, on the other hand, were assembled in the plain at the base of a high hill called "Mount Tabor," which dominates a large part of the valley. We do not know how many men were mobilized in the coalition led by Barak. "Forty thousand in Israel" are mentioned by the Deborah poem (Judg. 5:8); while the prose account speaks only of ten thousand (Judg. 4:6). But whatever the size of their army, the highlanders had no chariots; and the prospects were not any too bright in their favor. When they beheld in the distance the Canaanite host moving toward them, the oncoming chariots of Sisera must have seemed as terrible as did the German tanks to the French infantry.

Just as the opposing armies began to move toward each other— while they were yet a long way apart—a phenomenon of nature took place which occurs unexpectedly in that region: a black cloud arose over the Mediterranean and came rolling into the valley—as when, at a later day, King Ahab was caught here by a tempest and rode in his chariot swiftly to avoid the rain (I Kings 18:44, 45).

The sudden storm caught the Canaanite chariots in a sea of mud, throwing the army of Sisera into confusion. The river Kishon, ordinarily a small stream, overflowed its banks and swept away part of the Canaanite host; while the remainder were defeated by the highland militia of Israel. The conflict thunders out from the Deborah poem—the storm, the frightened horses, the flooding river: "The clouds dropped water. . . . Then were the horsehoofs broken by the prancings of their mighty ones. . . . The river Kishon swept them away. . . . The stars in their courses fought against Sisera. . . . So let all thine enemies perish, O Yahweh" (Judg. 5:4, 20–22, 31).

We have referred to the poem as Ephraimite, revealing the house of Joseph as the central force in the coalition; while credit for cooperation is given to the enslaved Issacharites in the valley, as well as to the men who came from Zebulun and Naphtali, north of Esdraelon: "Zebulun and Naphtali were a people who jeoparded their lives unto the death in the high places of the field" (Judg. 5:18). "The princes of Issachar were with Deborah; even Issachar and also Barak" (Judg. 5:15).

But there is a prose account by a Jewish writer who seeks to deprive the Josephites of all glory by describing the battle as if the Israelite militia consisted, not of men from Joseph, but of recruits from Zebulun, the maternal brother of Judah through the hated wife Leah and from Naphtali, the offspring of the slave girl Bilhah (Judg. 4:6, 10; cf. Gen. 30:8, 19–20). Barak, the leader of the host, is taken away from Issachar and located in Naphtali (Judg. 4:6, 10); while the slave tribe Issachar itself, begotten shamelessly by Jacob, when "hired" with Leah's *dudaim*, drops out of the narrative entirely.

Battle of Esdraelon milestone

There was no standing army in Israel at this time and consequently no effective means to follow up the victory. But the general effect of the battle was undoubtedly immense in an age when superstition was rampant everywhere among all peoples. That it would give courage to the small but growing nation of Israel is a natural inference. Not only was the victory accredited to the valor of those who slew the Canaanites, but it was also regarded as an overwhelming manifestation of Yahweh on behalf of Israel through his power to bring a storm upon the foe at the right moment. The Canaanites had long worshiped their Baal-gods as rainmakers and patrons of good crops; but now it was clear that the local deities were inferior to Yahweh, since he could engulf the followers of Baal in a flood of waters from heaven. Having been a god of the wilderness, he was evidently becoming acclimated as a deity of Canaan, able to bring rain and fertilize the crops which made the country "a land flowing with milk and honey." Identified thus far with obscure hill clans from the desert, Yahweh had now entered the great valley of Esdraelon—the lowlands where walled cities proclaimed a more advanced phase of civilization. The idea of a divinity with a "growing reputation" seems rather startling and questionable at first, but it is a Biblical idea: "What one nation in the earth is like thy people, like Israel, whom *elohim* [divinity] went to redeem for a people to himself, to make him a name" [that is, a reputation] (II Sam. 7:23).

Thus, the expanding conception of Yahweh was not an independent idea revolving in some abstruse theological orbit isolated from the world of common, daily life; it was bound up with secular affairs and was part of the social evolution by which the house of Joseph and its allies grew slowly into a greater Israel—the objective Hebrew nation of Canaan. The older "inhabitants of the land," although not completely exterminated, were never again to rally and seek the downfall of the race which had recently invaded the central hills and imposed itself as a master class upon the Canaanite population of that area.

Northward expansion of Israel

As we go along, accumulating evidence will show that the Israelite element was pressing northward. A significant item occurs in the Deborah poem itself, which mentions a village called Meroz, already established in the valley of Esdraelon. This village was located where it could have been of help to the coalition army. Yet, like the inhabitants of other places mentioned in the song, it held back and remained neutral. The reason may well have been that although founded by Israelite emigrants, it lay in a region still mainly Canaanite, and was restrained by considerations of prudence. The poem, however, takes the view that only one right course was open to the villagers: "Curse ye Meroz, said the angel of Yahweh; curse ye bitterly the inhabitants thereof, because they came not to the help of Yahweh—to the help of Yahweh against the mighty" (Judg. 5:23).

To speak of Yahweh as needing help was the equivalent of saying that Israel needed help. The fate of both went hand in hand. Thus, when the Assyrian empire was at the height of its power the god Asshur loomed as a great figure in the imagination of his votaries and in the minds of subjugated peoples. But when the Assyrian empire perished its god lost his "reputation." Likewise, Yahweh still had to "make him a name in the earth"; his cult was intimately involved in the fate of Israel as a secular community. In other words, at this period and for long thereafter Israel was neither more nor less "religious" than any of the surrounding peoples. If Yahweh were not first of all evolved and built up in a worldly sense, no basis would have existed later for spiritualizing "the idea of God." Theology arises out of experience; it does not appear in the mind as a projection from beyond the orbit of human life.

The sword of Yahweh and of Gideon, 1125 B. C.

The subject continues to unfold in line with the facts and principles already before us. The victory at Esdraelon was followed by a new, but slight, step toward unity and consistency amid the welter of jealous clans and clashing races which made up the picture of life in the "Judges" period. The land of Canaan was again attacked from the desert, as when the original Joseph-horde itself crossed the Jordan and came up into the central hill country. But in this case the invaders, led by the Midianites, did not follow the route into the highlands of Ephraim, for that would have brought them directly into collision with the militant Josephites, whose fastnesses they sought to avoid. For the clans of Midian had heard of the great battle in the plain, which resulted in the defeat of the older Canaanite population. Instead of directly attacking the house of Joseph, they broke into the eastern extension of the plain, the valley of Jezreel, and struck at the ancient inhabitants of the land, thinking perhaps that if they confined their campaign to this part of the country they might plunder at will, without fear of opposition: "Then all the Midianites and the Amalekites and the children of the east were gathered together, and went over [Jordan], and pitched in the valley of Jezreel" (Judg. 6:33).

But these new adventurers from the desert failed to reckon with the facts of a changing situation. For the great valley was no longer purely Canaanite. It was becoming more and more Israelite, or Josephite, in its general aspect. Here, as we have seen, were the formerly enslaved people of Issachar, whom we may assume to have been released from bondage to their baalistic masters; and in the immediate vicinity, just north of the valley, were the communities called Naphtali and Zebulun, prominent in the coalition which defeated Sisera. Here, too, was Mount Tabor, on whose lower slopes the army of Barak had been mobilized, which now seems to have become a regular Josephite outpost; for here at Tabor the invading Midianites put to death two men of the Abiezer clan, a subdivision of Manasseh. The news of their fate was quickly carried south across the valley and up into the central highlands to the village of Ophrah, where lived their brother Gideon, the son of Joash.

Immediately Gideon went into action:

The spirit of Yahweh came upon Gideon; and he blew a trumpet; and [the clan of] Abiezer was gathered after him. And he sent messengers throughout all Manasseh, who also gathered after him; and he sent messengers unto Asher, and unto Zebulun, and unto Naphtali; and they came up to meet them (Judg. 6:34, 35). "And Gideon sent messengers throughout all the hill country of Ephraim, saying, Come down against the Midianites [Judg. 7:24].

The battle cry was "The sword of Yahweh and of Gideon" (Judg. 7:20).

Several observations are to be made at this point: (1) The call to arms goes out, not from Naphtali, or Zebulun, or Asher, north of the valley, but from the house of Joseph, in which the initiative resides. (2) The Asherites, far away to the northwest, who were condemned by the Deborah poem for noncoöperation, have now significantly become converts to the cause of Israel. (3) The peasants of the Zebulun and Naphtali regions are loyal, as hitherto. (4) There is no mention of Benjamin, which, as we shall see presently, was preoccupied by trouble with the Moabites. (5) There is no reference to any tribe or community of Judah. (6) There is no word about coöperation by the Danites on the southwest, who were also absent from the battle of Esdraelon. (7) There is no recognition of the Reubenites, who are absent as hitherto. (8) The community of Gilead, on the other side of Jordan, is not only absent, as before, but in the outcome is hostile to Gideon. (9) There is no mention of the Issacharites, who were in the other action, but who, lying directly in the path of Midianite invasion, may have been wholly or partly exterminated.

In pursuing the Midianites, Gideon crosses the Jordan and passes through Gilead, where he is refused all aid by the rulers of Succoth and Penuel, chief cities in that region.

And Gideon . . . took the two kings of Midian, Zebah and Zalmunna, and discomfited all the host. . . . And he said unto Zebah and Zalmunna, What manner of men were they whom ye slew at Tabor? And they answered, As thou art, so were they. . . . And he said, They were my brethren, even the sons of my mother. . . . And Gideon arose, and slew Zebah and Zalmunna, and took away the ornaments that were on their camels' necks [Judg. 8:11, 12, 18, 19, 21].

Gideon becomes ruler, marries, 1125 B. C.

In driving away the Midianites, Gideon performed a service not only for his own people but also on behalf of the older, pre-Hebrew element in the land. His military activity protected both races, thus winning for him a prestige which extended beyond Israel and gave him authority in the eyes of the Canaanites. Symptomatic of this rapprochement, is the abrupt information that Gideon had a secondary wife, or "concubine," in the ancient, pre-Hebrew fortified city of Shechem, which had been standing, independent and unconquered, in the very heart of the Ephraimite hills, between Mount Ebal and Mount Gerezim, ever since the Josephites invaded the land at the beginning of the Judges period (Judg. 8:31). The Shechemite woman bore Gideon a son who was given the name Abimelech; and around this man revolves a chain of sanguinary events relating to the government of central Canaan.

Question of political ascendancy leads to destruction of Shechem, 1100 B. C.

As always happens when two or more ethnic elements are associated in the same geographical area, the question soon emerged whether governmental powers were to be controlled by the Shechemite aristocracy or by the elders of the Josephite clans in the hill country surrounding the city. The story is told in the ninth chapter of Judges; and in order to clarify the subject as we go along, it is necessary to observe that this chapter, in sharp contrast with material coming before and after it, refers to the citizens of Shechem by the old, Canaanite term *baal* (pl. *baalim*) sixteen times; whereas, the preceding and following narratives refer to the men of Israel in the open country, not by the term *baal,* but by *ish* ("man"; pl. *anashim*) or *zaken* ("elder"; pl. *zikanim*), or *adon* ("proprietor," "lord"; pl., *adonim*). The use of these other terms by the compilers of the Hebrew text proves their awareness that the word *baal* signified the pre-Hebrew, or Canaanite, master class before it was ever used with reference to the Israelite element which conquered the "enclave" in the central highlands. If this fact is held carefully in mind, it will help us to a better understanding not only of the Ephraimite, or "E," documents in the Bible, but of the later-coming Judaic, or "J," material.

The issue between Shechem and Israel was kept in the background by the personal prestige and influence of Gideon while he lived. "My father fought for you," said Jotham the son of Gideon to the Shechemites, "and adventured his life far, and delivered you out of the hand of Midian" (Judg. 9:17). But after Gideon had passed away the baalistic aristocracy of the city came out into the open. They subsidized the half-breed Abimelech to secure a gang of toughs, who went up into the hills, to the village of Ophrah, where they murdered the sons of Gideon; and thus the country people were terrorized, so that the city reactionaries were able to seize power. "And all the *baalim* of Shechem gathered together . . . and made Abimelech king" (Judg. 9:6). His kingship was not confined to the city; it related also to the Ephraimite hill district, though how extensively cannot be ascertained. The narrative merely states that after Abimelech was made king by the *baalim* of Shechem, he "reigned three years over Israel" (Judg. 9:22).

The story then goes on to say that after this brief period "*Elohim* [God] sent an evil spirit between Abimelech and the *baalim* of Shechem" (Judg. 9:23); whereupon Abimelech went over to the Israelite element, and led them in three regiments to attack the Shechemites.

And Abimelech fought against the city . . . and took the city . . . and slew the people therein, and beat down the city, and sowed it with salt. And when all the *baalim* of the tower of Shechem heard that, they entered into the hold of the house of the god Berith. And it was told Abimelech that all the *baalim* of the tower of Shechem were gathered together. And Abimelech . . . set the hold on fire upon them; *so that all the men of the tower of Shechem died also,—about a thousand men and women* [Judg. 9:45–49].

Shechemite catastrophe has economic basis

The destruction of this Canaanite city, as described in the foregoing narrative, appears to be unintelligible. It stands isolated in the book of Judges, without explanation by the writers of the narrative; and it has never been set in its true perspective by Jewish or Gentile interpreters of Hebrew history. But if it is checked against corresponding material in Genesis, the incident falls logically into place in the long evolutionary process which is here under survey.

We have already considered the Josephite need for more territory, as expressed in aspirations looking toward the great valley of Esdraelon; and in view of this tendency northward, it is clear that Shechem constituted a bar to what the house of Joseph considered its natural and rightful expansion. The *baalim*, like the aristocracies of other walled cities in ancient times, owned land outside the walls of Shechem and exploited the labor of slaves (*abadim*). Shechem was a fairly large place, whose inhabitants consisted not only of "the people" killed in the streets but also of "about a thousand men and women,"—the *baalim* and their wives, who had crowded into the stronghold, and who died "also," that is, in addition to the indiscriminate multitude which perished. A foreign city of such wealth, with extensive lands lying open and undefended in the country districts round about, could not fail to excite the avarice of surrounding hill clans whose numbers were multiplying rapidly.

But the immediate difficulty was that the Shechemites and the house of Joseph had been long settled side by side in peace. And if the land belonging to the city aristocracy might not be taken by force, the Israelites could possibly buy at least part of it from "the men of Hamor the father of Shechem" (Judg. 9:28). Here are found the conditions for a legend about Jacob's acquisition of the land, not "with sword and bow" (as in Gen. 48:22), but as a man of peace who buys land in a legal way: "And Jacob . . . bought a parcel of a field, where he had spread his tent, at the hand of the children of Hamor, Shechem's father" (Gen. 33:18–19). Whereupon, Hamor, the leading *baal* of the city, conceived the idea that Jacob and his sons would not only be a welcome addition to the labor force of the community, but good customers in the local real estate market. So the Shechemite chief, or mayor, said to the family of Jacob, "Make ye marriages with us; give your daughters unto us, and take our daughters unto you. And ye shall dwell with us; and the land shall be before you. Dwell and trade ye therein, and get you possessions therein." After which, Hamor and Shechem his son had a private and more subtle interview with the *baalim* of the city, saying, "These men are peaceable with us. Therefore let them dwell in the land, and trade therein; for the land, behold, it is large enough for them. . . . Shall not their cattle and their substance and every beast of their's be our's?" (Gen. 34, *passim*).

That the object of the Shechemite *baalim* was to reduce the neighboring Manassite hill clans to servitude is made clear by their massacre of Gideon's family, which put the city aristocracy in control of the taxing power and the courts—those two essential functions of government, the monopoly of which enabled all ancient cities to exploit the outlying populations, as in Babylonia, Assyria, Egypt, Greece, and Italy. The hostility of Shechem to the house of Gideon revolved around the question of government and shows how the political pattern of the community tended to follow the motivation of economic forces.

Shechemite story in Genesis confused

The form of the Shechem story in Genesis has obvious connection with the corresponding story in Judges; but its literary disposition differs from that of other legends in Genesis to such an extent that modern investigation long ago recognized it as a detached, isolated fragment which has been worked into hopeless inconsistency by a post-exilic redactor. In order to follow the pattern of the secular history in Judges, the Genesis tale about Shechem would have to revolve around an individual patriarch named Manasseh. But according to the orthodox legendary structure no such person has been born at the time contemplated by the Shechem story in Genesis; hence the figure of Manasseh was not available. The original outline of the story is evident in the background: "the sons of Jacob" are urged to make marriages with the women of Shechem (Gen. 34:9, 10); and "the sons of Jacob" spoil the city (Gen. 34:27). But within this general framework the editor has clumsily interpolated fantastic material regarding "two of the sons of Jacob, Simeon and Levi," who, as individuals, attacked the city "and slew all the males" (Gen. 34:25, *et passim*); after this the narrative reverts to "the sons of Jacob," collectively, who carry away the movable property and all the women and children, thus completing the devastation of the city. Whereupon Jacob complains to Simeon and Levi (but not to the "sons" as a whole), "Ye have troubled me, to bring me into bad odor among the inhabitants of the land, among the Canaanites and the Perizzites" (Gen. 34:30).

Climax of Josephite conquest of central highlands

The destruction of Shechem brings out into bold relief the downfall of the Canaanite baalistic regime in the central hill country. The smaller walled city, Bethel, as we have seen, had been reduced long ago by the Josephites, who "smote the city with the edge of the sword" (Judg. 1:22-25). And at about the same time, far down in the Jordan valley, Jericho and its *baalim* had been wiped out, as recorded by the Ephraimite, or "E," source, which attributes to Joshua the following words: "Ye went over Jordan, and came unto Jericho; and the *baalim* of Jericho fought against you . . . and I delivered them into your hand" (Josh. 24:11). The Ephraimite document uses the term *baal* for the master class at this point, as in most other cases; while the Judaic document, avoiding this term and using "ish" (man), gives the well-known, miraculous, fantastic version of Jericho's destruction, according to which the inhabitants remained within their walls and made no fight whatever, since "Jericho was straitly shut up, because of the children of Israel: none went out and none came in" (Josh. 6:1). This account assumes the existence of twelve tribes (Josh. 4:2) and is discredited by the E version, which adheres more closely to the secular conception of history.

The historical movement begun by the overthrow of Jericho and Bethel came to a logical climax in the fall of Shechem, far along in the Judges period. The destruction of this important central city not only gave Israel extensive landed areas, much needed by the rapidly multiplying hill clans, but also a vast amount of movable property:

The sons of Jacob came upon the slain, and spoiled the city. . . . They took their sheep, and their oxen, and their asses, and that which was in the city, and that which was in the field; and all their wealth, and all their little ones, and their wives took they captive [Gen. 34:27-29].

The catastrophe at Shechem, in fact, rounded out the Josephite conquest of the central highlands, which were now entirely free from the rule of walled cities, whose aristocracy regarded the soil as rightfully alienable. This part of Canaan had, in fact, become consolidated as the "inheritance" of Yahweh and of pastoral and agricultural clans averse to holding land as an item of commerce which might legally be sold or exchanged like movable property.

Israel "in bad odor among the inhabitants of the land"

Having gained favor in the eyes of the older, non-Hebrew population by settling down peacefully for a long period; having become natives of the country, instead of being mere foreign intruders, and finally, having won prestige through Gideon's exploit in defending alike the newer and older population against Midian, the house of Joseph now lost its painfully acquired position of esteem and found itself in "bad odor among the inhabitants of the land," as clearly expressed by the words attributed to Jacob. In a way, the destruction of Shechem, as viewed by the still unconquered Canaanite cities outside the Josephite enclave, was even worse than the fall of Jericho and Bethel. For these earlier catastrophes were such as might occur in any campaign of outright and open war. But in the case of Shechem there had been a state marriage between Gideon and a woman of the city, based upon a condition of peace by agreement, which in the prejudiced opinion of other Canaanite cities had been broken through the fault of Israel. These other cities, numbering nearly twenty, will come into view as the history unfolds.

Other incidents in period of Judges

Meanwhile, this period of Hebrew beginnings was marked by several incidents which, although local in their immediate bearing, had significance for the epoch as a whole.

The first involved an attack upon the Benjaminites (the people of the "south") by a pastoral nation, the Moabites, who lived east of the Dead Sea. The aggressors were defeated by the energy of a Benjaminite chief, Ehud, who rallied the militia of southern Ephraim. Hostilities required the use of territory pertaining to the Reubenites, who, it will be recalled, were blamed for noncoöperation in the Deborah battle. But in this case there is no mention of Reubenites whatever; which leads to the conjecture that they had now passed out of existence as a group, owing perhaps to the enmity of the Moabites, who could not have attacked Benjamin without assailing Reuben. These considerations place the clash with Moab after the battle of Esdraelon instead of before, as now indicated by the book of Judges (Judg. 4).

Another incident in this period was an attack upon Gilead, east of Jordan, by a tribe called Ammonites, whose territory lay farther toward the desert, eastward. The Ammonites were defeated in battle by a Gileadite chief, Jephthah. The people of Gilead had not coöperated in the battle of Esdraelon and were even yet hostile to the house of Joseph, which lay far away in the hills, west of Jordan (Judg. 11–12).

Still another community, related in some way to Israel, which, as already observed, had been among the "noncoöperators," was the Danites. This group, southwest of the Ephraimite hills, lay wedged between the house of Joseph and a militant power on the sea coast— the Philistines. The presence of the Danites in this region was a drawback to Philistine designs against the house of Joseph; and the folk tales about Samson, as a strong man of the tribe, may have some historical significance.[2]

Micah the Ephraimite and his "house of gods"

An interesting story in the seventeenth of Judges tells how a man of Ephraim, whose name was Micah, had a "house of gods" used by

[2] The statement that "three thousand men of Judah" betrayed Samson to the Philistines (Judg. 15:11) is part of a later folk tale and carries no implication that a tribe of Judah existed in Samson's time. The story means, at the most, only that men of the region later known as "Judah" gave up the Danite hero. And this agrees with the evidence that no sympathy or coöperation existed between the inhabitants to the south of Jebus and the clans of Ephraim. Samson was an Ephraimite, not a Judaic, hero. Moreover, as Professor Thatcher of Oxford observes, "the number of men thought necessary for his capture is evidently intended to enhance his reputation" (*Commentary on Judges*, London and New York, Oxford University Press, p. 132).

the people of his neighborhood as a temple, or church. In this building Micah placed a "graven image" and a "molten image," both of which were made of silver, dedicated to Yahweh. The temple also contained an *ephod*, or plated image made from gold, such as Gideon had made from the jewelry of the Midianites (Judg. 8:26–27). The ephod-idol was used for casting lots in order to learn the attitude of the divinity toward a given course of action. The equipment of Micah's temple included wooden images called *teraphim*, representing household, or family, gods. These idols were similar to the ones which Rachel is said to have stolen from her father (Gen. 31:19f.). That they were in the form of human beings is revealed by an instructive passage relating to the house of David (I Sam. 19:11f.). These references prove that Micah's temple, instead of being peculiar, was in accordance with current religious customs. He consecrated one of his sons to be priest (*kohen*); but this, again, was not unusual, for the sons of King David were priests, or *kohanim* (II Sam. 8:18); and there was originally no priestly class in Israel whatever.

One of the functions of the *kohen* was to cast lots (called *urim* and *thummim*) before an image in order to find out the attitude of *elohim* (divinity) with reference to any question or proposed undertaking, just as superstitious people toss a coin. The priestly function in Israel eventually began to be specialized in a class called Levites; but whether such persons had any relation to a tribe called Levi, or whether any such tribe or clan really existed as an organized entity, cannot now be ascertained.

At this point in the story another interesting fact emerges. A certain Levite applied to Micah, the man of Ephraim, seeking the priestly office already held by the son of Micah; and he secured the position on account of prestige already associated with Levites in contrast with ordinary laymen who became priests. The matter is illustrated by Micah's remark in the verse which concludes the story: "Then said Micah, Now know I that Yahweh will do me good, seeing that I have a Levite to be my priest" (Judg. 17:13).

Another instructive item of the Micah story is the emergence for the first time of a village called "Bethelehem of Judah," which is given as the home of the Levite. It is true that three thousand "men of Judah" are said to have delivered Samson to the Philistines (Judg. 15:10f.); but the fantastic Samson tales are by a very late writer, who speaks only of men from the region which in that writer's day had become known as Judah. The presence of population in the territory south of Jerusalem throughout the Judges epoch is not denied, but only that an Israelite tribe named Judah existed in that early period.

Now, however, the situation begins to take on a different aspect. Bethlehem is a concrete reality which has an important place in the literature and history of Israel. Here, as we shall see later, are the little beginnings of the kingdom and tribe of Judah, which was eventually recognized as integral to the Hebrew nation. How this part of Israel came into existence will be suggested further along in our study.

Danites migrate across Ephraim

The story of Micah is a kind of prelude to another story about the migration of the Danites from their earlier home southwest of the central highlands. They had been wedged between the Philistines on one side and the house of Joseph on the other, and finding that the resources of their locality were insufficient for the needs of an increasing population, they decided to leave in a body. So the people of Dan, to the number of six hundred armed men, with families and cattle, set out northward across the hill country of Ephraim. Stopping at Micah's "house of *elohim*," they robbed him of his "*ephod*, and *teraphim*, and graven image, and molten image," and also kidnaped his Levite priest; whereupon they continued their march, while Micah and his family stared, helpless and astonished. The strong-arm methods of the Danites may have been the background on which developed the tales of Samson the strong man.

Pressing onward, the emigrants marched north until they finally reached a city called Laish, about one hundred miles distant from the point where they started. The people of Laish were massacred, and the city was destroyed by fire. Then the Danites built a new city in place of the old one and called it Dan. "Howbeit, the name of the city was Laish at the first" (Judg. 18:29). Here they established a new temple, equipped with the material stolen from Micah the Ephraimite. The story concludes with a statement which has been very embarrassing to orthodox Christians and Jews for many centuries: "And Jonathan, the son of Gershom, the son of Moses, he and his sons were priests to the tribe of Dan until the day of the captivity of the land" (Judg. 18:30).

The spelling M-o-s-e-s in translated Bibles is a Greek form. In the Hebrew text the name is always Moseh, or Mosheh—the consonants being M-s-h. But since the general drift of the foregoing narrative is contrary to the orthodox view of what Hebrew history in the land of Canaan should have been, a very daring thing was done by some late, post-exilic Jewish editor, whose theology was outraged by the actions of the Levite. Such a priest, he thought, could not have descended from the orthodox, post-exilic, magnified figure which in later times came to be reputed as the author of the Torah, or Pentateuch. Accordingly the affronted scribe undertook to insert the letter n between the M and the s—making it read M-n-s-h, or Manasseh. But being unable to place the n on the same line with the rest of the name, he crowded it part way in and left it suspended above the line, like this: M-^{n}s-h. In other words, he did not venture to erase, but only to deface, the name so as to make it something less objectionable than Moseh. The general text of the narrative had already become a part of tradition and could not be altered too violently.

The King James, orthodox, English Bible renders the name incorrectly as Manasseh without the slightest explanation to the reader who does not know the Hebrew text. On the other hand, the American and English revised versions translate correctly "Moses." Still another way of handling the embarrassment is taken by the Jewish English Bible, issued by the Jewish Publication Society of America at Philadelphia (1917, p. 318): The name Manasseh appears in the main text, but its force is neutralized by a footnote which says, "M-n-s-h, with *n* suspended, indicating an earlier reading Moses." This is what might be called "oblique honesty."

Another instructive point relates to the name of the city which was destroyed and then rebuilt by the Danites: they called it Dan; but originally, the text says, it was Laish. If we now turn to Gen. 14:14, the following passage will be found significant: "And when Abram heard that his brother was taken captive, he armed his trained servants, born in his own house, three hundred and eighteen, and pursued unto Dan." But, as we have seen, the city was not called by that name until well into the Judges period, long after the Israelites had settled in Canaan. Hence, the Abram passage, quoted from Genesis, comes to us through a writer who knew of the city by its later name, not by the name which it bore during the earlier period.

Another important fact, bearing upon the literary chronology of the Bible, is the statement that the family of Jonathan the Levite were priests to the tribe of Dan "until the day of the captivity of the land." The captivity referred to is that in which the "ten tribes of Ephraim" were carried away by the Assyrians and lost forever—about 721 B. C. Hence, this passage in the book of Judges comes to us through a writer who lived after the Assyrian destruction of the Ephraimite kingdom, that is to say, from three to four centuries later than the time of Micah the Ephraimite.

Story of another Levite

The book of Judges concludes with a somber story about another Levite. This tale comes to us through the hands of a very late editor, who looks back at the early period from the standpoint of his own time, when the current theory was that early Israel consisted of twelve tribes which composed a united nation. The Levite of the second story lives in the highlands of Ephraim, but obtains a concubine, or subordinate wife, in the village of Bethlehem-judah, which thus again momentarily emerges into view, as in the other tale. Setting out on the return journey to Ephraim late in the day, with his concubine and also a man slave, the Levite passes along by the walls of the still unconquered Canaanite city of Jebus (Jerusalem). And although the day was far spent, he said, "We will not turn aside hither into the city of a foreigner, that is not of the children of Israel; we will pass over to Gibeah" (Judg. 19:12).

Going on, then, through the gathering darkness, they arrived in "Gibeah of Benjamin" as the sun was going down. Entering the city, they met an old man of Ephraim, who had migrated into Benjamin and was now established as a householder in Gibeah. This man invited them into his home, and they gladly accepted his offer. But as they were preparing to retire for the night, the men (*anashim*) of the city beset the house roundabout, and beat upon the door, and called to the man (*ish*), the master (*baal*) of the house, demanding, "Bring forth the man that came into thine house, that we may know him" (Judg. 19:22). The predicament of the householder was the same as that of Lot in the city of Sodom, when he took strangers into his home for the night:

And . . . the men (*anashim*) of that city, even the men (*anashim*) of Sodom, compassed the house round. . . . And they called unto Lot, and said unto him, Where are the men which came unto thee this night? Bring them out unto us, that we may know them [Gen. 19:4–5].

What the men of Sodom were proposing was to commit the unnatural crime which is called, from the name of their city, "sodomy." Incidentally, the narrative in Genesis comes from the "Judaic" document of the Pentateuch, J, which calls the citizens of Sodom by the term "men" (*anashim*), while the narrative about Gibeah of Benjamin uses not only *anashim*, but also *baalim*, with reference to the men of that place, because Benjamin, the only uterine brother of Joseph, was reckoned with Ephraim and was, in fact, as we have seen, the southern extension of Joseph. This remarkable distinction between J and E material will emerge more clearly, and will be explained more fully as we go along.

But meanwhile, then, it is evident that what the men of Sodom proposed in the case of Lot's visitors was what the *baalim* of Gibeah proposed in the case of the old man's guests. The progress of the story illustrates further what we in our day should regard as the very peculiar ethics of an already tangled moral situation: the master of the house in Gibeah sought to dissuade his fellow *baalim* from their nefarious design by offering them the use of his own daughter and also the concubine belonging to the Levite. Here again there is a marked resemblance between the stories about Gibeah and Sodom; for Lot also tries to dissuade the men of Sodom, saying, "I pray you, brethren, do not so wickedly. Behold now, I have two daughters which have not known man. Let me, I pray you, bring them out unto you; and do ye to them as is good in your eyes" (Gen. 19:7–8). In the Gibeah case the Levite settled the matter by surrendering his feminine property: "So the man took his concubine, and brought her forth unto them; and they knew her, and abused her all the night until the morning; and when the day began to spring, they let her go" (Judg. 19:23–25).

The woman then went and fell at the door of the house "where her lord (*adon*) was" and lay there till it was light. But by that time she was dead. And her lord rose up and found her at the door, with her hands outstretched upon the threshold. And he said, "Up, and let us be going." Not until then did he find that the unfortunate creature had expired; after which he took her body and loaded it upon his beast of burden and set out for Ephraim. The description of what followed when the man reached his home proves that the narrative was written at a time far distant from the Judges period. For the Levite is alleged to have taken a knife and cut the body of his concubine into twelve pieces, according to the number of the tribes of Israel; whereupon he sent out the fragments over the hill country.

That the material is being exploited for ulterior purposes by a late writer, or several writers, becomes increasingly evident as the narrative proceeds. It may be based ultimately upon some obscure incident relating to village toughs; but the story grows more and more fantastic and impossible. The fragments of the woman's body are said to have impelled the Israelites "from Dan to Beersheba" to assemble "as one man" at a place called Mizpeh, where there was an altar of Yahweh (Judg. 20, *passim*). Here, it is alleged, an army was mobilized consisting of four hundred thousand men out of all

Israel except Benjamin; whereas the Benjaminites are alleged to have had an army of twenty-six thousand, seven hundred. At this point the Israelites "asked counsel of God, saying, Which of us shall go up first to the battle against the children of Benjamin? And Yahweh said, Judah shall go up first." Thereupon the huge army of Israel fights the comparatively small army of Benjamin in two battles on two successive days and is defeated each time by the latter, which kills altogether forty thousand men of Israel. But on the third day the tide of battle turns in favor of the Israelites, who slay twenty-five thousand Benjaminites and set the city of Gibeah on fire; "and when the flame began to ascend out of the city, the Benjaminites looked behind them, and behold, the flame of the city ascended up to heaven."

In this absurd and fantastic enlargement upon what may have been a real occurrence the purposes of the late Jewish compilers and editors are quite clear: Gibeah of Benjamin was the home of Saul, the first king of Ephraim. There was violent antagonism between Saul and the Judean King David, as well as between Judah and Ephraim. This hatred, as we have seen, gave the historical pattern for hostility between Leah, the mother of Judah, and Rachel, the Ephraimite mother. The Jewish writers, by exploiting the outrage at Gibeah, were able to do two things: (1) to blacken the tribe of Saul by painting it in the darkest colors, and (2) to atone for the absence of Judah from the Judges epoch by imaginatively putting Judah ahead of all Israel in the war against the Benjaminites—"And Yahweh said, Judah shall go up first." The Benjaminites in the Judges tale are castigated and their city is burned by their fellow Israelites; but in the tale of Sodom the Jewish theological editors go further and put the matter completely into the hand of Yahweh, who rains fire and brimstone out of heaven upon the offending city (J source, Gen. 19).

"Judges" Ephraimite, with Jewish redaction

The fundamental matter in Judges consists of hero tales about Barak, Deborah, Gideon, Ehud, Samson, Jephthah, and others, whose exploits are entirely outside and north of the territory which later became identified with the tribe of Judah. The "judges" themselves are local heroes, not rulers over a united Israel of twelve tribes, or even over the Joseph-Ephraim clans. The stories about them were collected into a roll, or "book," by a writer-compiler belonging to what is called the Deuteronomic school, of which more in due time. This writer, to whom we owe a tremendous debt of gratitude, produced the original book of Judges, which begins at the sixth verse of chapter two of our present book and continues to and through chapter sixteen.

The Deuteronomic writer, living at a late period, long after the establishment of the Hebrew Monarchy, could not imagine that the people called "Israel" had been anything less than a united nation from the very beginning of Hebrew history in Canaan. Consequently he took the local hero tales and strung them together—one after the other—in a framework of his own personal comments based on the assumption that "all Israel" periodically forsook the worship of Yahweh and served the Baalim, or gods of Canaan; for which cause Yahweh brought foreign invaders into the land as a punishment; whereupon the people as a whole repented, and Yahweh raised up a "judge" who "saved" all Israel by expelling the alien aggressor.

But the hero-material enclosed within the framework of editorial comments does not bear out the compiler's interpretation of the early history. There is no united people of Israel anywhere in view. There is no evidence of periodical defection from the worship of Yahweh. There is no indication that foreign foes enslaved or oppressed "all" Israel at any time in the Judges epoch. On the contrary, the stories prove that there were highly independent clans, isolated from each other for the most part. They show that the "Josephites," at least, regarded Yahweh as their deity right along; the defections to Baalism being imputed to early Israel in view of conditions at a later period in the time of Amos and Hosea, when the original Josephite "core" had coalesced with Canaanite elements. While the stories do not show any general enslavement of Israel, they undoubtedly point to local invasions of the land, here and there, which were defeated by the local chiefs.

Being a Judaic writer, the Deuteronomist naturally wanted to find some hero from Judah in the south of Canaan, whose adventures, like those of Gideon, could be placed within the framework of editorial comments in the early history. But no Judaic hero could be found, because no tribe of Judah existed at that time. So the writer tried to invent a "judge" by the name of "Othniel ben Kenaz," without noticing that the family of Kenaz were descended, not from Jacob, but from Esau, and hence was, not Judaic, but Edomite (Gen. 36:11, 15, 42). Since there was no actual story with interesting details and local touches concerning Othniel, his name appears only as a part of the editorial framework of comments as a mere abstraction.

After the original "Deuteronomic" book of Judges had been thus created (that is, Judg. 2:6–Judg. 16, inclusive), another Judaic writer took charge of it, using some authentic old material, which was pieced out, as we shall see, by his imagination. This enterprising scribe added an "Appendix" containing the stories about Micah, the Danites, and the outrage at Gibeah of Benjamin (Judg. 17–21). Those chapters obviously stand outside the Deuteronomic structure which composes the original book of Judges. The same observation applies to material which was added as a prologue, or introduction, and which now appears as chapter one plus the first five verses of chapter two. The Judaic atmosphere of this preface, or introduction, is just as unmistakable as that of the appendix: the children of Israel ask Yahweh who shall go up against the Canaanites, to fight against them; and Yahweh answers "Judah shall go up!" (Judg. 1:1–2). The question and answer are precisely the same as those in the appendix to Judges, where Israel asks Yahweh who shall go up first against the Benjaminites, and is told that Judah shall go up (Judg. 20:18). The only difference is that in chapter one it is the Canaanites who are the object of attack: the tribe of Judah goes into action, slays ten thousand Canaanites, takes Jerusalem, smites it with the edge of the sword, and sets it afire (Judg. 1:4, 8); whereas, in reality, the city was not conquered or burned, but continued to be inhabited by the Jebusites throughout the Judges period and into the reign of David. The Jewish introduction, or preface, to Judges not only tries to exalt and magnify Judah but also seeks to belittle the Josephites by telling how "the house of Joseph, they also went up" and merely took the central highlands, while failing to take some twenty walled cities of Canaan which lay beyond the hill country of Ephraim (Judg. 1:22–33). The Josephites, in truth, did not conquer these twenty cities; the fact is that the house of Joseph never undertook to reduce them—with the exception of Shechem; which makes the Judaic editor's comparison wholly gratuitous and beside the point. He therefore shows unmistakable bias against the objective truth of history by seeking prestige for Judah in a wholly fictitious and imaginary destruction of Jerusalem as contrasted with the solid, though limited, achievement of the Josephites in taking the central hill country and maintaining the power of Israel in that region while the Hebrew people were slowly preparing to go forward into another stage of their evolution.

Conspectus of Judges period

Looking back over the earliest age of Hebrew history in Canaan, the epoch at first appears to be a time of confusion, without any pattern of events holding the promise of consistency or design. But when the situation as a whole is examined closely, certain definite facts begin to stand out; while an underlying logic thrusts itself more and more into attention. No actual movement of nationalism has taken form yet; but the growth of the house of Joseph reveals an urge in that direction. The extraordinary battle of Esdraelon brings into view a limited coöperative tendency under Josephite, or Ephraimite, leadership; yet the circumstances of the time have not thus far thrown up onto the surface of history any outstanding individual as the steadfast center around which the energies of nationalism can find expression.

During all this period a large number of "pre-Hebrew" fortified cities outside the Josephite "enclave" continue to be independent centers of old Canaanite baalistic aristocracy and the Baal cults—that is, Jebus (Jerusalem) to the south of the Josephites; the Gibeonite confederacy on the west; Megiddo, Beth-shan, Taanach, and other places in or near the valley of Esdraelon; Acco, Zidon, Rehob, and similar cities farther north (Judg. 1:27–35). The existence of these urban strongholds throughout the Judges epoch must be carefully borne in mind as we go along, not merely because they were a part of the total situation in Canaan, but because they were destined to have a profound effect upon the later course of Hebrew history. Each of them had suburban villages—for instance, "Taanach and her towns" (Judg. 1:27). These old Canaanite centers of population, as a matter of fact, controlled more territory during the Judges epoch than did the house of Joseph.

Israel and Yahweh growing in power

But in spite of their apparent superiority, the Canaanites were declining in strength. The destruction of their army in the great battle, when "the stars in their courses fought against Sisera," was a frightful blow from which there was no recovery; for the Canaanite cities never again mobilized in opposition to the rising might of Ephraim. The unforgettable portent of sudden storm, which flooded the valley, engulfing chariots, horses, and infantry, became a tradition which built up the prestige of Israel and Yahweh in the evolving political and religious ideology of Canaan. Contributory to the same psychological structure was Gideon's defeat of the Midianites: "The sword of Yahweh and of Gideon." The effect of these victories was further enhanced by the fall of Shechem, which in the blurred retrospect of popular imagination counted as an outstanding achievement of the Ephraimites and their deity. The northern adventure of the Danites, involving the destruction of Laish, the rebuilding of that city under the new name Dan, and the instituting of a new shrine to Yahweh—this exploit was another substantial item in the growing sense of Israel as a people of Canaan and of Yahweh as "god of the land." Hebrew influence was expanding in the great valley of Esdraelon and the hills north of it, where no resistance was forthcoming to the passage of the Danite warriors and their families.

Crystallization of rural aristocracy

Another aspect of the political and religious process during the Judges epoch was the consolidation and wider extension of a landed rural aristocracy. Factors in this development were the extensive lands and cattle of the destroyed Shechemite *baalim*, taken over by the Josephites, and the lands confiscated by the Danites from the slaughtered *baalim* of Laish. At the same time, outside the Ephraimite hills, the peasantry, in bondage to the Canaanite baal class, but liberated, like the Issacharites, by the rising power of Ephraim, would naturally accept the cult of Yahweh, thus becoming Israelite. Social transformations like this have occurred, in one form or another, during the evolution of all peoples. Thus, the Greek conquest of the prehistoric Aegean civilization did not exterminate completely the earlier elements. The incoming Greeks gradually imposed their language and gods on the resulting social mass which arose by intermarriage and coalescence. Such changes go forward silently in the hidden depths, unstressed by the records of history; and such a process was initiated in the land of Canaan during the Judges period.

The Hebrew peasantry which thus began to evolve in the rural districts of Canaan arose, of course, in the house of Joseph, and slowly became generalized throughout the country. Its ruling economic principle was that the land should not be made an article of commerce, but should of right continue forever under the control of any rural family which by any means found itself in possession. The title to a given piece of soil might rest on conquest, or on purchase from aliens, or on the intermarriage of Israelite and non-Hebrew elements, or on the mere association with Israel of liberated

Canaanite peasantry, such as the Issacharites, who became worshipers of Yahweh. The development of "Israel" in Canaan was more complex than appears on the surface of history.

The essential fact is that whatever may have been the circumstances entering into the rise of any given family, the inalienable relation of such a group to the soil was described in Hebrew as *mishpat*—comprehending the idea of "right" or "justice," the divine symbol of this ethical order being Yahweh. Thus, for example, we find in the valley of Esdraelon the peasant Naboth, already mentioned, whose racial, tribal, and family history is unknown to us and who may even have been ultimately of Canaanite origin. But he was a worshiper of Yahweh; and when asked to sell his land, refused vehemently in the name of Yahweh (I Kings, 21: 1–3). Unless we fix firmly in mind the gradual evolution of such a rural aristocracy, we shall be unable to envisage or understand Bible history. The social class which thus emerges into view is the root of Hebrew ethical and religious development; and the establishment of this class in Canaan was nothing less than a revolution.

———

The article in the Appendix, under the heading "Land and Mishpat," should be examined in this connection and referred to frequently.

V. NATIONALISM AND MONARCHY

LEAVING BEHIND US the difficult early period represented by the book of Judges, we pass into the age of Hebrew nationalism. The history continues to revolve amid familiar scenes in the hill country of Ephraim—the proper territory of the "house of Joseph." The beginnings of Hebrew nationality and the core of the future Israel are to be found in this region—the central highlands of Canaan, the Josephite enclave. It was here that the Israelite consciousness originated and took characteristic form, as distinct from the Jewish consciousness, which is a later fact of history.

The main sources for the new period consist of documents very unequal in fact value, combined so as to make the book, or books, of Samuel. The materials with which this writing begins are fundamentally Ephraimite, as in the case of Judges. Here again Judaic editors, while performing the invaluable service of compilation, have interjected observations and whole passages which are later than the basic Ephraimite sources and are intended to mold and manipulate the history and influence opinion in the interest of Judah.

New era of Hebrew history

On the coast of the Mediterranean sea, southwest of Ephraim, the Philistines lay athwart the trade routes between Egypt, Asia Minor, and the Tigro-Euphrates basin. From the Philistine standpoint the migration of the Danites into the north was an alarming portent, for it suggested the rise of a strong Hebrew power, based not only upon the highlands of Ephraim but also upon the hills of Galilee north of the valley of Esdraelon. Such a power, if once organized, could easily dominate the trade routes and become the strongest factor in policing and laying toll upon the rich commerce that flowed through Canaan. This danger had not been threatening while the house of Joseph lay divided in the hill country as independent clans engaged in shepherding and agriculture. But a hint of coming peril was given by the Josephite coalition at the Deborah battle in the great valley, when the Galilean peasantry of Naphtali and Zebulun answered the call of Deborah, while fresh hazard loomed when additional recruits came down from Asher in the north to coöperate with Gideon against the Midianites. Now the tribe of Dan had left its old home where it could be held in restraint by the Philistines and had augmented the forces in Galilee by which the power of Ephraim was extending northward.

Before going further into the relation between Philistine and Hebrew history, several topics must be considered.

Shiloh temple appears abruptly in history

At the very beginning of Samuel we are abruptly confronted by a temple at a village called Shiloh in the hill country of Ephraim, an outstanding sanctuary for annual pilgrimage and sacrifice to Yahweh. No such institution appears in the book of Judges, where sacrifice takes place at several shrines, one of which, belonging to Micah the Ephraimite, was robbed of its ecclesiastical equipment and its priest by the Danites en route to the north, where they set up a new temple as a center for worship in that region. The temple at Shiloh was evidently not intended as the only, or exclusive, place of worship. Yet when it looms up suddenly in the new era of nationalism it has already acquired some special prestige, just as a given shrine to the Virgin Mary obtains unusual prominence for some special reason. The Shiloh temple, appearing in connection with the rise of Hebrew nationalism, was the religious phase of the secular movement leading toward consolidation and monarchy. It is not mentioned in the Genesis legends of the patriarchs; and the modern archaeological excavations on the site reveal no remains of an earlier Canaanite shrine. Shiloh, in fact, was not complicated with any local, narrow allegiances or loyalties, and hence it was fitted to be a center where the gathering force of Ephraimite nationalism could find expression.[1]

Yahweh the deity of early Israel

Aside from libelous claims made by Judaic (Deuteronomic) redactors of Judges, there is no evidence that in the restricted enclave-area of the central highlands the early house of Joseph worshiped the Baal-gods of Canaan. At a later time these local cults complicated the religious life of Israel, when the framework of Hebrew monarchy had been extended to include the twenty or more Canaanite walled cities which lay beyond the original frontiers of Ephraim. With reference to this very important point, many modern scholars who have done good work in promoting the application of critical methods to the Hebrew Bible have joined the Judaic redactors in charging Baal worship to the account of an imaginary "Israel" from the very beginning of the Judges epoch. The alleged ground of this imputation is that from the very start "Israel" fell under the seductive sway of Canaanite Baalism because the local, native deities were gods of good crops and of sexual fertility. That a syncretized Yahweh-Baal cultus actually became a feature of the Hebrew scene at a later time, in the days of Hosea, is indeed one of the outstanding facts of Bible history. But there is no more warrant for projecting the Canaanite cults into the Josephite enclave during the Judges epoch than there is for throwing back into the same period the conception of a twelve-tribe united Israel or the completed priestly system of the Pentateuch. The Judaic redactors distorted the history of Ephraim with respect to Baalism for two reasons: (1) to teach

---

[1] It is a curious fact that the patriarchal narratives have no mention of Shiloh, the one great Israelite sanctuary of which we can say with certainty that it had no Canaanite predecessor. The excavations at Shiloh show no trace of a pre-Israelite sanctuary. Pottery remains suggest that Israelites were the first to occupy the site, that the main period of their residence came to an end in the eleventh century, and that it ceased altogether about 900 B.C. See T. H. Robinson, *History of Israel*, (London and New York, Oxford University Press, 1932), I, 52, 159, 161, in footnotes.

their Jewish contemporaries a lesson with regard to their own Baalistic idolatry practiced in Judah and Jerusalem, and (2) for the
purpose of defaming the hated Ephraimites from the very first, in
the same spirit which exploited the scandal at Gibeah in order to
blacken the character of the Benjaminites, who belonged to the
house of Joseph and hence to Ephraim.

Contrast between redaction of Judges and of First Samuel

The books of Judges and First Samuel reveal an editorial contrast
which has escaped notice in its bearing on the history and religion
of Israel. The Deuteronomist who compiled Judges lays down the
principle that the various oppressions of Israel by foreign conquerors during that period were in reality punishments by Yahweh
for the sin of Baal-worship (Judg. 2:6–19). The body of that book
is therefore a manipulation of history into a generalized pattern of
successive cycles which are assumed to illustrate the Deuteronomic
thesis that oppression of Israel is evidence and proof of apostasy
from Yahweh to Baal.

But when the work of redaction moves on to the sources dealing
with the times of Samuel and Saul, the cyclical framework method
vanishes abruptly. The Philistines defeat Saul and reduce the Josephites to slavery—a catastrophe which according to the Deuteronomic philosophy is proof positive that Israel had been worshiping
Baal and that Yahweh was now inflicting punishment for apostasy.
But as a matter of fact the compiler of First Samuel makes no such
claim, because he is operating under the stress of a new historical
pragmatism: he is magnifying the southern hero David, who must
by all means be represented as the legitimate successor of a Yahweh-
loyal Saul who, in turn, had ruled over a Yahweh-loyal nation. It
would not do to have David follow a king who had been any less
than "the Anointed of Yahweh." Hence the redactor departs insensibly from the philosophy upon which his theological school
constructed the book of Judges. Hence, for the first time the sources
relating to the Judges period are allowed to stand in the foreground,
exhibiting the Ephraimite highlanders in the premonarchic era as a

community of clans whose ritual devotion comes to a center upon the temple at Shiloh, where the fruits of the ground are offered to Yahweh as the deity who gives them (I Sam. 1:1f.).

This glaring redactional difference between Judges and Samuel has not been sufficiently considered in its bearing upon the general subject of Bible history. Since the cyclical framework appears only in Judges, while its disappearance coincides with the sudden flashing into view of a Yahweh-loyal Ephraim (not a twelve-tribe "Israel"), the Deuteronomic picture of the Judges period falls to the ground. The books of Judges and Samuel, in fact, were produced independently, by writers whose purposes were not the same. The former work projects into the distant past the views of the prophet Hosea, who lived in the middle of the eighth century B. C.

Yahweh the deity of early Ephraim

During the early period, Yahweh, therefore, was the deity of that "little Israel" which had been slowly consolidating in the hill country of Ephraim. During the long struggle for possession of the highlands the house of Joseph had exterminated the *baalim* of Jericho, Bethel, and Shechem. The annihilation of the Canaanite ruling classes in this particular area necessarily carried with it the downfall of local Baal worship. The Baal cults were the symbols of a social-economic regime which had reduced land to the commercial category of sale and exchange, while enslaving peasants and shepherds under the Canaanite master class of Bethel, Shechem, and Jericho. But these three cities were now engulfed in destruction, and with them had perished their legality, their courts, and their gods. A Baal-god symbolizing Jericho, Bethel, or Shechem was just as obnoxious and reprehensible in the eyes of an Ephraimite peasant as were the human *baalim* who had lived in these places and fattened on the decaying and corrupt system of pre-Hebrew Canaan.

On the other hand, Yahweh stood for the *mishpat*, or law, which regarded land as a noncommercial thing; which removed land from the category of sale and exchange; and which guaranteed its continued, inalienable possession in the family that owned and used the

soil as a means of life. Thus, the fruits of the ground, fertilized by
Yahweh, were brought to the sanctuary at Shiloh by the house of
Joseph as an offering to the deity who gave it; meal and wine were
presented in sacrifice by Hannah, the wife of Elkanah the Ephraimite (I Sam. 1:24). That Yahweh caused rain to fall upon the soil
of Canaan was never questioned after the storm that flooded the
battlefield of Esdraelon (Judg. 5:4). It was believed that Yahweh
sent dew upon Gideon's fleece of wool, leaving the surrounding
earth dry, and that on the following night he left the fleece dry
while causing dew to cover "all the ground" (Judg. 6:36f.). The
"shewbread" that stood before the altar of Yahweh at Nob was
the fruit of the soil (I Sam. 21:6). Bread and wine were carried to
the holy place at Bethel (I Sam. 10:3). The mythical patriarch Isaac
sows the soil of Canaan; and the earth, blessed by Yahweh, brings
forth a hundredfold (Gen. 26:12). "The smell of my son is like
the smell of a field that Yahweh hath blessed" (Gen. 27:27).

Yahweh-loyalty of Ephraim necessary

It is necessary to stress the indispensable function of the house
of Joseph, or Ephraim, in the development of Yahwism. The Josephites were a little embryonic nation which evolved a standardized
peasantry correlated with an ideological norm of Yahweh as a
divine symbol of soil possession and soil fertility. The practice of
mishpat, or primitive kinship justice in landholding, and the idea of
divinely endowed soil fertility went along together in a single "complex." During the early epoch the house of Joseph necessarily became identified with Yahweh-loyalty and Baal-antipathy, because
otherwise the great prophets (primarily Ephraimite) would have
had no psychological starting point. In other words, the prophets
could not have appeared as factors on the background of an essentially Baalized Israel. While prophecy did not, of course, take its
departure from a written Torah, as imagined by orthodox theology,
neither did it operate in a spiritual vacuum on the basis of "genius,"
as imagined by modern critics in the nineteenth century. The prophets, as we shall realize in due time, had a starting point of common

understanding with the plain peasantry on the ground of an ideology rooted in the Judges period.

It would be a great mistake, however, to assume that the standardized norm attained in early Hebrew history by the Josephites was identical with later prophetic doctrine. It was merely a starting point, or springboard, for the prophets—not their conclusion. For in itself the primitive Hebrew ideology of *mishpat* was provincial and narrow, like the little community in which it became the norm of practice and thought. It was only a beginning. Its energy lay, not in the realm of abstraction, but in the rural aristocracy's will to live. Judged from the modern ethical standpoint, it was far from perfect. Its origin and constitution were like the corresponding element in all nations. Its cherished estates in Ephraim were acquired by military conquest, which exterminated the previous Canaanite landholders in the central hill country and confiscated their slaves (*abadim*).

This little upland region, as we have already seen, was the spoil of war, which the militant Jacob, with sword and bow, took out of the hand of the Amorite, or Canaanite (Gen. 48:22). The legendary Jacob, indeed, follows the pattern and represents the ideal of the Ephraimite aristocracy: "And the man increased exceedingly, and had much cattle, and camels, and asses, and men-slaves (*abadim*) and women-slaves (*shifahoth*)" (Gen. 30:43). The legendary Isaac also stands for the same system: "And the man waxed great, and went forward, and grew until he became very great; for he had possession of flocks, and possession of herds, and great store of slave-service (*abudah rabbah*). And Isaac's slaves (*abadim*) digged . . . a well" (Gen. 26:14, 15, 19). Likewise the same aristocratic social class is reflected in the legends of Abraham, as revealed in the words of his eldest slave: "I am Abraham's slave (*ebed*). And Yahweh hath greatly blessed my master (*adon*); and he is become great; and he hath given him flocks, and herds, and silver, and gold, and men-slaves (*abadim*), and women-slaves (*shifahoth*), and camels, and asses" (Gen. 24:34, 35).

Terms "adon" and "baal" in the Judaic and Ephraimite documents

It will be noticed that the slave speaks of his owner, or master, as *adon*. This term is used eighteen times with relation to Abraham in the chapter from which the foregoing quotation is taken (Gen. 24), and in each case the modern versions render it "master." But sometimes precisely the same term, *adon*, is translated "lord," as when Sarah speaks of Abraham as "my lord" (Gen. 18:12).

The peculiar distribution within the Hebrew sources of the terms "adon" and "baal" as designations of the Hebrew aristocracy is a matter of great importance to the interpretation of Hebrew history and literature.

The source yielding the above quotations about Abraham is commonly called by critics the J, or Yahwistic, document, because it employs the divine personal name "Yahweh" more frequently than the plural term "Elohim" (generally translated "God"). Equally important, or perhaps more so, the Judaic source is also distinguished by the term *adon*—a fact not yet assimilated by Biblical criticism.

On the other hand, the cardinal source generally known as E, or the Elohistic document, makes use of the term "Elohim" (God) more frequently than it uses "Yahweh." The E document is also known as "Ephraimite," because it relates primarily to the hill country of Ephraim. And while E does use the term *adon* of the Hebrew master class, this document is characterized by the term *baal* as applied to the Hebrew aristocracy and the Canaanite gods.

Because of the foregoing considerations we shall speak of E not only as the Ephraimite source but also as the baal-document, in distinction from the J, or Yahwistic, element, which will be referred to as the *adon* source. The importance and full meaning of the *adon-baal* contrast between J and E cannot be fully explained here, but will become increasingly evident as we proceed. We shall find the Ephraimite, or E, source to be earlier than J, just as Ephraim, or Joseph, is the original core of the Hebrew nation, identified with that part of Canaan where Hebrew history begins; the J, or Judean, source trailing the Ephraimite in general, but varying from it in certain minor details which the Judaic redactor introduces to the supposed advantage of Judah.

Judaic redactors of Samuel distort Ephraimite history

Our only sources for the rise of the Ephraimite kingdom are the books of Samuel, which are even more confused in literary structure than Judges. The Judaic redactors have systematically distorted the facts, discrediting Saul, the first Ephraimite king, and glorifying David, the creator of the tribe and kingdom of Judah and the first ruler of the united Hebrew monarchy. The books of Samuel contain fundamental Ephraimite sources, the same as Judges; but this material—especially in I Samuel—is an inconsistent patchwork of documents from various writers who interpret the history in such a way as to make it a theological masquerade.

Saul ben Kish becomes king, 1015 B. C.

That the house of Joseph should go on from the position of advantage and prestige acquired in the Judges epoch, and consolidate into a kingdom, was inevitable. The situation called only for the stimulus of a definite event or exigency to crystallize the hill clans into a more definite political form. The occasion came when certain tribesmen, called Ammonites, living on the edge of the desert, made hostile demonstrations against Gilead, east of Jordan. The men of Gilead themselves, as we recall, had never been friendly to the Josephites west of the river; but a certain distant kinship had always been asserted theoretically; and now, in spite of past coolness, the Gileadites appealed frantically by messengers who made their way across Jordan and up into the hills of the central range, going from village to village, coming at length to Gibeah of Benjamin.

The scene was characteristic of the times. The highlanders, consisting of shepherds and farmers, did not live in separate households. They were collected in villages which, even when devoid of walls, afforded some degree of protection against attack by man and beast.

A large part of the population, including women, went out at day-break to work in the surrounding country, sometimes going several miles away. Not only was the outdoor work done by slaves but also in this primitive economy the landed proprietors themselves (the *adonim*) labored alongside their slaves in a kind of simple, democratic aristocracy.

Among the leading families in Gibeah was that of Kish, whose descent could be traced as far as the Judges period (I Sam. 9:1). The cemetery outside the village contained the graves of at least four generations of ancestors and relatives in a direct line leading up to Kish. This man is called in Hebrew a *gibbor hayil*, which means a man of consequence, with landed possessions and slaves, who is liable to military service in case of war. The family of Kish included a son whose name was Saul, "a choice young man, and a goodly; and there was not among the children of Israel a goodlier person than he,—from his shoulders and upward higher than any of the people" (I Sam. 9:2).

When the excited messengers from Gilead hastened along the highway toward Gibeah, the people at work in the fields caught sight of the approaching strangers and poured into the village, where they raised a great outcry upon hearing the news. The commotion was increasing when Saul, the son of Kish, came following the oxen out of the field and asked, "What is the matter with the people that they weep?" The story of the Gileadites roused him so greatly that he took a yoke of oxen, hewed them in pieces, and sent the fragments throughout all the coasts of Israel by messengers, proclaiming, "Whosoever cometh not forth after Saul and after Samuel, so shall it be done unto his oxen" (I Sam. 11:7).

These quotations are from the Ephraimite source, which gives a peculiar basis for comparison with the other story of Gibeah in Judges, wherein the Levite divides the dead body of his concubine and sends the pieces over the country. In Saul's case the oxen are merely "cut into pieces"; but the story in Judges refers to "twelve pieces," according to the twelve-tribe conception of Israel which arose and became orthodox at a later period of history under the united monarchy. The contrast between the two stories affords interesting evidence of the otherwise well-attested fact that the house of Joseph in the Judges period and in Saul's day was not a twelve-tribe nation and that the Gibeah tale in Judges (not the incident upon which it is based, but the tale itself) comes from a much later period than the actual, historical narrative about Saul's cutting his oxen in pieces and distributing them throughout the hill country.

The response to Saul's appalling summons was immediate: "The fear of Yahweh fell on the people; and they came up with one consent" (I Sam. 11:7). The foregoing statement is enlarged upon by a Judaic interpolation saying that three hundred and thirty thousand fighting men (330,000), including Judah, answered the call to war. The editorial hand is betrayed here both by the fantastic figures, which exceed any statistical possibility of that period in the central highlands, and by the writer's anxiety to designate Judah specifically, without mentioning other tribes by name. Much more consistent with the general situation at that time is the picture of Saul's army suggested by another Ephraimite source, which puts the number at four thousand (I Sam. 13:2).

Crossing the Jordan and advancing into the east country, the militia of Ephraim inflicted a severe defeat upon the Ammonites and saved Gilead, which thus became firmly attached to the cause of Israel and to the house of Saul.

This exploit, which brought Saul into prominence, led to the immediate choice of him as king by the people—that is, by the landed aristocracy, or *adonim*. "And all the people went to Gilgal; and there they made Saul king before Yahweh in Gilgal; and there they sacrificed sacrifices of peace offerings before Yahweh" (I Sam. 11:15).

Saul's kingship founded upon popular election

The foregoing natural and simple narrative is the Ephraimite explanation of the circumstances leading to the establishment of monarchy in "Israel,"—that is, in the house of Joseph. A number of important facts call for notice: (1) Saul is made king, not by a priest, or a prophet, or any sort of special religious functionary, but by popular election, on the basis of purely secular events, which are intelligible at this late date without any recondite interpretation. (2) The expression rendered "before Yahweh," or, in the King James version, "before the LORD," occurs in the Hebrew text simply as *liphnae Yahweh*. This means literally "to-the-face-of Yahweh" and indicates the fact of a permanent altar standing at whatever place is mentioned in the text, as for instance, here at Gilgal. Such altars turn up frequently in the Ephraimite sources, proving that sacrifice could be offered anywhere, as we have seen in the case of Micah the Ephraimite, and of the Danites who appropriated his paraphernalia to furnish their new church in the far north. Thus, although some special prestige was attached to the temple at Shiloh, it could not have been the one exclusive sanctuary where sacrifice to Yahweh was legal. (3) The people themselves offered sacrifices at the election of Saul without the help of a priestly minister. (4) The Ephraimite source describes the events in religious terms precisely as corresponding secular occurrences are explained in the history of other ancient peoples: the agitation of Saul when hearing the news brought by the messengers from Gilead is told by saying that "the spirit of *Elohim* rushed upon him" before he hewed the oxen in pieces. But this does not constitute redactional interference; it is merely the conventional, popular way of expressing any unusual secular happening in antiquity, which leaves the natural cause-and-effect relationship of the events in full view. To destroy valuable property in such fashion was an extraordinary occurrence which, in primitive thought, implies the action of some supernatural spirit or demon; but from our modern point of view all these events are natural and secular. The Jewish redactional comments and interpolations, however, always remove the entire train of circumstances beyond the natural orbit, superimposing upon the events an artificial, theological, or ecclesiastical explanation which disconnects them from the realm of cause-and-effect as we understand it in our daily life. (5) Like the triumphs of the early Josephite invaders and the Deborah battle and the exploits of Ehud and Gideon, the victory of Saul over the Ammonites had the religio-psychological effect of heightening the prestige of Yahweh, as declared by Saul in the verse completing the martial narrative: "Today Yahweh has wrought deliverance in Israel" (I Sam. 11:13).

Philistines undertake to throttle Hebrew power

The Philistines were naturally aroused upon hearing that Saul had collected an army and had gone to war against Ammon. His campaign and election as king must have taken more time than seems to be implied in the condensed narrative which constitutes I Samuel 11. The entire following chapter (I Sam. 12) is a hortatory insertion by a redactor of the Deuteronomic school and has no bearing upon the historical problem before us. But immediately after this, we again reach good Ephraimite material, which comprises about half the ensuing chapter (that is, I Sam. 13:2–6, and the second sentence of vs. 15 through vs. 18). This matter, with most of chap. 14 (also Ephraimite), brings the Philistines into view in a most interesting, and indeed astounding, situation, which is not explained by any of the preceding portions of Samuel or even by the modern critical school, but which takes a logical place in the history.

Unable any longer to endure the portentous consolidation of the Josephite *adonim* in the hills of Ephraim, and hearing of their preoccupation with the campaign against Ammon, the Philistines invaded the country during the absence of Saul and his militia, and when he returned they were already established in garrisons. The invasion may, indeed, have been part of a conspiracy by which the Ammonites drew off the attention of Ephraim while the Philistines came up into the hill country. But the intruders did not long maintain their position. For the crown prince, Jonathan, led an ambush against them, followed by a running battle in which King Saul and six hundred men expelled them with great slaughter from the highlands: "So Yahweh saved Israel that day . . . and they smote the Philistines that day from Michmash to Aijalon . . . and the Philistines went to their own place" (I Sam. 14:23, 31, 46).

Saul attacks Gibeon

As a country landlord, brought up in the open life of the fields, King Saul shared the prejudices of his class against the walled cities of Canaan. When pushing the Philistines back into their own country, he passed by a number of Canaanite, or Amorite, cities, the chief of which was a fortified place called Gibeon, lying directly west of the Benjaminite frontier. This place is not to be confused with the Benjaminite village Gibeah. Perhaps the king was elated by his victories over the Philistines and Ammonites; perhaps he wanted to obtain control over Gibeon so as to secure his own frontier against the Philistines; or perhaps he recalled the Josephite destruction of Shechem and thought he could equal that exploit. But in any case, he attacked Gibeon; and although he did not destroy the city, he slew some of its people. The event is explained vaguely thus: "Now the Gibeonites were not of the children of Israel, but of the remnant of the Amorites; and the children of Israel had sworn unto them; and Saul sought to slay them in his zeal for the children of Israel" (II Sam. 21:2).

The more we explore the records, the more the unconquered, Baal-worshiping cities of pre-Hebrew Canaan come into view outside the Josephite enclave, persisting on through the Judges epoch into the times of the Israelite monarchy. Some of the Hebrew documents generalize them as "Canaanite," and others call them "Amorite"; but both terms mean the same. That an accommodation of some kind should be reached between the Israelites and these older "inhabitants of the land" (as the Bible quaintly calls them) would be a natural tendency after the force of invasion had spent itself and the newcomers had subsided into peaceful settlement. But reconciliation was not easy. The master classes, the *baalim*, in the walled cities followed a "way of life," as we now express it, which differed from the way of life habitual to the Ephraimite landed aristocracy, the *adonim*, whose *mishpat* was unlike that of the effete and immoral cities of the ancient oriental world. Gideon, as we have seen, had sought to heal the breach between the two elements by marry-

ing into the Shechemite aristocracy. But this gesture did not prevent
the ultimate annihilation of Shechem by the Josephites. Now Saul,
in his attack on Gibeon, was maintaining the old attitude of destructive military conquest. The onflowing tide of history, which
was creating the Hebrew nation, presented a frightful dilemma: If
all the earlier "inhabitants of the land" had met the fate of Shechem,
their fields and farms would then have become the property of rural
Israelite *adonim*, the followers of Yahweh in the country villages.
But on the other hand, if the Canaanite cities were taken into the
evolving Hebrew nation, then the Canaanite *baal* class, with its
alien way of life, would, so to speak, be in a position to "bore from
within" and exert a subversive influence. That neither horn of the
dilemma spelled any final or satisfactory conclusion will be clear as
the swiftly moving drama of Bible history unfolds before us.

Nature of source-material in book of Samuel

In the first book of Samuel the Ephraimite narrative about Saul's
campaign against the Ammonites in chap. 11 is an outstanding landmark. The material preceding and following chap. 11 is largely devoted to building up an obscure seer, Samuel, as the direct priestly
and prophetic intermediary of heaven, enjoying detailed conversations with Yahweh, not as a local deity of Israel, but as God of the
Universe. Acting as mouthpiece for the Almighty, Samuel first
anoints Saul as king; then rejects him; and then transfers the celestial
unction to the Judahite David, whom he anoints king of Israel when
but a youth. In this transcendent atmosphere the Philistine war is
conducted, not by human administration, but by the immediate intervention of God, who thunders upon the Philistines, driving them
away from Israel into their own country: "So the Philistines were
subdued; and they came no more into the coast of Israel; and the
hand of Yahweh was against the Philistines all the days of Samuel"
(I Sam. 7:10–13).

Nevertheless, the Ephraimite material following Saul's victory
over the Ammonites in chap. 11 shows not only that the Philistines
invaded the country and put garrisons there, as already noted, but

also that all this occurred during the lifetime of Samuel himself, who took part in concurrent events: "And there was sore war against the Philistines all the days of Saul" (I Sam. 14:52; for Samuel's activity during this period see I Sam. 15:1–35; 16:1–30; 19:18–22; 25:1). At the same time, the ark of Yahweh is said to have been carried into Philistia by the enemy, where it is alleged to have caused so much damage by its mere presence that it was brought to a place called Kirjath-jearim: "And the men of Kirjath-jearim came, and fetched the ark of Yahweh, and brought it unto the house of Abinadab in the hill . . . and it came to pass, while the ark abode in Kirjath-jearim, that the time was long, for it was twenty years" (I Sam. 7:1–2). Accordingly, twenty years later, after David had become king, he sent for the ark, "and they set the ark of *elohim* upon a new cart, and brought it out of the house of Abinadab" (II Sam. 6:3). Nevertheless, while the ark was quietly resting in the house of Abinadab (according to one source), it was somewhere else according to another document: "And Saul said unto Ahiah, Bring hither the ark of God. For the ark of God was at that time with the children of Israel" (I Sam. 14:18).

Most of the material with reference to Samuel in the book bearing his name is the product of Judaic manipulation, and is not only inaccurate but also fantastic when judged from the standpoint of the more sober Ephraimite sources, which are, as it were, crowded into the background. The Judaic writers, much against their inclination, are compelled to acknowledge that the Hebrew nation and monarchy arose in the hill country of Ephraim. But they accept this fact with bad grace and have succeeded in distorting the history in such a way that the religious ideas of Jews and Christians alike have been regimented for nearly two thousand years.

If the question be raised why such discrepancies were allowed to remain in such a book as the Bible, we recur to observations made in the opening chapters of the present work: The writings which are now before us in collected form as "the Bible" were not primarily "Bible" in any sense, but were at first private rolls containing matter copied from various preëxisting sources. The owners were at liberty to intersperse comments between the lines, on the margins, or at the beginning or end of the material already copied onto the rolls. If the owner disagreed with certain statements or narratives, he did not destroy them, but merely prefixed another account giving a different story, as we saw in the case of the Judaic prologue to our present book of Judges (Judg. 1–2:5). Later, when the roll was copied by other scribes or came into the hands of new owners, the added matter was written regularly into a continuous text by scribes who were not concerned with niceties of historical criticism. But at length, after many rolls were brought together into a single collection and edited and then officially accepted by the religious authorities of later generations, no further changes were allowed; whereupon began the process of interpretation which has continued in some form, orthodox or critical, up to our own day.

David becomes actor in history

Not until the region later known as Judah is invaded by the Philistines does David of Bethlehem come upon the stage of history. He is already an independent chief with an army of six hundred men (I Sam. 23:13; 25:13). Hated by Saul, he has nevertheless won the king's younger daughter, in the hope, doubtless, of ultimately gaining prestige toward uniting southern Canaan with Ephraim in a single Davidic state. The conflicting stories about personal relations between David and Saul result from the Judaic manipulation to discredit the latter and give authority to David as the favorite of Samuel, magnified from a local seer into an august and imposing vice-regent of heaven.

The opening scene of David's public military career is staged in an old Canaanite town, Keilah, with gates and bars, whose burghers are twice called *baalim* in the Hebrew text, whereas a country aristocrat in the vicinity is called *adon* (I Sam. 23:7, 11, 12; cf. 25:10, 14, *et passim*). The narrative is partly as follows: "Then they told David, saying, Behold, the Philistines fight against Keilah. . . . So David and his men went to Keilah, and fought with the Philistines . . . and smote them with a great slaughter" (I Sam. 23:1, 5).

That Bethlehem, the home of David, was related in some vague way to Ephraim, becomes apparent as we proceed. No tribe of Judah is heard of at first, but only Bethlehem-judah (Judg. 17:7, 19:1; I Sam. 17:12). No individual "Judahites" from any other village or city come into the picture, but only David and his relatives and townsmen of Bethlehem. The region south of Ephraim is much higher above sea level than the territory pertaining to the house of Joseph; and it has a physical independence which isolates it from the hill country of Ephraim. That the self-reliant David had a comprehensive policy of his own with reference to this area in southern Canaan is hinted by his move protecting the city of Keilah against the Philistines. He next posted his men to guard the property of Nabal, a non-Israelite, Edomite landlord against marauders from the desert, not in the interest of Nabal, but for David's own purpose. The death of this man gave the enterprising David another opportunity: he married the widow and also another woman from Jezreel —not the place of that name in the valley of Esdraelon, but a southern Jezreel (I Sam. 25). His rapid progress toward power now became so alarming to Saul that he took his daughter away from the ambitious Bethlehemite.

Incompatibility between David and Saul

While the post-exilic writers have thrown a mantle of artificial sanctity over the life of David which obscures the actual events, nevertheless the underlying secular history still remains visible when the interpolations of the compilers are set aside. David and Saul were great men—each in his own way. Saul was a provincial farmer, whose main object was to hold back the Philistine menace, which made necessary the consolidation of Ephraim under strong monarchic authority. "There was sore war against the Philistines all the days of Saul; and when Saul saw any strong man, or any valiant man, he conscripted him" (I Sam. 14:52). These laconic observations from the Ephraimite source bring the essential case into view. The king wanted men who would not be too self-important and would obey orders. But David was an independent, self-reliant personality; and there could be no real coöperation between a man of his characteristics and a leader like Saul, facing the problem of Ephraim in the central highlands.

Nor was it a mere difference of individual talent. The two men were not natives of the same locality. David was born outside Ephraim and had a different outlook on Canaan as a whole. Judged from the narrow standpoint of Saul's provincialism, David was not "patriotic"; and why should he have been? From the beginning the southern part of Canaan had never made common cause with Ephraim, as we learned when studying the great battle of Esdraelon in the time of Deborah. David's outlook tended to be international. He became friendly with the Ammonite King Nahash, who made the attack on Gilead which brought Saul onto the stage of Hebrew history in the first place (I Sam. 11:1, II Sam. 10:2; 17:27ff.). This attack from the east, as already intimated, may have been timed by agreement between Nahash and the Philistines, enabling the latter to steal a march into Ephraim. Nahash, then, was "Public Enemy No. 1" on Saul's calendar; and when David's friendship with Nahash became known, the news was enough to give Saul a startling vision of "encirclement" by Ammon on the east, the Philistines on the west, and the forces of David on the south.

David aligns himself with Philistines

The suspicions of Saul ripened into certainty when word came that David and his army of six hundred men had left the southern hill country and entered into alliance with Achish, king of the Philistine city of Gath (I Sam. 27–30). Saul was now fast approaching his doom. The Philistine army, with David's force of six hundred men, marched north along the Mediterranean coast and turned into the valley of Esdraelon. Pausing here, the Philistine commanders held a council of war with reference to their new ally; and in spite of earnest protestations by the king of Gath, it was decided to order David off the field, lest in the heat of battle he might go over to the help of Saul. But David was under no obligations to the Ephraimite king. There was not in existence at that time any Hebrew nation covering the larger part of Canaan and giving the name

"Israel" to the entire country. The post-exilic writers who created the book of Samuel assumed a relation between Ephraim and southern Canaan, of which there is no proof. The fundamental Ephraimite sources in Samuel do not give any clear indication that David ever coöperated with Saul in Ephraim. It is not until the Philistines attack southern Canaan that we begin to hear about David as a warrior chief; even then he is not aligned with Saul, but goes with his own army to help the Canaanite city of Keilah. It is undoubtedly true that Saul's younger daughter was one of David's wives. But so was the daughter of Talmai, king of Geshur in the northern part of Canaan (II Sam. 3:3). Neither of these marriages made David a subject of either father-in-law. The conclusion, therefore, holds that as an independent chieftain in the south, with his own standing army, David had a right to enter into relations with the Philistines and that in so doing he was not a traitor. After the council of war decided to keep his forces out of the impending action, David and his men returned to Philistia and avoided the scene of conflict. The battle might not have been lost by Saul if David and his six hundred men had fought for the house of Joseph on that fateful day.

Philistines defeat Saul at Mount Gilboa, 1008 B. C.

Having disposed of David, the Philistine commanders now ordered their troops across the valley of Esdraelon into Jezreel, where they chased the Ephraimites onto the slopes of Mount Gilboa. The pursuit was inexorable and swift, the Philistine archers pausing at intervals to send clouds of arrows into the retreating Ephraimites. King Saul and his sons, hard pressed by the bowmen, fell on their swords and perished. The victors carried the royal corpses across the valley to the Canaanite city of Beth-shan, where they fastened them to the city wall in a ghastly row. The Philistines wanted to keep the fortified cities of pre-Hebrew Canaan from entering into political union with the Ephraimite highlanders; and by this dramatic form of publicity they held up to general notice the body of the man who had attacked the Canaanite city of Gibeon and had slain some of its people.

Thus ended ingloriously the first kingdom of the house of Joseph.

VI. CREATION OF JUDAH

THE BATTLE of Gilboa was followed by great confusion. The Philistines were masters of the hill country and could oppress the Israelite highlanders at will. But what now had become of the power of Ephraim's deity? The prestige of Yahweh had steadily increased in the Judges period and throughout most of Saul's reign. Yet the outcome of Gilboa seemed to cancel the promise of the past and make the Philistine gods victorious.

If the Judaic editors and compilers had followed their usual custom, at this point in the story they would have been compelled to assume that the misfortunes of the house of Joseph were the result of "serving other gods." It would have been necessary to insert a statement like the following: "Now the children of Israel did evil again in the sight of Yahweh; and therefore Yahweh delivered them into hand of the Philistines for . . . years." Saul was defeated at the end of I Samuel, in chapter 31; and such a formula would naturally have occurred somewhere in the neighborhood of the battle narrative—provided the compiler followed the method used in the book of Judges. But he was already afoul of his own method, because in the earlier part of I Samuel he had inserted a long passage containing the statement, "Then the children of Israel did put away the Baalim and Ashtaroth, and served Yahweh only" (I Sam. 7:4). And on the view of the compiler this testimony about Israel's faithfulness held good throughout the reign of Saul up to the end; so that when reaching the catastrophe at Gilboa, the usual Deuteronomic formula could not be brought forward. The chief reason for this conspicuous omission, however, is quite evident: The editorial manipulators, by the terms of their own thesis, are estopped from the claim that Saul and Israel have forsaken Yahweh and served Baal, because the compilers and redactors themselves are building a structure of piety around the figure of Saul as "the anointed of Yahweh," whose authority is destined to devolve upon the Judaic hero David.

Accordingly no claim is made that Saul and his people apostatized after the fashion of Israel's alleged idolatry at earlier times. The fundamental Ephraimite sources so unequivocally and clearly depict Saul as an adherent of the Yahweh-cult that the redactor simply cannot distort the documents by libeling the Ephraimite monarch in Deuteronomic fashion. So the sins alleged of Saul, which cause Yahweh to reject him in favor of David, are ritualistic offenses (I Sam. 13, 15, 28). Nothing reveals more clearly the factitious and casual nature of Judaic manipulations than the documents covering the passage of Hebrew history from Saul to David. The post-exilic editors conveniently forget their emphasis upon Baal-worship in their intense preoccupation with the rise to power of the Bethlehemite chieftain.

David creates kingdom and tribe of Judah, 1008–1001 B. C.

After the defeat of Saul, David and his army left the Philistine country and went up into southern Canaan, where they established themselves for seven years in the country villages around the Kenizzite, non-Judaic city of Hebron (II Sam. 2:1–3). The fact that David was able to make this move without opposition from the Philistine conquerors of Saul shows that they did not suspect the design which he cherished. By posting his army around Hebron, but not in the city, David was able to impress the inhabitants and win them over to his plan of organizing a little kingdom in the south of Canaan. The opening chapter of his new career is described simply in the following passage: "And the men of Judah came, and there they anointed David king over the house of Judah" (II Sam. 2:4). Not through Samuel, then, but through his own initiative and the votes of the elders did David become king over the southern territory. But the process by which the kingdom of Judah came into existence was more complex than appears upon the surface of the history.

We have seen that the house of Joseph, expanding southward, gave birth to a new tribe, "Son of the South" (Ben-yemen, or Benjamin). That the migratory movement of Ephraimites in the same direction gave rise to Bethlehem and brought this village into the light of history is the best explanation of its origin. Bethlehem was David's native place and the germ of his first kingdom. It was not only called Bethlehem-judah, but also Bethlehem-ephratha (Ruth 4:11; Micah 5:2; and elsewhere). David's father, Jesse, is called an Ephrathite in the Hebrew text (I Sam. 17:12); while Samuel's father, Elkanah, in southern Ephraim, is called by the same term (I Sam. 1:1). These data give no positive proof; but the suggestion is that Bethlehem was Ephraimite in origin and that the term "Ephrathite" was an ancient designation common to inhabitants of both places.

Bethlehem lay but five miles to the south of Jebus (Jerusalem), which was still an independent, non-Hebrew, Canaanite city at the period we have now reached. And such being the case, Judah— whatever this name signifies—did not extend much north of Bethlehem. Nor could it have extended far westward, because when David went to the Canaanite city of Adullam, west of Bethlehem, and took refuge in its fortress (not "cave"), a reference to "the land of Judah" locates Judah east of Adullam (I Sam. 22:1–5). At the same time the city of Hebron, about twenty miles south of David's birthplace, is identified with Caleb, brother of Othniel and son of Kenaz; while Kenaz, in turn, is a son of Esau, "who is Edom" (Josh. 15:17; Judg. 1:13; Gen. 36:1, 11). The Kenizzites (descended from Kenaz) are mentioned, among other foreigners, as inhabitants of Canaan before the arrival of Israel in that country (Gen. 15:19–21).

In view of these data it is instructive to observe again how the legends of Genesis follow the history and reflect the evolution of Judah from non-Hebrew clans in south Canaan. Symbolizing

David, the mythical patriarch Judah (*Y'hudah*) is said to separate himself from his brethren and "go down" to Adullam, where he has a friend; and while there he sees a Canaanite woman, whom he marries and by whom he has three sons (Gen. 38:1–12).

Elements entering into completed kingdom of Judah

In the extreme south of Canaan, called "the Negeb," were certain clans known as Kenites and Jerachmeelites; in the center, around Hebron, were the Calebites, a branch of Edom; in the west were the Canaanite cities of Adullam and Keilah; while in the northern section, adjoining the territory of Canaanite Jebus, was Bethlehem-judah, or Bethlehem-ephratha, which, being the home village of David, gave one of its names to the new kingdom.[1]

Judah, as a whole, was on higher ground than Ephraim and was not so agricultural; nor was it near the trade routes which went through or around the central highlands of Ephraim, or Joseph. While some agriculture was practiced in southern Canaan, Judah was mostly pastoral; and through the semi-nomadic elements that haunted the Negeb, it was in closer touch than Ephraim with the *mishpat* ideology followed by wandering clans in the desert.

These considerations must be carefully fixed in mind; because, in the final outcome, as we have seen, the cultural burden of Israel was to be carried onward through the ages, not by Joseph, but by Judah.

---

[1] Practically the same view of the rise of Judah is taken by Professor T. H. Robinson, of University College, Cardiff, in an article, "The Origin of the Tribe of Judah," reprinted without date from *Amicitiæ Corolla*.

VII. KINGDOM OF UNITED ISRAEL

AFTER a long period of uncertainty and confusion following the battle of Gilboa, the elders of Ephraim, seeing no other escape from Philistine oppression, elected David king over the house of Joseph: "So all the elders of Israel came to the king to Hebron; and king David made a league with them in Hebron before Yahweh; and they anointed David king over Israel" (II Sam. 5:1-3). Two important facts are to be noted: (1) Precisely as when David became king of Judah, he was chosen and inducted into this office, not by Samuel or by priestly validation of any kind, but by vote of the people,—that is, the landed proprietors, the *adonim*, composing the rural aristocracy of Ephraim. (2) The ceremony took place "before Yahweh." This expression is the translated form of a Hebrew phrase indicating the presence of an altar, which meanwhile had been set up at Hebron.

David takes Jebus (Jerusalem), 1001 B. C.

Having become king of the new, united Hebrew nation, David needed a strong capital, but he could not wait for one to be slowly constructed. For this purpose he chose the still Canaanite city of Jebus, which lay almost on a line between Judah and Ephraim, about five miles to the south of the Benjaminite frontier. To the conventional Bible student the fact comes with a shock that this characteristic city of Scripture was not captured or destroyed at the time of the original invasion, but had remained Canaanite, or Amorite, throughout the Judges period, the reign of Saul, and the seven-year reign of David over Judah at Hebron. The situation is described in the second book of Samuel:

And the king and his men went to Jerusalem unto the Jebusites, the inhabitants of the land, which spake unto David, saying, Except thou

take away the blind and the lame, thou shalt not come in hither. . . .
Nevertheless, David took the fort of Zion. . . . So David dwelt in the
fort, and called it the city of David. And David built round about from
Millo and inward [II Sam. 5:6–7, 9].

It is important to make sharp and clear the difference between
the capture of Jebus by David and the earlier conquest by which
the Josephites took the central highlands of Canaan, to the north
of Jerusalem. That earlier movement was marked by the utter
destruction of Jericho in the Jordan valley and of Bethel and eventually of Shechem in the hill country, so that a uniform aristocracy
of rustic landholders, or *adonim*, consolidated gradually throughout the "enclave" area, in allegiance to Yahweh. But in the case of
Jebus, David's men effected an entrance and captured the fort of
Zion which commanded the city, and in which David lived as a
conqueror without putting the Jebusite inhabitants to death. If
there is any uncertainty about this point an old source in the book
of Joshua makes the circumstances clear: "As for the Jebusites, the
inhabitants of Jerusalem, the children of Judah could not drive
them out; but the Jebusites dwell with the children of Judah at
Jerusalem unto this day" (Josh. 15:63). Consideration of the foregoing facts will have to be postponed on account of the startling
portent which now appears on the horizon of David's newborn
kingdom.

Philistines attack and are defeated

David's quick work in organizing the new kingdom, followed
by his prompt capture of Jerusalem as headquarters, threw the
Philistines into panic and impelled them to equally decisive action.
Coming up from the sea through the hills of northwestern Judah,
they found that David had already left Jerusalem and occupied the
fortress in the Canaanite city of Adullam, to bar their advance.
Scarcely had they discovered where David was, when he skillfully
deployed his forces and avenged Gilboa by shattering the Philistine power in a fierce engagement which restored the prestige of
Yahweh as a "god of hosts, mighty in battle."

Application of Canaanite term "baal" to Yahweh

Hardly noticed by conventional readers and expounders of the Bible is an arresting passage which refers to David's triumph over the Philistines in terms full of significance. The field of battle, covered with dead and mangled corpses, rose before David's imagination as a breaking-forth of Yahweh upon the foe: "And David said, Yahweh has broken forth upon mine enemies like a breach of waters. Therefore he called the name of that place "The Breakings-forth-of-Baal" (*Baal-perazim*, II Sam. 5:20). Strictly speaking, of course, the name should have been "*Yahweh-perazim.*" But the application of the term "Baal" to Yahweh bears ominous witness to the rising influence of Canaan upon the religious ideas of Israel.

Gilboa disaster explained by David

David's victory over the Philistines was not enough, in his eyes, to retrieve the prestige of Yahweh from the humiliation suffered through the shameful defeat of Saul at Gilboa and the exposure of his body on the wall of Beth-shan. Some equally striking demonstration must be made in order to wipe out the discredit which Israel incurred through Saul's attack upon Gibeon and the slaughter of certain people belonging to that Canaanite city. Anxious as David had been to curry favor with the *adonim* of Joseph as the successor to Saul, "the anointed of Yahweh," he was no less eager to placate the non-Josephite, pre-Hebrew "inhabitants of the land," whose fealty he was also desirous to secure. He had begun his career in Saul's time by defending the Canaanite city of Keilah against the Philistines; he had associated with the Canaanites of the city of Adullam, who gave him the protection of their fortress; he had captured the Canaanite city of Jerusalem and was now using it as his capital. These places in the south had become part of Judah. But there were many other independent, non-Hebrew cities —particularly in and near the great plain of Esdraelon—whose good will was vital to the success of the new monarchy engineered by David.

To secure the allegiance of Canaanites north of Judah, the king announced that Saul's defeat was not due to the superiority of the Philistine gods over Yahweh, but was caused by the anger of Yahweh at Saul's perfidious massacre of the Gibeonites, with whom Israel had sworn peace in the name of Yahweh. Accordingly David arrested seven men of Saul's descendants, giving them over into the hands of the Gibeonites, who slew them by hanging before an altar of Yahweh erected at Gibeon. This horrible transaction was carried through as a matter of state policy which gave dramatic evidence of David's good faith toward the Canaanites, "the inhabitants of the land."

The story of the Gibeonites is casually tucked away in the latter part of II Samuel. The compiler, living centuries later, scarcely understood the incident or knew where to place it in the chronology of the new reign. Perhaps it was even incorporated by some scribe who found it in an old manuscript and copied it into Samuel as an appendix. The nature of the event, however, is not casual in the least, because it stood connected with two very important matters—the status of the Canaanite cities in the political structure which David was rearing against the Philistines, and the reason for the triumph of the Philistine gods over Yahweh at the battle of Gilboa. These matters were pressing enough to call for David's attention as quickly as possible after he secured the throne of Israel; hence they are considered at this point, on the view that Gibeon (and by implication the other Canaanite cities) were promptly appeased by the new king.

Oracle of Yahweh manipulated

To bring out the technical phase of the Gibeonite incident, certain aspects of pre-exilic Hebrew religion, and of early religion in general, call for stress. The story begins by stating that in the days of David there was a famine which lasted three years. But in the history itself we hear nothing of such a tremendous misfortune as a three-year famine. Some occasion, or excuse, had to be found by David in order to set going the train of circumstances demanded by royal policy. The cause actually alleged by David may have been distorted into something more formidable when the story came to be written. The significant point is the statement that "David enquired of Yahweh; and Yahweh answered, It is for Saul and for his bloody house, because he slew the Gibeonites" (II Sam. 21:1f.). Literally interpreted, Yahweh seems to be conversing with David and making quite a complicated explanation. But as a matter of fact, "enquiring of Yahweh" merely consisted of "leading" questions aimed at an ephod-image before which a priest cast lots —that is, "*urim* and *thummim*." Hence, the issue was in reality raised by the inquirer himself, who in this case put the question, "Is it on account of Saul and his bloody house because he slew the Gibeonites?" If the answer of the sacred lot suited the inquirer, he could go ahead and act in accordance with it; but if the lot came out otherwise, the questioner could wait awhile and try again.

The ephod was, not an article of wearing apparel, but a metal image, such as Gideon made from golden earrings (Judg. 8:26–27). The priest of David was Abiathar, who came "with an ephod in his hand" (I Sam. 23:6). "And David said to Abiathar the priest, 'Bring hither the ephod'"; whereupon leading questions were asked in the name of Yahweh (I Sam. 23:9–12). The technique emerges more clearly in the case of Saul and Jonathan; the king says to the priest, "Cast lots between me and Jonathan my son" (I Sam. 14:42). The Greek text of the passage is even more explicit: "And Saul said, O Yahweh, god of Israel. . . . If the iniquity be in me or in my son Jonathan, Yahweh, God of Israel, give *urim*, but if . . . in thy people Israel, give *thummim*." The sacred lot is referred to briefly by the single term *urim*, as in the following passage, where it is mentioned among three methods of communication with God: "And when Saul enquired of Yahweh, Yahweh answered him not, neither by dreams, nor by *urim*, nor by prophets" (I Sam. 28:6).[1]

The execution of Saul's descendants was regarded as necessary

---

[1] "Religion in antiquity, particularly official religion, usually gave its oracles in accordance with royal or priestly policy," says G. S. Goodspeed (*History of the Babylonians and Assyrians*, New York, p. 288; cf. Breasted, *History of Egypt*, New York, pp. 522–23). R. C. Jebb says, "There were occasions on which an oracle became, in a strict sense, the organ of a political party"; and he adds, "Apollo, in short, kept up a series of most urgent leading articles" (*Essays*, pp. 156f.).

in order to overcome the psychological effect of the Philistines' exposition of the bodies of Saul and his sons at Bethshan after the disastrous battle of Gilboa. The Philistines, by this appalling procedure, carried the significance of the battle to extreme potency; and we can be sure that in an age when there were no newspapers or other ordinary means of publicity, the mind of every adult Canaanite was reached and influenced in terrible fashion. The subsequent seven years, in which the Philistines held sway and the Ephraimites lay quiet, bear eloquent witness to conditions prevailing after Gilboa.

The situation rankled in the mind of David; and his act, matching that of the Philistines in horror, must have been equally effective in the opposite direction. The seven dead bodies, hanging for months at Gibeon, were inevitably discussed all over the country; and the appalling spectacle no doubt canceled the psychological effect produced by the Philistines' treatment of the royal corpses. David's good faith was thereby impressed upon the *baalim* of every non-Josephite walled city in Canaan; and under cover of public policy he could also vent his personal grudges against Saul.

After the bodies had been exposed for many months, David ordered that they be taken down; while at the same time, he himself went to Jabesh-gilead for the remains of Saul:

And David went and took the bones of Saul and the bones of Jonathan his son from the *baalim* of Jabesh-gilead, who had stolen them from the street of Bethshan, where the Philistines had hanged them, when the Philistines had slain Saul in Gilboa. And he brought up from thence the bones of Saul and the bones of Jonathan his son; and they gathered the bones of them that were hanged.

All the remains thus collected were buried in the sepulchre of Kish, the father of Saul (II Sam. 21:12–14).[2]

None of these matters—highly important for understanding the history—are taken up in conventional Bible study; instead, they

[2] Notice that the bodies of the hanged men were not disposed of by David "until water was poured upon them from heaven" (II Sam. 21:10–13). The victims were sacrificed to Yahweh; and the power of Israel's deity to cause rain was now fully established.

have been ignored as completely as if they had no place whatever in the Bible. Yet it is from such material that insight is obtained into the actual course of events; whereas the "orthodox" interpolations and remarks of post-exilic editors get the spotlight of attention so generously that the fundamental facts are buried in oblivion.

David takes other non-Israelite wives

David's policy of appeasing the Canaanite cities was consistent with his many marriages to non-Israelite women from these places. "David took him more concubines and wives out of Jerusalem after he was come from Hebron" (II Sam. 5:13). His third son, the notorious Absalom, was born of Maacah, the daughter of Talmai, king of Geshur (II Sam. 3:3). Geshur was a small principality in the far north of Canaan which remained independent: "The children of Israel expelled not the Geshurites nor the Maachathites; but the Geshurites and Maachathites dwell among the Israelites until this day" (Josh. 13:13).

David's policy promotes intermarriage

David's policy of matrimonial connection with Canaanite women was foreshadowed by Gideon, who, as we recall, had a concubine in the Canaanite city of Shechem (Judg. 8:31). The fusion of the newer Israelite element with the older Canaanite "inhabitants of the land" was practically inescapable under the circumstances demanded by David's policy; it could not have been avoided unless, indeed, the entire non-Israelite population had been slaughtered outright. The proposal credited in Genesis to Hamor, prince of Shechem, reflects the pattern of actual conditions which arose during Hebrew history: "Make ye marriages with us. Give your daughters unto us, and take our daughters unto you; and ye shall dwell with us. And the land shall be before you. Dwell and trade ye therein; and get you possessions therein" (Gen. 34:9-10). Accordingly one of the Deuteronomic authors of Judges writes as follows in a passage previously quoted: "The children of Israel dwelt among the Canaanites, Hittites, and Amorites, and Perrizites, and Hivites, and Jebusites; and they took their daughters to be their wives, and gave their daughters to their sons" (Judg. 3:5).

Political and social amalgamation of Israelites and Canaanites was necessary in face of the Philistine danger. It was the Philistine pressure, indeed, that brought the nation of "united Israel" into existence; and beginning in David's reign, the fusion-process went forward until eventually the two elements were merged into an indistinguishable race.

Ethnic paradox in Bible history

For the simple reason that the Israelite element supplied the political symbol (Yahweh) under which the Hebrew nation evolved and because Yahweh was "the god of Israel," the fused population eventually called itself "the people of Israel" and ignored its Canaanite ancestry. The logic of the situation is entirely clear, although its implications are complex and confusing unless carefully scrutinized and held in mind as a key to the unfolding problem of Bible history. The Canaanites had no single, outstanding deity around which the new nation could rally; because "the inhabitants of the land" were independent city-ruled groups in which every province worshiped its own local Baal as a religious reflex of the human *baalim* in the urban centers. Obviously, then, no single one of the local Baal-gods could serve as an outstanding symbol of David's new state.

Thus it came to pass, in course of time, that the Hebrew people in Canaan advanced out of the melting-pot epoch and evolved a homogeneous, unitary Israel-consciousness. And since the Canaanite, or Amorite, name fell out of current use, a mistaken idea naturally arose that the Canaanites had been completely exterminated by the incoming Israelite conquerors from the wilderness.

In view of these facts we are now able to understand why the sources in the Old Testament disagree in their approach to the national history. Some of the documents are based upon the idea that the earlier inhabitants of Canaan were wholly swept away;

while others know that only a fraction of the previous population was destroyed and that the actual, historic Hebrew people evolved at the point of assimilation with earlier stocks.

Even so, however, certain qualifying explanations are called for with reference to the Ephraimite, or Josephite, element in the central highlands.

House of Joseph maintains original "purity"

The house of Joseph, as we have seen, developed on the ground of a local conquest, culminating in the destruction of Shechem, which cleared the central highlands of a baalistic city proprietary. The result was a consolidated rural class of pro-Yahweh *adonim*— an aristocracy of Israelite landholders and slave-owners. This whole section of the country was for the time being eclipsed by the house of Judah through the personality and work of David. While the assimilative tendencies to which the Davidic policy gave expression were in the long run irresistible, yet the course of Hebrew history, in its larger spiritual outcome, was determined by Josephite antagonism to those very tendencies. The great prophetic movement originated, not in Judah, but in Ephraim, where the house of Joseph continued as a kind of primitive enclave, reacting against the Canaanite, baalistic influences, which grew more and more powerful as the stream of history rolled onward.

David appropriates Josephite "ark of Yahweh"

Long before David became king, the ark of Yahweh, which was at first kept in the temple at Shiloh, had been taken by the Philistines to the Canaanite city of Kirjath-jearim (I Sam. 6:21; 7:1). Meantime this place had entered more and more into friendly relations with Israel; and by the time of David's reign it was called by the alternative name "Baal Judah," or "Kirjath-Baal which is Kirjath-jearim" (Josh. 15:60). The ark was now appropriated by the king and placed under cover of a tent within the fort of Zion, so that whatever mysterious potency or prestige it possessed might be conferred upon David's capital city (II Sam. 6). This object was probably not the only ark of Yahweh; but as part of the Josephite legend it had political value. That the city of Kirjath-jearim underwent a change of name to include the term "Baal" while the ark remained there is a noteworthy fact.

David conquers and enslaves Edomites

The policy of assimilation put the man power and wealth of Canaanite cities at the disposal of David, augmenting the strength of his armies; and one of the first moves which he made after sub-duing the Philistines was to turn his forces against the nation called Edom, directly to the south of Judah. The Edomites were a more primitive people than Israel, occupying territory which lay close to the desert and afforded less plentiful subsistence. Emigrants from Edom had already, before David's time, entered the territory of Judah and settled around Hebron, where we have seen them in history as the Kenizzite clan of Caleb. This community, however, as already shown, was incorporated into the kingdom of Judah by David. And although there is no record of any further incursions from Edom, such a possibility existed and probably explains David's move against the Edomites.

But this motive may have been colored by a more personal im-pulse: we find an Edomite by the name of Doeg in the province of Benjamin long before David became king, whose conduct was very obnoxious. This man was a slave (*ebed*) of Saul, and he held the position of overseer of all the slaves who tended Saul's cattle. He also acted as spy on David and reported his whereabouts to Saul (I Sam. 21:7; 22: 9–11). Moreover, at Saul's command this Edomite slew eighty-five priests of Yahweh in the Benjaminite vil-lage of Nob, for the simple reason that they were friendly with David. The massacre was thorough. But one priest, named Abi-athar, escaped and became an official of David (I Sam. 22:9–23). Thus, both David and his priest had the most personal reasons to abhor the Edomite slave, and perhaps their hatred for him had some influence toward the attack on his people, which is reported in a single brief sentence describing one of David's most important military adventures as follows: "And he put garrisons in Edom. Throughout all Edom put he garrisons; and all they of Edom became slaves (*abadim*) to David" (II Sam. 8:14).

Hebrew mythology creates "Isaac" and explains Edomite slavery

The two national groups, Israel and Edom, formed an almost continuous belt of population, beginning in the north with Dan and running southward into the wilderness below the frontier of Judah. That a legend of kinship should arise was but natural under the circumstances of time and place. Israel was descended from the mythic patriarch "Jacob"; while Edom was the progeny of "Esau." A list of Edomite monarchs appears in Genesis under the caption "Kings that reigned in the land of Edom before there reigned any king over the children of Israel" (Gen. 36:31). According to this document the Edomites achieved nationality prior to Israel and were therefore an older nation. The nature of the relationship between them takes form symbolically in the legend which makes them "brothers" linked by descent from a patriarch who now emerges in the evolving mythology of Israel as "Isaac" (Yitschak, Gen. 25).

But the enslavement of the older nation by the younger was of such a scandalous nature that it called forth five explanations, or excuses: (1) The best known is that which consigns the Edomites to bondage because they picked out the wrong ancestor, Esau, who "despised his birthright" and sold it to his younger brother, Jacob, for a mess of pottage (Gen. 25:29–34). (2) Another explanation, or alibi, is found in the story that Jacob deceived his father Isaac, who gave the younger son the blessing that should have been given to the first-born: "Let people serve thee, and nations bow down to thee. Be lord over thy brethren, and let thy mother's sons bow down to thee" (Gen. 27:1–29). (3) A third story makes the brothers twins, and when Esau, the elder, is delivered, his heel, or *aqeb*, is taken hold of by the younger, who is therefore called *"Ya-aqob"* (Jacob), that is, "he who grasps the heel," or, symbolically, "he who supplants" (Gen. 25:24–26). (4) Another mythic tale has it that when their mother was pregnant she was troubled by so much uterine commotion that she "enquired of Yahweh," who said that within her were two nations at war and that the elder was destined to serve the younger (Gen. 25:21–23). (5) Finally Esau, in tears, begs a blessing from Isaac. But his father says that he has already made Jacob lord over Esau, who must therefore serve Jacob (Gen. 27:30–40a). But in view of the historical fact that after Edom had been in slavery to Israel for a century or so and the united kingdom had split into "Israel" and "Judah," "Edom revolted from under the hand of Judah unto this day" (II Kings 8:22)—in view of this fact, Isaac is made to add, as it were, a postscript, wherein he says, "It shall come to pass . . . that thou shalt break his yoke from off thy neck" (Gen. 27:40b). Thus the legend, or myth, follows the track of history and evolves according to the pattern of actual events.

David conquers and enslaves the Moabites

Turning eastward in his new career of conquest and imperialism, David subjugated the people of Moab, east of the Dead Sea. "And he smote Moab. . . . And the Moabites became David's slaves (*abadim*), and brought tribute" (II Sam. 8:2). The nature of this relationship is indicated by another source pertaining to the time of Ahab: "And Mesha king of Moab was a sheepmaster and rendered unto the king of Israel an hundred thousand lambs and an hundred thousand rams, with the wool" (II Kings 3:4). Conquerors always look down upon those whom they subjugate and who pay them tribute. An example of this attitude is found in the Hebrew mythology relating to these Moabites, who are said in the book of Genesis to have originated from incest between the drunken Lot and his elder daughter; while the Ammonites, who were also subdued by David, are said to have had the same origin from Lot and his younger daughter (Gen. 19:30f.).

David conquers and enslaves the Syrians

Going still farther afield and venturing into the region that lay northeast of Israel, David extended his conquests to include the Syrians: "And David put garrisons in Syria of Damascus; and the Syrians became slaves (*abadim*) to David, and brought tribute" (II Sam. 8:6).

The circumstances in this case were unlike the conditions relating to the subjugation of Edom; and so the myths and legends about Syria took a different form. Unlike Edom, which was practically contiguous to Israel, Syria was farther away and more populous; therefore that region could not be dominated so completely by Jerusalem. Traditions were already afloat that Israel had migrated from Syria in the patriarchal, or prehistoric, age; that Syrian women had been afterward secured and brought into Canaan as wives for Isaac and Jacob; and that Jacob himself, on a visit to Syria, had obtained a harem consisting of Rachel, Leah, Bilhah, and Zilpah.

But so far as concrete historical events are concerned, the further back in time the legendary material goes, the more inconsistent and wavering it becomes. For example, Jacob's excursion to Syria is treated in two different ways: The Ephraimite document sends him out of Canaan at the secret behest of Rebekah his mother, merely to avoid the anger of Esau at the loss of his birthright: "Flee thou to Laban my brother until thy brother's anger turn away from thee, and then I will send and fetch thee from thence" (Gen. 27:41–45 *passim*). The intention here is a round trip, going and returning, to be entered upon secretly without the knowledge of Esau and without any reference to a wife. But in the P, or priestly, source Rebekah complains to Isaac that unless Jacob goes to Syria for a wife, he will marry some foreign girl in Canaan, as Esau has; whereupon, both parents command Jacob to visit Syria for the express purpose of getting a wife; and his expedition is known to Esau, who now undertakes to find a wife in the family, so as to curry favor with his parents (Gen. 27:46–28:9). In the

Ephraimite document, as we have already seen, Benjamin is born in the land of Benjamin in Canaan (Gen. 35:16–20). But in the P document, Benjamin is born in Syria, at Padan-aram, hundreds of miles distant from Canaan (Gen. 35:23–26).

The exploitation of Syria through David's conquest is reflected in the stories about the despoiling of Laban, the Syrian, through the sharp practice of Jacob, who steals away with a huge herd of cattle "unawares to Laban the Syrian" (Gen. 31:20). The entire herd is claimed by Laban upon overtaking Jacob: "And Laban answered and said unto Jacob. . . . The flocks are my flocks, and all that thou seest is mine" (Gen. 31:43). The size of the herd is not stated; but the story says that Jacob deducted exactly five hundred and eighty beasts as a present for his brother Esau; after which he still had "enough" remaining for himself (Gen. 32:14, 15; 33:11). According to the legend, therefore, Jacob took a large number of cattle out of Syria into Canaan; and the implication is that Jacob (that is, Israel) obtained from the Syrians the same kind of pastoral tribute that is received from the shepherd-king of Moab.

David king of kings

The conquests of David entitled him to be known as "king of kings" and also carried the conception of Yahweh, god of Israel, into the realm of imperialism as "god of gods." At the same time, the god "Baal-zebub," of Ekron, the Philistine city nearest to Israel, underwent a curious and obscure process of parallel evolution (II Kings 1:2). Representing the power that sought implacably to enslave Israel forever, Baal-zebub at length appears in the New Testament as "Beelzebub, the prince of demons"—an alternative title for "Satan" (adversary). Thus, in the book of Luke the titles are associated as follows:

But some of them said, By Beelzebub the prince of the demons casteth he out demons. . . . But he, knowing their thoughts, said unto them, Every kingdom divided against itself is brought to destruction. . . .

And if Satan also is divided against himself, how shall his kingdom stand? because ye say that I cast out demons by Beelzebub [Luke 11:15–18].

Thus gradually come into view the outlines of a mighty Biblical epic. The secular history, here a little and there a little, slowly puts the Baal-idea forward as a foil against which the idea of Yahweh evolves.

David's military forces

David began his career as an independent chieftain during the time of Saul with an army of six hundred men (I Sam. 23:13; 25:13). This force continued to be the central base of David's power throughout his kingship, first over Judah, and then over united Israel (II Sam. 15:18; 20:7). The individual soldier in this organization was called *gibbor* ("strong one" or "mighty one"; pl., *gibborim*). Their leader was a very important officer, Benaiah ben Jehoiada (II Sam. 8:18; 20:23). At the same time, the regular army, or "host," was commanded by David's nephew, Joab ben Zeruiah (II Sam. 8:16). The army was mobilized on warrant of the king and consisted of many thousands, drawn mostly from the landed proprietors (*adonim*). A man of this class was called *gibbor hayil*, or "mighty man of valor." Such were Gideon (Judg. 6:12); Kish, the father of Saul (I Sam. 9:1); Jephthah the Gileadite (Judg. 11:1); Jeroboam ben Nebat (I Kings 11:28). These men were not professional soldiers, like the plain *gibborim;* but Israel's power as a nation depended upon how many of the landed proprietors and their sons could be mustered into the "host."

Taxation under David

The fiscal department of David's administration was in charge of an officer named Adoniram, abbreviated sometimes to Adoram (Heb., The adon is exalted). The text merely says, "Adoram was over the tribute" (II Sam. 20:24). But this means in Hebrew that he was in charge of the "forced labor" (*mas*). In other words, he was not a collector of money, because the taxing power of the state was not at first exercised in terms of cash payment, as in modern times, but rather in terms of labor service rendered by the landed proprietors or by their slaves, which was a drain upon their economic resources in either case.

Thus it is clear that labor service and military duty were forms of taxation affecting the mass of the people precisely as if they paid money to the government; and eventually, as we shall see in due course, the exactions upon the *adonim* became progressively heavier and caused a serious economic problem.

David's revolting crime against Canaanite "baal"

David's capture of the Canaanite city Jerusalem brought him into contact with a certain resident named Uriah, who was a Hittite. This non-Hebrew became a noted soldier in David's army, belonging to the second class of knights (II Sam. 11, entire, and 23:39, *passim*). He was the owner of a house located below the hill on which a palace had been erected for David by the king of Tyre (II Sam. 5:11). While Uriah was absent in the army at war, David walked one day on the roof of the palace; and as he looked around over the ancient Canaanite city, congratulating himself on his good fortune and personal greatness, his attention was arrested suddenly by the sight of a beautiful woman washing herself in the courtyard of a house near by. Inquiring into her identity, the king found that she was Bathsheba, the wife of Uriah the Hittite. He then deliberately sent men to kidnap the woman and bring her to the palace, where David seduced her and then allowed her to return home.

After this David sent a message ordering Uriah to bring news of the war. Having heard the report from the husband of Bathsheba, the king told him to go down to his house. The term "down" occurs four times in the narrative, showing that the house was below the palace. But because Uriah's comrades were at war, he refused to follow this order and slept at the door of the palace with the slaves of the king. Then presently Uriah was ordered back to the army with a sealed letter telling Joab, the general, to set the hapless Hittite "in the forefront of the hottest battle." This, of course, was an indirect way of murdering the poor man so that he would be disposed of "legally" and the king could obtain "legal" possession of his wife.

The effect upon Bathsheba of Uriah's inevitable death is told as follows in our English Bibles: "And when the wife of Uriah heard that her husband was dead, she mourned for her husband" (II Sam. 11:26). But the Hebrew text runs thus: "And when the wife of Uriah heard that Uriah her *ish* was dead, she mourned for her *baal*." The translators are not to be blamed for using the one word "husband" when putting these two Hebrew terms into a modern Bible. Nor could they merely transliterate the Hebrew letters of the two words into corresponding modern letters, as above. Because if they had attempted anything different from what they have actually done, they would have been compelled to make wordy explanations in footnotes or on the margins; which, in any event, would be confusing to the laity, who, as a rule, use the Bible for devotional purposes only. Moreover, the translators themselves knew nothing about the problem which they have innocently obscured here and elsewhere in the Bible. If they had been asked for an explanation of the two words, they would merely have replied (without scientific accuracy) that *ish* and *baal* are simply two different Hebrew words for "husband."

The real situation, however, is that *ish*, which primarily means "man," or "a man" as a member of the community, is also the earlier "Israelite" word corresponding in a loose way to the modern term "husband." That is, an Israelite woman's husband was originally referred to as her "man"; while she was his "woman." Accordingly, the term *ish* is characteristic of the J, or Yahwistic, document in the Pentateuch, as expressing the relationship which we indicate by the word "husband."

On the other hand, the word *baal*, indicating "husband" or simply referring to a man, does not occur in the J document, but is frequently found in the Ephraimite, or E, document and in other sources relating to the Josephite part of the country. Although the house of Joseph exterminated the Canaanite *baalim* of Jericho, Bethel, and Shechem and thus cleared a space in the central highlands for the evolution of an upper class called *adonim*, and while these Ephraimite *adonim* held out as long as possible against Canaanite customs, nevertheless the population in that part of the country was at length engulfed in the religious and economic usages of Canaan: "When Ephraim became guilty in Baal, he died" (Hosea 13:1). The term *baal* is equated with *ish* in the passage about the death of Uriah simply because it refers to a foreigner who lived in the Canaanite city of Jebus (Jerusalem) before the place was captured by David.

The same Uriah story furnishes another instructive piece of evidence with regard to the problem which is developing under the surface. Uriah's death was caused by an order commanding him to take up an exposed fighting position close to the wall of a city, where the enemy's arrows were fatal, and in the story the manner of his death is compared to the death of Abimelech, the son of Gideon, in the Judges period, who was destroyed by a missile thrown from a city wall. The point of interest here is the treatment of Gideon's alternative name which was given to him because he had previously destroyed an altar of Baal, and thus earned the epithet "Jerub-baal," which means "Let Baal contend," that is, let Baal fight for himself now that his altar is demolished. Later in Hebrew history, under the influence of the great prophets, the name Baal, as applied to a god, was looked upon more and more as a term of shame (*bosheth*, or *besheth*). Therefore one of the post-exilic editors of the book of Samuel deliberately changed Gideon's nickname to "Jerub-besheth." (Compare Judges 9:1, "Abimelech the son of Jerubbaal," with II Sam. 11:21, "Abimelech the son of Jerubbesheth.") But the editors of Judges did not change the name from Jerubbaal in that book, either because they were not so daring or because the documents in Judges originated at an earlier period and acquired prestige and sanctity prior to the sources in Samuel.

The sin of David against the Jerusalemite *baal* Uriah reverberates in the Bible and has echoed through the ages. That the king repented is hardly probable. "When the mourning was past, David sent and fetched her to his house; and she became his wife, and bare him a son" (II Sam. 11:27). Bathsheba became the first lady of the kingdom and the mother of the successor to David. The writers of the Old Testament do not in any way seek to extenuate the king; and while the long story about the condemnation of David by Nathan the prophet cannot be taken literally, it nevertheless represents Israel's growing ethical sense in reaction against the royal crime. The king had already appeased the Canaanite walled cities by his general policy of conciliation and assimilation; but in committing this monstrous wickedness against a Canaanite *baal*, he began to alienate both his non-Hebrew subjects and the Israelite masses. The alleged penitence of David cannot be linked with Psalm 51, which is a post-exilic prayer of contrition.

Growing social discontent under David

David enjoyed enormous prestige through delivering the country from bondage to the Philistines and through his conquest of Edom, Syria, Moab, Ammon, and so forth. His reign brought "glory" to Israel; but the glory was tawdry and sordid, paid for by forced labor and military service, which inevitably reduced the level of Hebrew well-being. The condition toward which the nation was drifting is pictured by a speech put into the mouth of Samuel by a late editor who had in view the experiences of Israel under the kings:

This will be the *mishpat* of the king that shall reign over you: He will take your sons, and appoint them for himself, for his chariots, and to be his horsemen; and some shall run before his chariots. And he will appoint him captains over thousands, and captains over fifties; and will set them to ear his ground, and to reap his harvest, and to make his instruments of war, and instruments of his chariots. And he will take your daughters to be perfumers, and cooks, and bakers. And he will take your fields, and your vineyards, and your oliveyards, even the best of them, and give them to his servants [i. e., the nobles who surround the throne]. And he will take the ten per cent tax of your seed, and of your vineyards, and give to his officers and to his nobles. And he will take your menservants (*abadim*), and your maidservants (*shifakoth*), and your goodliest young men, and your asses, and put them to his work. And he will take the tenth of your sheep; and ye shall be his slaves (*abadim*) [I Sam. 8:11–17].

That a king had power over the disposition of land is taken for granted in a remark said to have been made by Saul when he realized the ambition of David to be a ruler: "Hear now, ye Benjaminites! Will the son of Jesse give every one of you fields and vineyards, and make all of you captains of thousands, and captains of fifties?" (I Sam. 22:7).

The foregoing generalization is illustrated by the case of Prince Absalom, a son of David. Not only did this personage have a residence in Jerusalem (II Sam. 14:24, 28), he also comes into view as an extensive landholder and slaveowner in Ephraim at a place called Baal-hazor (II Sam. 13:23–29; 14:30, 31); in these passages the word *abadim* [slaves] occurs five times, wrongly translated "servants." Another instance is that of the general, Joab, a relative of David, who was born in Judah and had a house "in the wilderness [of Judah]" (I Kings 2:33–34). But after David's rise to the throne of Israel, Joab also had an estate in Ephraim at Baal-hazor, near the property of Absalom (II Sam. 14:30).

Since these men were neither natives nor previous residents of Ephraim, they could have acquired land in the central hill country only by one of two methods, either of which would have been objectionable to the Ephraimite peasant aristocracy: (1) They might have invoked in their own behalf the exercise of the royal power of condemning or confiscating land, which would have been contrary to the traditional usages, or *mishpat*, of the Ephraimite *adonim*; or (2) they might have used pressure to buy land, which would also have outraged the moral feelings of the Josephite proprietary, who were strongly opposed to alienation of land by sale or by any other method.

David, like most kings, was completely surrounded by self-seekers who constituted, in modern parlance, a "ring." The most intimate ones were his own relatives, whose origins went back to the aristocratic families of Bethlehem. Joab, the general of the regular army, was the son of David's sister Zeruiah. Another of her sons, Abishai, was captain of several *gibborim*, or strong men, specially noted as adherents of David. Asahel, a third son of Zeruiah, was prominent in a group of thirty knights. Amasa, who was eventually appointed in Joab's place, was the son of another sister of David named Abigail (II Sam. 8:16; 19:13; 23:18, 24). A foreigner from the Philistine city of Gath, named Ittai, was a great friend of David and at one time commanded a third of the army (II Sam. 18:2; cf. 15:19–22). Another member of the ring was Hushai the Archite (II Sam. 16:16). But the wisest and most respected of all was a man whose name was Ahitophel: "The counsel . . . which he counselled in those days was as if one had enquired at the oracle of God" (II Sam. 16:23). Men such as these must be "taken care of" by a ruler if he is to have a government. The cases of Joab and Absalom, noted above in some detail, are only examples of what went on under the surface of Hebrew history.

There were ample opportunities for building up a "machine" responsible, not to the people, but to the king, who, in spite of having been elected, became increasingly despotic. One of the means at hand for taking care of the king's adherents was the tribute which flowed steadily into Israel from Edom, Moab, and other conquered countries. These incoming streams of wealth were not in any way under popular control, but accrued to David and were dispensed as best suited the king's purposes. Another source was found in the tariffs, formerly collected by the Philistines on the commerce passing through Canaan, which now became a perquisite of the Hebrews (I Kings 10:15). Also, the exactions of the king upon his own subjects, by the methods noted in the alleged address of Samuel, were an element in a situation containing many dark possibilities.

When a small, powerful group in the upper levels of an ancient oriental kingdom could be enriched through so many channels, the small and medium proprietors of the country found themselves at a growing disadvantage. The owner of a comparatively modest farm, having a few sons and one or two slaves, could be called into military service along with his elder offspring, and the affairs of his household would suffer more in proportion than the estate of some wealthier member of the aristocracy who had a larger number of slaves or enjoyed surreptitious favors through connections with the court. All the social and economic forces were at work under David by which the fortunes of privileged groups are always promoted, while at the same time the mass of smaller property holders are inevitably depressed into a lower condition. The process had not gone far as yet; but its beginnings are clearly discernible.

Directly involved in this problem was the necessity of appeal to the king's court at Jerusalem in legal disputes which were formerly settled by reference to the local elders, who understood better the claims of the litigants. These cases related mostly to land or to debts. And so the aggrieved parties had to sue for *mishpat* in an ancient, Canaanite, walled city. Thus, the narrative says, "David executed *mishpat* and righteousness unto all his people" (II Sam. 8:15). But the actual condition was that along with all the other business of government which demanded the king's personal attention the law cases piled up in arrears because the king did not appoint special judges to hear them. In view of these facts it is instructive to observe what was done by Absalom, the most favored of the royal princes:

Absalom rose up early, and stood beside the way of the gate; and it was so that when any man that had a legal dispute came to the king for *mishpat*, then Absalom called unto him, and said, Of what city art thou? And he said, Thy servant is of one of the tribes of Israel. Then Absalom said unto him, Look! Thy matters are good and right; but there is no man deputed by the king to hear thee. And Absalom said, Oh that I were made a judge in the land; so that every man that hath any dispute might come unto me. And on this manner did Absalom to all Israel that came to the king for *mishpat*. So Absalom stole the hearts of the men of Israel [II Sam. 15:2–6].

"Rebellion of Absalom" social uprising

There is no doubt that Absalom was ambitious and that he was what we now call a demagogue. But his personal traits do not explain the history with which his name stands connected. His ambition found a channel in the growing popular protest against the centralizing tendencies of the government. That Absalom himself was in the little circle of royal favorites and that an estate had been carved out for him in the house of Joseph would not count against him in the eyes of a crude constituency, blinded by the prestige of a prince daring enough to step forth and take the part of "the people" against a royal father who was more and more incurring the dislike of the masses. "There was none to be so much praised in all Israel as Absalom for his beauty:—from the sole of his foot even to the crown of his head, there was no blemish in him" (II Sam. 14:25).

Another high-placed leader in the movement seeking to depose David was the king's counsellor, Ahitophel of Giloh. This man's coöperation may be explained by a fact in his family history, for he was the father of Eliam, who, in turn, was the father of Bathsheba (II Sam. 23:34; cf. 11:3). Thus the queen was the granddaughter of Ahitophel. But in view of the popular resentment against the murder and adultery committed by David, it is reasonable to infer that Ahitophel had viewed his personal connection with the throne as a doubtful honor and that he had been awaiting the opportunity to bring the royal crimes back upon the king's head. "And the conspiracy was strong; for the people increased continually with Absalom. And there came a messenger to David, saying, The hearts of the men of Israel are after Absalom" (II Sam. 15:12, 13).

A great battle took place between the adherents of David and the followers of Absalom. The tide was turned in the king's favor by the tough, mercenary *gibborim*, who were "chafed in their minds like a bear robbed of her whelps" (II Sam. 16:6; 17:8; 18:6, 7). The peasantry were slain by thousands; Absalom himself losing his life; and while this battle appeared to decide the issue, the real animus of the uprising comes into relief as a kind of postscript. For the revolt was continued under the stimulus of a new leader, a Benjaminite by the name of Sheba ben Bichri: "He blew a trumpet, and said, We have no part in David! Neither have we inheritance in the son of Jesse! Everyman to his tents, O Israel! So every man of Israel followed Sheba ben Bichri; but the men of Judah clave unto their king" (II Sam. 20:1, 2). The house of Joseph was reasserting itself; this new phase of the mutiny called for the services of both Joab with his peasant conscripts, and Benaiah ben Jehoiada with his *gibborim* who must have been still more "chafed" in their minds at the prospect of additional war duty. The rebellious Benjaminite was pursued "through all the tribes of Israel" into the far north, where the Josephite uprising was finally crushed (II Sam. 20:6f.). But the outcome of the civil war did not presage well for the future of the Davidic dynasty.

Ambitions of Adonijah

The failure of Absalom brought into play the ambitions of another son of David: "Then Adonijah exalted himself, saying, I will be king. And he prepared him chariots and horsemen, and fifty men to run before him" (I Kings 1:5). This prince's name in Hebrew means "Yahweh is my *adon*." The latter term is familiar as an early and primitive designation of the Hebrew master class in the rural districts; whereas in contrast with *adon*, the term *baal* refers to the Canaanite, or Amorite, master class driven into the walled cities by the Israelite invasion. We have seen that David called Yahweh a *baal* after the battle of Perazim (*supra*, p. 107); and it will become clearer that the application of these terms to Yahweh is involved in a significant phase of Hebrew psychology. The name Adonijah ("Yahweh is my *adon*") may have been given to the prince by David, or it may have attached itself to Adonijah because he opposed the baalistic tendencies of David, just as many Hebrew names grew out of concrete occasions. Let us notice, then, the elements for and against Adonijah's claim to the throne.

Coöperating with him was Abiathar, the Josephite priest. This man was the only survivor of the northern priests massacred by Doeg the Edomite at the command of King Saul (I Sam. 22:20, 21). Another assistant was the doughty general Joab, who was now out of favor with David (I Kings 1:7). But on the other hand, Captain Benaiah and his *gibborim* were not with Adonijah; nor was the sinister priestly figure Zadok (*Tsadok*) on the side of the new aspirant. This priest became the real or symbolic father of the *Tsadokee* (or Sadducee) priesthood which represented everything aristocratic and undemocratic in the religion of Israel clear down into the New Testament period and was never popular with the Israelite masses at any time (I Kings 1:8, 10).

Bathsheba intervenes to promote "Sh'lomoh"

Alarmed at the course of events, Bathsheba, ex-wife of Uriah the Hittite, now entered upon a palace intrigue to thwart the ambition of Adonijah and promote the fortunes of her son, called in Hebrew *Sh'lomoh* (rendered inaccurately "Solomon"). In consequence, David, whose throne was founded originally upon election by the people, made use of his prestige, without the slightest warrant in public opinion, to deliver the kingdom to the son of his union based upon adultery and murder. Summoning Zadok, the priest, and Benaiah, captain of the *gibborim*, David ordered Zadok to anoint the son of Bathsheba king, and the proceedings were guarded by the police (I Kings 1:15f.).

What the house of Joseph thought about this high-handed affair may well be imagined. They were not even consulted, and they were forced to submit for the time being. But the eventual result, the permanent separation of Israel from Judah, was more certain than when Sheba ben Bichri led the Ephraimite revolt against the rule of David.

New king native of Canaanite walled city, 970 B. C.

The successor to David was born in the Amorite city of Jebus (II Sam. 5:14; 12:24). Out of touch with the standpoint of the Israelite masses, he was wholly surrounded by machine politicians and kept in power by professional, hired strong men. He ordered their captain, Benaiah, to go and "fall on" Adonijah and slay him. The same procedure was followed in the case of Joab, the old commander of the national army; after which Benaiah was promoted to be head of the host in Joab's place. The Josephite priest Abiathar was ordered back to the village of Anathoth in the Ephraimite province of Benjamin, and his position as head of the Jerusalem sanctuary was given to Zadok (I Kings 2:24, 25, 26, 28–34). Equally important, Adoniram, David's fiscal officer, continued as chief tax collector and overseer of the *mas,* or labor-gangs (I Kings 4:6).

Twelve districts appointed for taxation

As might be expected, the arrangements of the new king to exploit the people were more systematic and thorough than those of David. The country was marked out into *twelve* districts for purposes of taxation and forced-labor, which may have suggested the idea of twelve tribes in the still unsettled and fluid legends of Israel. The names of several very important Canaanite walled cities, unconquered in the Judges epoch, now appear casually in the tax map as organized into the kingdom of Israel. These fortified cities were mostly in or near the plain of Esdraelon, to the north of the central highlands, which were the proper home of the house of Joseph. Their names are Shaalbim, Bethshemesh, Taanach, Megiddo, Beth-shan (I Kings 4:9, 12; cf. Judg. 1:27, 33, 35). In view of developments that will shape the history presently, it is important to observe that no fortified cities are mentioned as existing in the central highlands at this time and that the tax officer of the region is listed as being in general charge without having headquarters at some city stronghold, thus, "Ben Hur in the highlands of Ephraim" (I Kings 4:8). In other words, that section of the country continued as it had been in the earlier periods—an agricultural and pastoral community of hill villages on an irregular plateau averaging about 2,400 feet above the sea.

Hebrew nation forced into framework of despotism, 970 B. C.

A small group of machine politicians who have the services of a conscienceless, paid police can frequently seize the agencies of government and for awhile hold in subjection a large, unorganized, inert community. This is precisely what happened after the death of David. The Josephite bulk of the nation, having already risen against the growing centralization of government, waited in silence for an opportunity to throw off the still worse autocracy established by the son of Bathsheba. The outlines of the new system of tyranny rise into view as we examine the fundamental sources used by the compiler of the books of Kings.

Referring to the twelve officers placed over the twelve districts marked out for purposes of taxation, the following statement is instructive: "And those officers provided victual for king Sh'lomoh, and for all that came unto king Sh'lomoh's table, every man in his month: they lacked nothing" (I Kings 4:27). A sample of the commissary department's work for one day is given thus: "thirty measures of fine flour; threescore measures of meal; ten fat oxen; twenty oxen out of the pastures; an hundred sheep, beside harts, roebucks, fallow deer, and fatted fowl" (I Kings 4:22, 23).

In line with the address placed in the mouth of Samuel, the following is very suggestive:

And king Sh'lomoh raised labor gangs out of all Israel; and the levy was thirty thousand men. And he sent them to Lebanon,—ten thousand a month by courses; a month they were in Lebanon, and two months at home. And Adoniram was over the labor gangs. And Sh'lomoh had seventy thousand that bare burdens and eighty thousand hewers in the mountains, beside the chief officers which were over the work, three thousand and three hundred, which ruled over the people that wrought in the work [I Kings 5:13–16].

All this tremendous human exertion was related to various undertakings, partly described as follows:

(1) A huge royal palace in Jerusalem, which was thirteen years in course of construction, the dimensions and plans of which are

not given (I Kings 7:1). (2) A great edifice called The House of the Forest of Lebanon—a hundred cubits long, fifty cubits broad, and thirty cubits high, resting upon four rows of cedar pillars, which upheld cedar beams. Here was placed the throne of ivory, overlaid with gold, and having six steps guarded by twelve lions. And here also was the judgment seat of the Supreme Court, presided over by the king, who, following the example of his father, monopolized the *mishpat* of the nation (I Kings 7:2–7; 10:18–20). (3) Another palace, of unspecified size and plans, for the daughter of Pharaoh, king of Egypt, whom the king of Israel took as chief wife (I Kings 7:8; 9:24). (4) A temple to Yahweh, seven years in course of building, as contrasted with the king's personal palace which required thirteen years. The temple was much smaller than the House of Lebanon, that is, sixty by thirty by twenty cubits, the cubic contents being 36,000, while the Lebanon house was 150,000, in addition to the unknown size of the palaces for the king and for the daughter of Pharaoh (I Kings 6:1–10, 15–38). (5) Repairs to the stone walls of ancient Canaanite cities coming down from the pre-Hebrew period, such as Jerusalem, Megiddo, Hazor, Gezer, and other cities (I Kings 9:15). Other items of royal magnificence are given as one thousand, four hundred chariots, forty thousand stalls for horses, and twelve thousand horsemen (I Kings 4:26; 10:26).

Along with all the wealth arising out of taxation and forced labor were the imposts on mercantile caravans going through the land in many directions (I Kings 10:15). This lucrative source of income had, no doubt, passed entirely out of control by the Philistines, who had now sunk into a little nation of agriculturists and fishermen. A basis can be seen here for the growth of legends in which the Philistines are a weak people who regard the Hebrew patriarchs respectfully and make treaties with them (Gen. 21:32; 26:8, 14, 28, 29).

Having power over international commerce, the new government naturally entered into alliance with Tyre, the great Phoenician emporium, whose fortified port lay on the Mediterranean just west of Dan, the northern Hebrew city. An Israelite navy was built on the shores of the Red Sea, in the land of Edom, which had long ago become a tribute-paying dependency under David. The vessels, however, were not navigated by Hebrews, who knew nothing of water transportation, but by Tyrian shipmen who had knowledge of the sea and were obtained from the Phoenician king (I Kings 9:26, 27). This flotilla made regular voyages to foreign countries, bringing gold, silver, ivory, apes, and peacocks for the son of Bathsheba (I Kings 10:22).

The climax of the new extravagance was the royal harem, which exceeded anything known in the times of David. The statistics are no doubt exaggerated; but a late source declares that, in addition to Pharaoh's daughter, this amorous monarch had seven hundred wives and three hundred concubines. Such a ménage would require a huge income arising from the systematic exploitation and enslavement of the Israelite masses.

Jewish redactors glorify heir of David

The compiler of the books of Kings tells us categorically that the sources for this reign are to be found in a work entitled "The Book of the Acts of Sh'lomoh" (I Kings 11:41). Thus, the literary process by which the Hebrew Bible was constructed is put clearly on view. The book about this king was a work of reference available at one time, but now, unfortunately, lost. The method of the editor of Kings was to make excerpts from this earlier source and interpolate brief comments, as well as long passages, in which he vainly seeks to glorify the voluptuous heir of David.

The material about "the prophet Nathan" has the same literary and theological character as the interpolations with reference to Samuel: they seek to build up a structure of prestige around a figure which has extended conversations with Deity; and this figure is used retrospectively for the purpose of legitimizing a king who actually comes into power by purely secular means. Thus, Saul and David are alleged to have been chosen as kings by Samuel at the command of Yahweh, when, as a matter of fact, they were elected by the people. The son of Bathsheba was enthroned by means of a palace intrigue, not by Nathan the prophet, and his accession was thus a purely secular development.

Again, a long Deuteronomic interpolation occurs beginning at I Kings 8:14 and concluding with 9:9. This passage alleges that a categorical declaration was made by Yahweh, saying, "Since the day that I brought forth my people Israel out of Egypt, I chose no city out of all the tribes of Israel to build an house, that my name might be therein" (I Kings 8:15, 16). This is an obvious endeavor to discredit and throw into obscurity the Josephite house of God at Shiloh in the hill country of Ephraim, regarding which the prophet Jeremiah, of the tribe of Benjamin, says, "The word that came to Jeremiah from Yahweh, saying, Go ye now unto my place which was in Shiloh, where I caused my name to dwell at the first, and see what I did to it" (Jer. 7:1, 12). The sanctuary at Shiloh is described in the first book of Samuel as a "house" having "doors" (I Sam. 3:15); as a "temple" containing an "ark," which was lighted at night by a "lamp" (I Sam. 3:3); the narrative speaks of Eli the priest seated upon a seat "by a post of the temple of Yahweh" (I Sam. 1:9); there is also a reference to "the women that assembled at the door of the tabernacle of the congregation" (I Sam. 2:22); and it is stated that the establishment had a regular service of sacrifice (I Sam. 2:13f.). These details, together with Jeremiah's testimony, should be enough to discredit the Deuteronomic interpolator, who so clearly reveals his anti-Josephite bias and his desire to give the Jerusalem temple a character of uniqueness and sanctity wholly out of keeping with the fundamental sources in Kings itself.

The dimensions and furniture of the Jerusalem temple may be taken as authentic (I Kings 6 [except vss. 11–14]–7 [entire]). But the priestly details, the alleged assembly of the entire nation, and the supernatural glory (*kabod*) filling the temple—all these are insertions by the redactors (I Kings 8:1–13).

Enslavement of Edomites calls for special attention

Subjugation of Edom, "the elder brother of Israel," was accomplished, as we have seen, by military force. Hostility between the two nations prevailed for centuries; but the definite basis of the relationship did not come into view until recently, when certain discoveries were made by an archaeological expedition representing the American School of Oriental Research at Jerusalem, the Transjordan Department of Antiquities, and the Hebrew Union College at Cincinnati.[3]

About twenty miles below southern Judah and in midst of the now desolate land of ancient Edom the remains of a large fort were discovered in 1934. Standing on an elevation about ninety feet above the surrounding dry water courses, this place is called by the nomadic Arabs "The Ruin of Hamr Ifdan" (*Khirbet Hamr Ifdan*). A citadel of such magnitude implies that a powerful garrison was located here permanently. The reason for its existence became evident when the further disclosure was made that the fortress lay in a strategic position dominating several roads which go directly to ancient copper mining and smelter sites in the vicinity.

A striking example of these mining centers is found at a point five miles to the southeast of the citadel. It is called by the Bedouins "Ruin of Copper" (*Khirbet Nahas*). The word *nahas* (copper) corresponds to the Hebrew term *nehsheth*, meaning copper, or tin-alloyed copper, known as brass. The term *nehushtan* was applied to a copper or brass god (possibly a serpent) worshiped in Jerusalem for many centuries, until the time of King Hezekiah; "for unto those days the children of Israel did burn incense to it" (II Kings 18:4). A great deal of equipment in the temple of Yahweh at Jerusalem was made of this alloyed metal. The term *nehsheth* (translated "brass") occurs nine times in the schedule of work on the temple (I Kings 7:14, 15, 16, 27, 30, 45, 47). "Neither was the weight of the *nehsheth* found out" (I Kings 7:47).

[3] The expedition into Edom is described in full by Dr. Nelson Glueck, Professor of Biblical Interpretation, Hebrew Union College, in a volume entitled *The Other Side of Jordan* (New Haven, 1940). Dr. Glueck is not only an archaeologist, but he understands the literary and historical approach to the Hebrew Bible.

The precise economic nature of the connection between Israel and Edom thus begins to clear up. The "Copper Ruin" was a mine where the ore was not only dug but also smelted. The site is covered with large buildings, furnaces, miners' huts, and great piles of copper slag. At one end of the area is an enclosure 76 meters square (about 50,000 sq. ft.), surrounded by walls about 6 ft. thick. In this enclosure are the remains of more furnaces, miners' huts, and copper slag heaps. Similar centers are found within a radius of a few miles on roadways commanded by the central fortress.

Here, then, emerging from the mists of dim antiquity three thousand years ago, is the objective background of the Biblical narrative saying that David conquered this country and "put garrisons in Edom, throughout all Edom put he garrisons; and all they of Edom became David's slaves (*abadim*). And Yahweh preserved David whithersoever he went" (II Sam. 8:14). Although a palace was built in Jerusalem for David, the postponement of the temple until the next reign seems to indicate that in David's time the general situation was not fully organized. But the successor of David sent for a Phoenician overseer of metal work, whose labor gangs took the smelted copper into the Jordan valley, where suitable clay was found for the huge molds, or matrices, into which the melted metal was poured (I Kings 7:13, 14, 46).

Copper was wanted, not simply for manufacturing temple equipment but also as a commercial product having great value in the channels of international trade. Exportation of this metal on a huge scale to pay for merchandise imported from distant lands explains the fleet of ships constructed at the port of Edom on the Red Sea. "And King Sh'lomoh made a navy of ships in Ezion-geber which is beside Eloth, on the shore of the Red Sea, in the land of Edom" (I Kings 9:26). Here, again, rich archaeological deposits were awaiting the spade of modern scholars.

Going southward from the fortress and mining sites described above, the explorers finally arrived in the vicinity of Edom's port on the Red Sea. And here was unearthed the complicated ruin of an ancient city, surrounded by huge walls from seven to twelve feet thick, the topmost height of the walls being on the level of today's desert, while the entire city was buried in the drifting sand of ages. Enclosed within this fortification was a remarkable manu-facturing center, laid out in streets, having brick houses and a series of industrial plants for smelting copper and iron and making metal-lic goods. A forced draft system was used in operating refineries and complex flues and air-channels. The city is a most impressive sight.

All these discoveries, taken in connection with the Biblical sources, help us to realize how complete was the conquest of Edom and how drastic was the bondage of its inhabitants under the yoke of Jerusalem. Slave labor mined and smelted the vast quantities of copper which constituted the main stock in trade of the Hebrew monarch. The prodigal scale on which this laboriously produced wealth was used in the purchase of luxuries not only proves how little the legal owners of it cared for the toiling masses, held down by military garrisons, but it also throws light on the ultimate col-lapse of David's dynasty, which resulted from the revolt of Ephraim. The flotilla that set sail from Ezion-geber was loaded with copper, and it

came to Ophir, and fetched from thence gold, four hundred and twenty talents, and brought it to King Sh'lomoh . . . Now the weight of gold that came to Sh'lomoh in one year was six hundred three score and six talents of gold . . . And King Sh'lomoh made three hundred shields of beaten gold; three pounds of gold went to one shield; and the King put them in the House of the Forest of Lebanon (at Jerusalem). More-over, the king made a great throne of ivory and overlaid it with the best gold . . . And all his drinking vessels were of gold, and all the vessels of the House of the Forest of Lebanon were of pure gold; none were of silver; it was nothing accounted of in the days of Sh'lomoh [I Kings 9:28; 10:14, 17, 18, 21].

And Sh'lomoh gathered together chariots and horsemen; and he had a thousand and four hundred chariots, and twelve thousand horsemen, whom he bestowed in the cities for chariots and with the King at Jeru-salem" [I Kings 10:26].

Stables for three hundred of these horses have been unearthed by excavators at the important hill-city of Megiddo, commanding the plain of Esdraelon.[4]

Thus, at length, it becomes possible not only to understand the organization of Hebrew power which oppressed Edom and other small nations; but at the same time we can see how the Davidic aristocracy ruled the masses in Israel. The successor of David has been called a man of peace; but while it is true that he waged no actual wars, he possessed expensive and well-equipped military forces by which Israelites and foreigners alike were held in subjection. This regime was the basis upon which were built the splendid royal palaces at Jerusalem and the ornate sanctuary of Yahweh.

House of Joseph moved by stirrings of revolt

The arrogance of the Davidic monarchy grew more and more unbearable. The house of Joseph, in the hill country of Ephraim, began to realize that it was now given over into a condition of permanent slavery to the house of Judah. Herein lay a vivid suggestion toward a legend that in dim antiquity the mythical patriarch Judah proposed the sale of Joseph into bondage: "And Judah said unto his brethren . . . Come and let us sell him to the Ishmeelites. . . . And his brethren were content . . . and sold Joseph to the Ishmeelites for twenty pieces of silver" (Gen. 37:26, 27, 28). Unless the people of Ephraim rose up and made a Declaration of Independence, backed by deeds, they would never again be free.

The king unwisely placed an Ephraimite, Jeroboam ben Nebat, "over all the burden of the house of Joseph" (I Kings 11:26f.). This man is described as *gibbor hayil*—one of the upper class of landholders, or *adonim*, who could be called into military service. As an Ephraimite, he would naturally know about the discontent smoldering throughout the central hill country; and his official position as overseer of all the forced-labor service imposed upon the Josephites gave him an opportunity to realize more clearly the

[4] Guy, *New Light from Armageddon* (Chicago, 1927–29).

spirit of insubordination which was gathering force among his countrymen. His legal duty, of course, demanded that he sell out his neighbors; but he chose the opposite course. Entering into a conspiracy, Jeroboam "lifted up his hand against the king," that is, he secretly took an oath to renounce the house of David.

The oppression of Joseph by Judah brought Hebrew prophecy forward in defense of Ephraimite national integrity against usurpation. The religious forces of the central highlands found a leader in prophet Ahijah from the ancient sanctuary village of Shiloh. Thus it came to pass, upon a certain day, when Jeroboam, wearing a new uniform, went forth from Jerusalem, "the prophet Ahijah the Shilonite found him. . . . And Ahijah caught the new garment that was on him, and rent it in twelve pieces; and he said to Jeroboam, Take thee ten pieces: for thus saith Yahweh, the god of Israel, Behold, I will rend the kingdom out of the hand of Sh'lomoh, and will give ten tribes to thee" (I Kings 11:29–31).

The foregoing material is complete in itself, and comes ultimately from some Ephraimite source which, in the name of Yahweh, validates the political and religious independence of the house of Joseph, precisely as in the days when altars to Yahweh stood at Shiloh, Ramah, Gilgal, and other Ephraimite villages. That is to say, in conspiring with Jeroboam for the political independence of the Josephites, the prophet Ahijah also expected a correlative religious independence carrying with it the legal right to worship Yahweh at altars in the central highlands. The two things necessarily went along together in the objective, secular life of antiquity; because, in ancient society the one was impossible without the other; the Josephites could not separate themselves politically from Judah without at the same time separating religiously.

But this, of course, was not satisfactory to the Judaic editor through whom we get the books of Kings; and so, after using the material quoted above he immediately puts into the mouth of Ahijah a long Deuteronomic passage, pro-Davidic in tone, emphasizing that Jerusalem was the city chosen by Yahweh to put his name there, thus, by implication, preparing the way for the doctrine that the religious separation of the Josephites from Judah constituted the sin of ecclesiastical schism (I Kings 11:32–39). But this doctrine was far ahead of conditions and ideas prevailing in the time of Jeroboam, because the temple of Yahweh at Jerusalem was at first only a gorgeous royal chapel and was not regarded as the *only* place where an Israelite should rightfully and legally worship Yahweh.

Following this interpolation, the compiler once more quotes from early material showing that the Ephraimite conspiracy became known to the government at Jerusalem; which thereupon sought the life of Jeroboam, who fled into Egypt, where he was given hospitality by Shishak, the king of that country. Thus, for the time being the plans of the conspirators failed.

VIII. RENASCENCE OF JOSEPH

THE POWERFUL political and military machine which upheld the Davidic throne was able to suppress discontent and mutiny while the son of Bathsheba lived, but his death precipitated one of the most important, though little understood, epochs in Hebrew history. The heir to the throne, Rehoboam, did not venture to assume power by dictatorial proclamation, as did his father. Instead, he came up into Ephraim, where he expected the people to go through the form of electing him king. The following statement is said to have been made by "all Israel," that is, the elders, representing the landholders, or *adonim*: "Thy father made our yoke grievous. Now therefore make thou the grievous service of thy father, and his heavy yoke which he put upon us, lighter; and we will serve thee" (I Kings 12:4).

But this reasonable request of the elders called forth a reply which reveals all the concentrated arrogance and perfidy accumulated in the dynasty of Jerusalem through the reigns of two kings for seventy-five years: "My father made your yoke heavy; and I will add to your yoke. My father chastised you with whips; but I will chastise you with scorpions!" (I Kings 12:4, 14). Then the scion of the house of David commanded Adoniram, the overseer of labor-conscription, to proceed with his duties. "But all Israel stoned him with stones, that he died"; and they answered Rehoboam in the words used by Sheba ben Bichri at the time of the revolt against King David: "What portion have we in David? Neither have we inheritance in the son of Jesse! To your tents, O Israel! Now see to thine own house, David!" (I Kings 12:16, 18; cf. II Sam. 20:1). And so, after the reigns of only two kings the dynasty of David passed from the stage of history as an oriental power and reverted to the obscure status of a tiny principality in southern Canaan.

The story of the revolution comes from an Ephraimite source, which declares that "the cause was from Yahweh, that he might perform his saying, which Yahweh spake by Ahijah the Shilonite" (I Kings 12:15).

Josephite revolution largely misunderstood by Jews, Gentiles

The reassertion of Josephite power in Israel has been misunderstood, first, by post-exilian Judaic editors and compilers of the Hebrew Bible, because of their anti-Ephraimite prejudice and their lack of historical training; second, by orthodox Jewish writers and thinkers ever since; third, by orthodox Gentile students of the Bible; and last, by many Gentile "higher critics," who have investigated Bible history from literary and grammatical standpoints and, in most cases, have been subtly dominated by the orthodox legend. Yet we could not now possess the Old Testament itself without the faithful zeal of Judaic compilers, unknown to fame; nor would the writings have been physically preserved through ages of anti-Semitic persecution without the fanatical faith of Talmudists and rabbis; nor would the Hebrew text have been translated into foreign tongues without the devotion of orthodox Christian scholars; nor should we now be in a position to interpret the Bible critically from sociological and economic points of approach without the careful, sometimes capricious, labor of critics whose methods of operation were primarily literary and grammatical. More than one type of worker and more than one ideology are necessary for the progress of scientific knowledge. The Bible in your home is woven into an almost incredible process of history, beginning far back in oriental times and extending throughout the ages until today.

Germinal ideas for growth of Hebrew legend

When the Josephites came out from under bondage to the tyrannical dynasty seated in the old, pre-Hebrew stronghold of Jerusalem, the sense of release was overwhelming, and it made an impression upon Israelite psychology never to be effaced. That no adequate conception of it has been conveyed to us by the Jewish makers of the Hebrew Bible is not strange in the least when we consider the post-exilic Jewish point of view: Ephraim was largely alien and foreign and had vanished into captivity hundreds of years before the Jewish compilers began to create the Bible.

Although the national sense of liberation from "the house of bondage" has not been definitely transmitted to us in so many words by the unsympathetic editors of the Old Testament, they have nevertheless copied out from ancient Ephraimite sources Hebrew legends formed on the pattern of actual Josephite slavery in Canaan. Thus, the following facts of history are to be considered as germinal in the evolution of bondage myth: the levy of thirty thousand "out of all Israel"; the long and arduous construction in Jerusalem of the royal palace, the house of the forest of Lebanon, the temple of Yahweh, and the palace for the daughter of Pharaoh, king of Egypt; the strengthening of ancient Canaanite city walls; and the flight of Jeroboam the Josephite into Egypt and his eventual return from Egypt. All these living facts in Hebrew history furnished raw materials on which the legend-building faculty of the house of Joseph exercised itself in the new epoch following liberation from Davidic tyranny.

Thus stories originated telling how Joseph was sold into slavery in Egypt (Gen. 37); how the other tribes of Israel came into Egypt as an afterthought (Gen. 46); how the Israelites were downtrodden in Egypt and compelled to work in labor gangs under Pharaoh (Exod. 1:11); how they escaped from Egypt and carried with them the bones of Joseph" (Exod. 13:19). But the total mass of legend has no internal consistency. According to one account Jacob goes into Egypt "few in number," having with him seventy-two souls (Gen. 46:27; cf. Deut. 26:5); but according to earlier material Jacob is, not the head of a small household, but the conqueror of the central highlands of Canaan and military head of an army equipped with swords and bows, the territory having been given to Joseph (Gen. 48:21, 22).

Again, according to one strand of the legends, the Israelites are said to have been established at first on the northeastern frontier of

Egypt, in the land of Goshen. Thus, Joseph instructs his brethren: "When Pharaoh shall call you, and shall say, What is your occupation? that ye shall say, Thy servants trade hath been about cattle from our youth even until now, both we and also our fathers,—that ye may dwell in the land of Goshen; for every shepherd is an abomination to the Egyptians" (Gen. 46:34; 47:1, 3, 4, 6). Then the legends allow for the passage of four hundred years (Gen. 15:13), after which the Israelites are still in the land of Goshen: "And Yahweh rained hail upon the land of Egypt . . . but there was no hail in the land of Goshen, where the children of Israel were" (Exod. 9:23, 26; cf. 8:22).

But according to other strands of the legends, the Israelites are intimately mingled with the Egyptians in Egypt proper, and when about to escape from the land every Hebrew man and woman "borrows" from Egyptian neighbors "jewels of silver and jewels of gold" (Exod. 11:2; 12:35, 36). Moreover, Yahweh proposes to slay all the first born of the Egyptians in the darkness of a single night, so that the Israelites, in order to protect themselves from what would otherwise be indiscriminate slaughter, are commanded to put the sacrificial blood of a lamb on the door posts of all their houses, which will enable the destroying deity to distinguish between Egyptian and Hebrew houses: "and when I see the blood, I will pass over you, and the plague shall not be upon you to destroy you when I smite the land of Egypt" (Exod. 12:13).

Another precedent for the bondage legend was furnished by the actual, historic deliverance of Israel from the king of Canaan, who had nine hundred chariots of iron, which were all swept away by the waters of the Kishon in the time of Deborah (Judg. 4:2, 3; 5:21). On this model, the king of Egypt, in addition to six hundred "chosen" chariots, had all the other chariots of Egypt—the entire number being swept away in the waters of the Red Sea (Exod. 14:7, 27, 28).

Our main object, of course, is to study authentic, secular Hebrew history in the land of Canaan. The legends are merely cited for the purpose of showing that the course of real experience in Canaan gave suggestive points of departure for the legend-building imagination, which, when operating in the void of prehistoric time, necessarily worked into fantastic and inconsistent forms.

That the actual, objective history had provided grounds on which the legends of Israel could originate and make a certain amount of progress prior to the break between Joseph and the house of Judah, has been pointed out in earlier chapters; that is, that Joseph and Benjamin were the "core" of the nation; that the mother of these boys, Rachel, was the beloved and favorite wife of Jacob; that he, himself, was "the man of Rachel" (*ish-rahel*, by elision "Israel"); and that the other "sons," or "tribes," were the issue of a less-regarded wife, or of slave girls.

But the definitive Josephite revolt against the house of David produced a new environment in which the legend could assume clearer forms along certain lines of crystallization. More than seventy-five years had passed since the Philistine oppressors of Israel had been defeated and reduced to impotence by David; and the gratitude which the people of that earlier day had felt was now obscured by the shameful tyranny which later-coming generations of Israel had suffered under the Davidic dynasty. Hence, conditions had arisen in which the idea could emerge that Judah, having been forced upon Israel, was hated for that very reason; had been endured for a time, and then thrust out. Thus, by a similar chain of ideas, Leah, the mother of Judah, is foisted upon Jacob against his will; but he is compelled to endure her presence in his tent for "one week" (Ephraimite source, Gen. 29:23, 25, 28b). Unable to change the substance of the legend, which had stood for a long time prior to the Babylonian exile, the Judaic editor then inserted a J passage, which gives Leah several sons by Jacob; whereat she vainly exclaims, "Now therefore will my husband be joined unto me" (Gen. 29:31–35). This Judaic detour is followed by another section of the Ephraimite source, wherein Jacob has put Leah out of his tent, so that she no longer has his company. It is in the days of wheat harvest; and Leah has procured a supply of certain fruit which even today ripens at that season in the east, and which the modern translations call "mandrakes." In the Hebrew text of Genesis, however, the fruit is called *dudaim*, which means "love apples," because of a supposed power over conception. Accordingly, when Jacob comes out of the field in the evening, Leah goes to meet him with her love apples, demanding that he perform the duty of a husband. She bears him two more sons, making six altogether, and exclaims, "Now will my husband dwell with me because I have borne him six sons" (Gen. 30:14–20). But Jacob is obdurate; and nothing can change the force of the legend, since Ephraim never again united with Judah.

Interpreted from still another standpoint, the regaining of Josephite independence was accomplished by the reaction of a rural community (the highland "enclave") against a corrupt oriental city, Jerusalem. This revolt, in turn, strengthened the long-standing Ephraimite hatred of walled cities which was manifest when the Josephites destroyed Shechem, Bethel, and Jericho in the Judges period. All the immediate patriarchs of Israel, without exception (i. e., Abraham, Isaac, and Jacob) are said to be men of the open country, who follow pastoral and agricultural pursuits. None of them inhabit walled cities; although urban life is everywhere about them in the world as a very sinister and ominous reality. Two cities in particular, Sodom and Gomorrah, are so very wicked that they have to be destroyed by fire from heaven (Gen. 13:13; 18:20; 19:24f.).

No claim is made here that the impressive Genesis legend of city versus country arose at the moment when Ephraim revolted against the rule of Jerusalem. The precise chronology of the legend cannot be discovered. The patriarchal figures reflect the sociology and ideology which became standard in the central highlands during the epochs covered by the books of Judges, Samuel, and Kings. The house of Joseph developed into a uniform, consolidated social mass, consisting of primitive, rustic landlords and slaveowners, animated by a definite sense of right and wrong (*mishpat*); and the mythical Hebrew forefathers are simply these lords, or *adonim*, projected against the murky background of patriarchal, prehistoric time. The sweeping condemnation of cities by the legend is, of course, based upon a provincial and contracted view of ethics and is too much a matter of simple right and wrong. But the house of Joseph, nevertheless, had experienced the bitter evils of city domination during seventy-five years under the rule of Jerusalem, the result being a slowly cumulative moral protest which was the point of departure for Ahijah of Shiloh and later-coming Hebrew prophets in Ephraim and Judah.

Condemnation of Josephite revolt beside point

It was the opinion of Cardinal J. H. Newman that the Ephraimite revolt from Judah was not only schism but "worse than schism"; that Israel, that is, the eleven tribes, "had no priesthood at all"; and that "the kingdom of Israel was cut off from the Temple." [1] To similar effect, an orthodox Jewish writer, Judge Mayer Sulzberger, speaks of "the audacious ambition" of Jeroboam in entering upon a movement against the Judaic dynasty. [2] These authors represent the "orthodox" view, both Christian and Jewish, which prevailed for many centuries regarding the disruption of David's united Hebrew kingdom.

But the opinions represented by Cardinal Newman and Judge Sulzberger merely reproduce the ideas of Jewish compilers and redactors who lived hundreds of years after the events in question and through whose devoted, but partly mistaken, labors we have received the Old Testament. The creators of the Hebrew Bible, as we have already seen, looked back upon Hebrew history in view of a long evolutionary process which, through concrete experience, led gradually up to a high, generalized monotheism; but since they were not scientific historians, they could only explain the process by projecting its outcome far back into the past, prior to the settlement in Canaan, and assuming that the doctrine of one true God, represented by one legitimate Altar and Priesthood, had been familiar to Israel from the beginning of the nation's life.

Every turn and phase of the history that we are studying involves this problem; hence the compilers, who bring the early

[1] *Apologia*, London, 1914, p. 171.
[2] *Labor in Ancient Israel*, Philadelphia, 1923, p. 29.

records together in forming the Hebrew Bible, are continually interjecting their *post eventum* comments and explanations, which uncritical readers of Scripture have accepted without question in all subsequent ages of the Synagogue and the Church.

At the same time, the redactors are continually embarrassed by the never-ending compulsion, which lies upon them like a nightmare, to reconstruct the history in the interest of their own theory. This unavoidable task becomes even more onerous after the break between Judah and the house of Joseph, because now, in place of a single filiation of events, they must carry along a double narrative concerning two lines of kings (those of Judah and those of Ephraim or Israel), going alternately from one to the other and explaining how or why this or that king did right or wrong "in the eyes of Yahweh."

For information regarding the two lines of kings the compilers largely depend upon two sets of state histories, called respectively "The Book of the Matters of the Times Pertaining to the Kings of Israel" (*Sefer Dibrae ha'Yamim l'Malkae Yisrael*) and a corresponding roll, "The Book of the Matters of the Times Pertaining to the Kings of Judah" (*Sefer Dibrae ha'Yamim l'Malkae Y'hudah*). These books, or manuscript-rolls, gave the secular facts; and the editors, in creating the Hebrew Bible, took from the secular sources what they felt to be essential, interjecting their own remarks, as already explained. Thus they frequently say to the reader, "The rest of the acts of king so-and-so—are they not written in the Book of the Matters of the Times Pertaining to the Kings of Israel?" In other words, the inquiring reader is referred, as it were, to the public library if he wishes to go into the course of events more fully. The earlier sources, if we had them, would carry us back into closer touch with Hebrew history as a secular process.

Editorial sentence of condemnation wholly beside point

The wide chasm between what the compilers thought the history should have been and what the history actually was comes into stark relief when the *post eventum* verdicts on the reigns of the various kings are considered. The editors cannot escape admitting that the popular worship at scattered altars in villages of the open country was the rule in Judah and Ephraim alike both before and after the erection of the temple in Jerusalem. The people of Judah, for instance, patronized the local "high places," or *bamoth*, at various rural centers outside Jerusalem for three hundred years after the break with Ephraim, and the editors were compelled to say again and again that the Judeans themselves "built high places . . . on every high hill and every green tree" (I Kings 14:23). "Howbeit the high places were not taken away: as yet the people did sacrifice and burn incense on the high places" (II Kings 14:4).

Consequently, since the people in the little principality of Judah continued to worship at the local high places, no point whatever is made by the interpolator who declares that Jeroboam's object in erecting Ephraimite high places was to keep the Josephites at home, so that they would not feel attracted by the Jerusalem temple. Utter lack of insight into the motives of Jeroboam is revealed by the following passage, which is not history, but mere animadversion:

And Jeroboam said in his heart, Now shall the kingdom return to the house of David. If this people go up to do sacrifice in the house of Yahweh at Jerusalem, then shall the heart of this people turn again to their lord, unto Rehoboam king of Judah. . . . Whereupon the king took counsel, and made two calves of gold, and said unto them, It is too much for you to go up to Jerusalem: behold thy *elohim*, O Israel! . . . And he set the one in Bethel, and the other put he in Dan. . . . And he placed in Bethel the priests of the high places which he had made [I Kings 12:26–32].

"Books of Chronicles" more "high church" than Kings

The books of Chronicles represent a Judaic recension of Hebrew history even more lofty and severe than that of Kings. The significance of the contrast between them will become clearer as we go along; but for present purposes it is enough to point out that the Kings editors criticize the history from the standpoint of the book of Deuteronomy, which was "found" in the temple in the time of

King Josiah shortly before the Babylonian exile and observed in his reign only; whereas the Chronicles editors approach the history from the point of view of ecclesiastical usages enjoined by the priestly document P, running mostly through the books of Exodus, Leviticus, and Numbers, the principles of which were followed in the second temple of Jerusalem after the reëstablishment of Judah in the post-exilic age. A comparison between Kings and Chronicles is instructive at this point, since it reveals even more clearly the manipulation of Hebrew history by the Biblical compilers.

After the break between Judah and Ephraim, the first king of Judah was Rehoboam, who was followed by his son Abijam: "And Rehoboam slept with his fathers. . . . And Abijam his son reigned in his stead" (I Kings 14:31). Abijam is described thus in Kings: "He walked in all the sins of his father, which he had done before him" (I Kings 15:3). Turning to Chronicles, we first identify this king, whose name is given a slightly different spelling: "And Rehoboam slept with his fathers. . . . And Abijah his son reigned in his stead" (II Chron. 12:16).

Bearing in mind the characterization of Abijah, or Abijam, in Kings and comparing with it the Chronicler's description of him, we find the contrast very startling:

And Abijah stood up upon mount Zemaraim, which is in mount Ephraim, and said, Hear ye, thou Jeroboam, and all Israel: Ought ye not to know that Yahweh, god of Israel, gave the kingdom over Israel to David forever, even to him and to his sons? . . . Yet Jeroboam the son of Nebat, the servant of Sh'lomoh [that is, "Solomon"] the son of David, is risen up, and hath rebelled against his lord. . . . And now ye think to withstand the kingdom of Yahweh in the hand of the sons of David. . . . But as for us, Yahweh is our god; and we have not forsaken him; and the priests which minister unto Yahweh are the sons of Aaron; and the Levites wait upon their affairs. And they burn unto Yahweh every morning and every evening burnt sacrifices and sweet incense. The shewbread also they set in order upon the pure table; and the candlestick of gold with the lamps thereof to burn every evening. For we keep the charge of Yahweh our god. But ye have forsaken him. . . . And Abijah waxed mighty, and married fourteen wives, and begat twenty-two sons and sixteen daughters" [II Chron. 13:4–21, passim].

The differences between Chronicles and Kings are vast. Not only were the books of Kings themselves written long after the history which they treat, but also the books of Chronicles were produced about three hundred years later than Kings. A comparative study of the two sets of Bible histories helps to show how the various writers and schools of writers did their work and how their ideas are more unreal and fanciful the farther away they stand from the facts. The chronicler begins with Adam, gives many genealogical tables, and regards the entire history as turning around the house of David; while he ignores the kingdom of Ephraim, or Israel, as much as possible, makes only one reference to the great prophet Elijah who worked in Ephraim, and ignores the other Ephraimite prophets entirely. Reference to the "Chronicles" is instructive as giving an extreme instance of the historical distortion toward which the Biblical writers constantly tended. The above speech placed in the mouth of Abijah, king of Judah, can only be pronounced completely baseless. Yet, living in an age when monotheism was fully established and the centralized priestly system was in operation, the chronicler could understand the early history only in terms of his own experience.

Hebrew kingdoms continue ancient hostility

Hatred between the two Hebrew kingdoms naturally existed from the first. The abortive revolt of Ephraim under Sheba ben Bichri was never forgotten; while the antagonism between David and Saul had become a settled feature of Israel's traditions. That there was continual war between Rehoboam, king of Judah, and Jeroboam, king of Israel, is claimed by one of the writers in Kings (I Kings 15:6); but as a report of actual hostilities the claim is very doubtful. The Deuteronomic editor (himself Judaic) has inserted a passage declaring that Rehoboam assembled a huge army of more than one hundred thousand men to fight against Israel, but that a prophet, Shemaiah, speaking in the name of Yahweh, persuaded the Judean king to call off the proposed expedition (I Kings 12:21–24).

But the actual circumstances were that Shishak, king of Egypt, invaded Judah and extorted from Rehoboam as tribute all the gold stored in Jerusalem (I Kings 14:25–28). The compiler of Kings tries to conceal the humiliation of his ancestors; although the later chronicler admits that the kingdom of Judah was enslaved under Pharaoh, but insists that the disgrace was a punishment for having "forsaken Yahweh" (II Chron. 12:1f.). Pharaoh Shishak was the king who had befriended and entertained Jeroboam as a Josephite conspirator against the Davidic dynasty (I Kings 11:40); and in order to understand Egyptian policy at this time it is necessary to recall certain aspects of the general situation.

The original and proper territory of "Joseph," as we have seen, was the central highlands of Canaan, the hill country of Ephraim, which was the only district ruled by King Saul. At the same time, the belt of Canaanite fortified cities, Taanach, Megiddo, and Bethshan, which lay at the north, in or near the plain of Esdraelon, were not included in "Israel" before the rise of the united Hebrew kingdom under the Davidic monarchy. Therefore the Josephites under King Saul found themselves between the pressure of non-Hebrew Jerusalem at the south and the alien cities at the north. What the Egyptian king now did was not only to terrorize Jerusalem but also to take captives out of Megiddo, Taanach, and Bethshan (as inscriptions on the temple at Karnak reveal), neutralizing these places as points of conspiracy against both Egypt and the house of Joseph.[3] The Esdraelon district had been under Egyptian control before the Philistine settlement on the sea coast and before the Israelite conquest of central Canaan; so that the campaign of Shishak restored Egyptian rule over the trade routes, while at the same time it threw the house of Joseph back into its older isolation as a community of rustic proprietors living in country villages free from involvement with fortified cities.

Dynasty of Jeroboam destroyed, 911 B. C.

The forces and conditions which produced the social-economic problem in Israel are clear and certain; but the political events are

---

[3] Cf. Breasted, *History of Egypt* (New York), p. 529.

often obscured by the inconsequential attitude of the narrative, which leaps over long spaces of time without giving notice and refers in a purely casual way to matters of great importance. Thus, it is recorded that Jeroboam was followed on the throne of Israel by his son Nadab, who reigned two years and was besieging the Philistine city of Gibbethon, when a man of Issachar, Baasha ben Ahijah, conspired against him, slew him, and reigned in his stead for twenty-four years. All this in a few sentences, leaving us to guess at the under-surface meaning of the events (I Kings 15:27f.).

Gibbethon was located somewhere southwest of Ephraim, in the lower hills beyond the more elevated plateau belonging to the house of Joseph. An attack upon this Philistine outpost by the successor to Jeroboam points to a decided change in the general situation over that prevailing when the break between Ephraim and Judah took place. The Philistines were now a very weak people, who could be attacked with impunity; and this invasion of their territory by Israel, when considered with regard to the population-increase during the twenty-three-year period, suggests that the house of Joseph needed more land. Added weight is lent to this conjecture by the fact that the conspiracy was led by a man from the district of Issachar in the valley of Esdraelon, located on the northern rim of the house of Joseph.

The frontiersman Baasha was able to hold the throne for twenty-four years. During this time he erected fortifications in southern Ephraim against the kingdom of Judah, to blockade all traffic; whereupon Asa, king of Judah, formed a league with Benhadad, king of Syria, whose capital was at Damascus, and the Syrian king straightway sent an army of occupation into the Galilean hills, threatening the northward expansion of Israel. Baasha then left off erecting fortifications against Judah, whereupon the Judeans took the deserted works and completed them as a protection against Ephraim (I Kings 15:16–22). Baasha was followed on the throne by his son Elah, who reigned two years. Still another generation of Ephraimite young people had now come upon the stage of history. Biological increase was continuing steadily. The admonitions of Yahweh to the legendary, prehistoric patriarchs, bidding them be fruitful and multiply, were but the reflected ideology of Israel itself in the land of Canaan; and the legend-building power was monopolized, as we have seen, by the Ephraimites, the sons of the favorite wife, Rachel: "I will multiply thy seed as the stars of the heaven and as the sand which is upon the sea shore; and thy seed shall possess the gate of his enemies" (Gen. 22:17). "All this land that I have spoken of will I give unto thy seed, and they shall inherit it forever" (Exod. 32:13). Accordingly, Isaac, on the Philistine frontier, says, "Now hath Yahweh made room for us; and we shall be fruitful in the land" (Gen. 26:22).

All these ideas, instead of being remote from the actual history that we are studying, originated in the very midst of that history. And it is instructive to observe that the notion of "increase" is linked closely with struggle to seize territory belonging to the enemy. The words just quoted from "Isaac" are said to have been uttered after a dispute with the Philistines at the frontier of that country. The Philistine city of Gibbethon had not been reduced by Nadab, the son of Jeroboam; and so the southwestern frontier of Ephraim had remained precisely the same throughout the period of the house of Baasha. The internal expansive energies of Israel were therefore still shut in and frustrated. There was no room for territorial increase northward or southward; the only possibility for expansion was west-by-south into Philistine country. Decision was accordingly reached that another attempt should be made against Gibbethon; and in this connection a new change of dynasty occurred which turned out to be more momentous than the one by which the house of Baasha displaced the house of Jeroboam.

Dynasty of Omri founded, 887 B. C.

The circumstances gave sinister promise of the degeneration which eventually overtook Ephraim. The army, under a general named Omri, was besieging Gibbethon. But King Elah, son of Baasha, was not at the front. Instead, he was attending a cocktail party in the house of his steward and was "drinking himself drunk" when an army officer, named Zimri, broke in and slew him.

And the people were encamped against Gibbethon, which belongeth to the Philistines; and the people that were encamped heard say, Zimri hath conspired, and hath also slain the king. . . . Then were the people of Israel [that is, Ephraim] divided into two parts: half of the people followed Tibni ben Ginath, to make him king; and half followed Omri [I Kings 16:8, 9, 15, 21].

The ensuing civil war lasted four years; and the nature of the struggle can only be guessed. But a possible clue may be found in the contrasting references to the leaders. "Tibni ben Ginath" was a man of publicly-known ancestral origin; that is, his father was "somebody." But on the other hand, Omri, the general of the army, is not called the "son" of anyone and was therefore a man of the people who rose by his own talents. The struggle between the two parties began "in the twenty-seventh year of Asa king of Judah" and only came to an end "in the thirty-first year of Asa" (I Kings 16:15, 23). "The people that followed Omri prevailed against the people that followed Tibni ben Ginath. So Tibni died, and Omri reigned" (I Kings 16:22).

New, fortified capital, "Samaria," 881 B. C.

If the faction, or party, which put Omri on the throne of Ephraim hoped for better things, that hope was disappointed sorely by events that followed the new dynastic revolution. Fifty years had now slipped away since the house of Joseph had separated from Judah. Persons above sixty could clearly recall the times of bondage under Sh'lomoh, of evil memory. The rule of the ancient Amorite city of Jebus (Jerusalem) was remembered as a hateful thing of the past. The attempt of the Davidic dynasty to naturalize Yahweh in Canaan as a deity under the generic name Baal had been defeated by the uprising of the house of Joseph. The bulk of the Hebrew nation had thus reverted to the rule of rustic proprietors, or *adonim*, living in country villages; and even the capital of Ephraim itself had been the little rural town Tirzah, scarcely known in Bible history (I Kings 14:17; 15:21; 16:6, 9). Here at Tirzah the new king, Omri, made his headquarters for the first six years of his reign (I Kings 16:23).

Now comes a change of mighty consequence, whose effects were to reverberate throughout Bible history. A magnificent hill in the midst of the central highlands arrested the attention of Omri. It was owned by a certain proprietor named Shemer. This man is called "the *adon* of the hill" (I Kings 16:24); and the narrative says that the king offered to buy the property for the large sum of two silver talents, equaling more than $4,000 in American money and having a much higher purchasing power than that sum. The proprietor of the hill was a very wealthy man!

It is to be observed at once that the proposal by King Omri contravened the settled *mishpat* of Ephraim, which required the rigid possession of land in the family owning it. This was a principle of the Yahweh religion, which forbade the treatment of land as an item of sale or exchange. But no exception to the proposal seems to have been taken by the *adon* Shemer in the name of Yahweh; this is all the more noticeable because when Omri's son and successor, Ahab, made a similar offer to buy land from Naboth, an indignant objection was at once interposed on religious grounds (I Kings 21:1–3).

The case of Omri and Shemer may be approached from several standpoints; but in any case the purchase of the land was an outrage on family ethics and current Ephraimite legality. The fact that Omri wanted the location for the purpose of erecting on it a fortified city, whereas Ahab wanted Naboth's land merely as a private addition to his palace, makes no difference in the long view; and the narrative skips over the entire transaction in a very casual way. Either there was some objection made by Shemer which is not recorded, or history had already reached a point where the old clan ethics was already in process of dissolution, as the Ahab-Naboth incident seems to argue. The difficulty cannot be avoided by assuming that Shemer could have acquired other land elsewhere; for this would have involved still another outrage upon *mishpat*, since it would merely transfer the locale of the problem without solving it.

Omri's capital entangled with commercial "baalism," 881 B. C.

"And he bought the hill from Shemer for two talents of silver, and built on the hill, and called the name of the city Samaria (*Shomeron*) after the name of Shemer, *adon* of the hill" (I Kings 16:24). The capital of Ephraim, therefore, was now hastily transferred from the unpretentious country town of Tirzah to the heavily-fortified city of Samaria, built *de novo* at enormous expense. And what was more natural than that Omri should seek to revive one of the outstanding features of Davidic policy, the alliance with wealthy, commercialistic Phoenicia? To this end Omri made a treaty with Eth-baal, king of Sidon, whereby the Phoenician princess Jezebel, or Isabel, was given in marriage to the Ephraimite crown prince Ahab; in connection with which a temple was built at the new capital for the worship of the Phoenician *Baal* (I Kings 16:31, 32). This, however, did not by any means bring with it the abandonment of Yahweh as the Ephraimite national deity; although it involved a strong tendency toward complicating the idea of Yahweh with legalistic usages contrary to the ancient *mishpat* of the country villages. The outlook, indeed, was not promising.

Samaria's rule imposed abruptly upon rural clans

Since breaking with the house of David, Ephraim had now gone through two violent changes of dynasty and a four-year civil war which placed a third royal family on the throne. And although the rule of Canaanite Jerusalem had been repudiated, Ephraim now found itself once more under a city despotism. What could the village proprietors do? The rural *adonim* were, indeed, helpless for the time being. The country was exhausted. The wars against Philistia and the civil struggle had been a drain on the community. The growth of numbers and the pressing need for expansion made necessary the dividing of land among heirs in smaller parcels. Also the burden of taxes and military service bore down with heaviest weight upon the poorer *adonim*, the smaller property holders, who were placed at a disadvantage as compared with others, wealthier, who possessed more than the average. Thus, in the long run a landholder like Shemer, "the *adon* of the hill Samaria," who was able to obtain for his real estate a price almost fabulous in terms of the prevailing social conditions, would naturally suffer less in proportion than some peasant with a few acres, one or two slaves, and a large family.

When political, economic, and geographical influences operate in a milieu such as that of the Ephraimite hill country at the period under consideration, the inevitable result is that the poorer landholders tend to become poorer, while those who are already more favored by fortune tend to become wealthier. In other words, the problem arises which the prophets of Israel presently attacked with vigorous language. We are dealing, therefore, not with mere conjecture, but with an actual, historic situation, whose outlines become clearer as we scrutinize the total evidence. The half century in Ephraim between the break with Judah and the rise of Omri followed upon ruthless exploitation by the Davidic dynasty, which had brought the house of Joseph into an impoverished and angry condition. The central hill country itself was less than 2,500 square miles, wedged in between Judah on the south, Canaanites, Phoenicians, and Syrians on the north, the Jordan river on the east, and Philistines and the Mediterranean on the west. In this comparatively small area, with its multiplying population, there had been, as we have seen, two unsuccessful attempts made upon Philistine territory; and finally a four-year civil war had ushered in the reign of Omri. All of which heavily burdened the poorer landholders, while at the same time the social and economic problem in this period was complicated further by important circumstances which the Old Testament compilers have largely, but not completely, ignored.

Revolt of Moab cuts revenue

We saw that among the conquests of David was the subjugation of Moab, whose large pasture lands east of Jordan were devoted to sheep raising. The enormous annual tribute coming in from this direction was one of the sources which built up the wealth of the united Hebrew kingdom. Two landholders whom we have observed in Ephraim (Absalom and Joab, at Baal-hazor) would inevitably have profited from the inflowing yearly tribute; and it is a reasonable conjecture that a certain portion of it was regularly allocated to the Josephite upper classes in order to prevent rebellion. But the sudden break-up of the Davidic state and the disturbances following the separation of Ephraim from Judah gave Moab a welcome opportunity to declare its independence and to withhold the annual tribute. Stoppage of so much regular graft in the form of sheep and wool affected living conditions in Ephraim to such an extent that Omri undertook decisive action.

Omri reconquers Moab

The Moabite king, Mesha, set up an inscribed stone of black basalt, two feet wide and three and one half feet high, which was found in the ruins of Diban in 1868 and is now preserved at the Louvre, in Paris. Its language is nearly the same as Hebrew, but in a different dialect, and it has been translated by Professor S. R. Driver, of Oxford University, for the *Encyclopedia Biblica*. A portion of the text follows:

"I am Mesha, son of [the god] Chemosh. . . . And I made this high place for Chemosh. . . . Omri, king of Israel, afflicted Moab for many days because Chemosh was angry with his land. Omri took possession . . . of Mehedeba and [Israel] dwelt therein."

Thus, the military forces of Omri broke into Moab and occupied part of King Mesha's territory, in which, as the inscription states, many Israelites came to settle. Also the tribute formerly paid in King David's time was now restored and is mentioned in a passage of the Old Testament which is very instructive when considered with reference to the foregoing quotation from the Moabite Stone: "And Mesha, king of Moab, was a sheepmaster, and rendered unto the king of Israel a hundred thousand lambs, and a hundred thousand rams, with the wool" (II Kings 3:4).

The circumstances which come before us in this interesting way give rise to several observations and queries: The conquest of Moab was expensive, requiring taxes and military service. How were these expenses met? What class in Ephraim profited most from the Moabite tribute and the seizure of Moabite land? Did the smaller and less important Ephraimite *adonim* reap the greater advantage? Or did Omri and his clique and the wealthier and more influential *adonim* derive the greater economic benefit from the adventure? Omri's expedition into Moab enslaved the masses of Moabite peasantry. Bible history is not commonly studied from this purely secular standpoint; and if the subject is not handled primarily on the lines of this method, the Bible will have less and less meaning for the modern world.

Incidentally, the Moabite Stone shows that the people of Moab had a cult similar to the religion of Israel. Their divinity, Chemosh, is recognized by several writers in the Bible (Judg. 11:23; Num. 21:29; I Kings 11:7; Jer. 48:7). His worshipers are said by King Mesha to be oppressed "because Chemosh was angry with his land," in the same fashion that Israel is said to have been oppressed by foreign powers "because Yahweh was angry with his people"; but this common "frame of reference" was put to a higher use by Israel's prophets.

Ahab enthroned, 876 B. C.

The house of Joseph was now enmeshed in economic, political, social, and international forces which were fast carrying the country beyond any effective control by the bewildered *adonim* in the rural districts and reducing them to a condition of dependence different in form, but similar in reality, to that which prevailed under the house of David. These forces were complicated with military attacks upon Ephraim and corresponding campaigns of defense—all of which required the conscription of thousands, who were taken away from their work in the fields and whose private affairs necessarily suffered, while the larger property holders and a ring of "insiders" grew richer. The reign of Ahab was marked by increasing friction between Ephraim and Aramea, or Syria, whose capital city, Damascus, was rising steadily in importance.

And Benhadad, the king of Syria, gathered all his host together; and there were thirty and two kings with him, and horses, and chariots; and he went up and besieged Samaria, and warred against it [I Kings 20:1]. . . . And the children of Israel were numbered, and were all present, and went against them. . . . And they pitched one over against the other seven days. And so it was that in the seventh day the battle was joined; and the children of Israel slew of the Syrians an hundred thousand footmen in one day [I Kings 20:27, 29].

In this narrative the expression "the children of Israel were numbered and were all present" gives a hint of the drain upon the peasantry caused by military service.

Ahab joins coalition against Assyrian empire, 853 B. C.

The drama of Hebrew history thickens as the action moves onward. A new and appalling danger was now slowly emerging over the northeastern horizon from the direction of Mesopotamia. The Assyrian empire was attempting to reach and control the Mediterranean coast, so as to dominate the trade routes running through Canaan. This would mean that the Ephraimites, Syrians, Ammonites, Phoenicians, Philistines, and all the little nations in the path of the oncoming monster would be eventually crushed and reduced to vassalage or bondage. The only way to meet the peril seemed to be a coalition of as many small peoples as could be prevailed upon to send forces into battle against the westward-moving invader. A combination was formed consisting of ten groups, to which King Ahab of Ephraim contributed 2,000 chariots and 10,000 foot soldiers to an allied host numbering around 50,000. The allies met the Assyrians near the city of Karkar, in the Orontes valley. The battle is described in terms of exaggerated self-praise by the Assyrian ruler, Shalmaneser III, on a large black obelisk. He claims a great victory over the coalition; but for the time being his westward advance ended, although he was within seventy-five miles of the Mediterranean. This crisis in the reign of Ahab finds no mention whatever in the Old Testament. Its effect upon the internal situation of Ephraim can only have been to intensify the already pressing social and economic problem.

The landed proprietor Naboth

That the Josephite influence had by this time penetrated more fully into the great plain of Esdraelon is evident from the fact that Ahab, whose capital city was in central Ephraim at Samaria, had a royal palace in Jezreel, at the eastern end of the plain; while adjoining his property was the land of a certain *adon* by the name of Naboth. Desiring this land as an addition to his palace grounds, the king, without anticipating what a storm he was about to raise, offered Naboth a better piece in exchange or the worth of it in cash. That the king's father, Omri, had bought land of Shemer, was a well-known fact in the history of the royal family; and Ahab supposed that Naboth, like Shemer, would be willing to part with his ancestral acres for a just consideration. The deep significance of this case has been missed for centuries by most readers of the Bible because from the standpoint of real estate practice in later Judaism and among Christian peoples the offer of the king seems perfectly normal and conventional, and there can be no doubt of his good faith in making it.

But we have seen that the country village folk, who composed the bulk of the population in Ephraim, were still in the clan stage of social evolution. Their primitive ideology, indeed, struck its moral roots deep down into the soil of that nomadic desert life whence Israel came. Moreover, a considerable part of the community calling itself "Israel" was in Gilead, east of the Jordan river, living in a half-settled, semi-nomadic state, in frequent contact with wilderness clans which came up to the frontiers to trade a few sheep, goats, or desert dates for fruits, vegetables, eggs, or bread. According to the moral code of this world outside the walled cities, a piece of land was a natural resource of life, conferred, or at least guaranteed in possession, by the deity of any given group; and it was to be held with tenacity as a means of mere, physical existence; if one were parted from "the inheritance of his fathers," he would be cut adrift and deprived of life. While this principle seems to have no relevance to the purely nomadic tribe in the wilderness, it applies among nomads with even more force than it does in settled communities; for every nomadic tribe feels that the general region, or district within which it roves, with all its oases and wells of water, belongs to the tribe as a whole.

But on the other hand, Ahab's proposal was in line with the practices of Tyre and Sidon, the great commercial cities of Phoenicia, to which he was allied and from which his queen, Jezebel, had come, and he was only asking Naboth to do as the *baalim* of Shechem did when, according to legend, they sold land to Jacob. Yet, when Ahab's innocent offer to Naboth is taken out of its context as a conventionality of "citified" civilization and regarded from the standpoint of Ephraimite history, we can see that it carried explosive possibilities, because it ran afoul of the more primitive moral code still vital in the hill country.

The king, indeed, could not have been ignorant of rural Israelite prejudices; and, as the sequel shows, his Phoenician wife may well have "stirred him up," as the Deuteronomic editor quaintly says (I Kings 21:25). The refusal of Naboth to sell or exchange his land was made in the name of Yahweh on the grounds of religion, and Ahab was, in fact, completely frustrated, without any legal recourse. But at this point Jezebel intervened, without his knowledge, and wrote forged warrants in the king's name, directed to the elders of Naboth's home city, requiring them to enter suit against Naboth on grounds of blaspheming "elohim and the king." The testimony of two false witnesses brought a quick sentence of death, which was executed not only upon Naboth but also upon his sons, who in the eye of the "law" shared his crime. It was necessary to put them out of the way, so that they might not cause trouble about inheriting the land, which was confiscated by the king on the technical ground of treason (I Kings 21:1f.; II

Kings 9:26). Ahab was virtually forced to make Jezebel's act his own, since disavowal of it might well imperil his alliance with Phoenicia.

Significance of the Ahab-Naboth case

Modern bourgeois piety has considered the Ahab-Naboth incident with relation to the murders and the prostitution of justice, while totally missing the broader significance of the tragedy. When the case is carefully scrutinized in relation to the political and economic history of Ephraim since the break with Judah and with relation to the problem soon to be reflected in the books of Amos and Hosea, there is but one scientific way of construing the facts: They are an extremely vivid, poignant illustration of what was going forward more and more in the life of Israel. Naboth's reaction against the treatment of his land as a mere article of sale or trade is a virtual protest against the rising tide of baalistic usage exemplified already by the sale of Shemer's hill on which a walled city had been built, where the wealthier section of the Ephraimite property class could reside in safety and a temple had been erected for worship of the Phoenician Baal. Back of Naboth's refusal to sell are the inexorable concentration of land in the power of a small wealthy group and the heartless reduction of the poor landholders into the lower class of slaves. "Now there cried a certain woman of the wives of the sons of the prophets unto Elisha, saying, Thy servant my husband is dead; and thou knowest that thy servant did fear Yahweh; and the creditor is come to take unto him my two sons to be slaves" (II Kings 4:1).

Elijah, first great prophet of Hebrew history

How far the government of Israel had gone in the direction of "totalitarianism" and absolutism is well shown by the fact that no prominent leader arose forthwith in Ephraim to denounce the outrage perpetrated upon the obscure Naboth and his family. The grounds for a general and organized resistance against the king were ample. But the masses of the people were inert, so the revolutionary impulse took its origin east of the Jordan river, in the hills of Gilead—"a land fit for cattle" (Numb. 32:1). The prophet Elijah suddenly appears in the narrative as a man of the people, whose family connections were so humble that he is referred to by his personal name without any mention of his father: "And Elijah the Tishbite was among the sojourners of Gilead" (I Kings 17:1). True in principle, if not in literal fact, is the dramatic story of his abrupt appearance before Ahab at the very moment when the king goes to take possession of the slain peasant's land.

And the word of Yahweh came to Elijah the Tishbite, saying, Arise, go down to meet Ahab king of Israel, which is in Samaria. Behold, he is in the vineyard of Naboth, whither he is gone down to possess it. And thou shalt speak to him, saying, Hast thou killed, and also taken possession? . . . In the place where dogs licked the blood of Naboth shall dogs lick thy blood, even thine! [I Kings 21:17f.]

The significance of the story is the growth in Israel of moral conviction that the death of an obscure peasant could not pass without the notice of Yahweh, who sends a messenger to denounce the haughty king and call down upon him the stroke of retributive justice.

Elijah type and reality of "Mosheh"

No writings have come down to us from Elijah; but in order to make such an impression on the spiritual consciousness of Israel, he must have been a man of tremendous personality. One thinks of the earlier figure, Ahijah of Shiloh, who in the name of Yahweh called upon Jeroboam to lead a revolution against the Davidic dynasty; yet the message of Ahijah dealt, not with ethics, but with the break-up of the united monarchy and the rise of another government. The Shilonite was only a political prophet; whereas the Tishbite was definitely a champion of justice and righteousness, the founder of a new prophetic type, without any predecessor in Hebrew history. The solid witness to his importance is the fact that all along through the post-exilic ages Elijah is the intimate, universal prophet, or *nabi*, of the Judaic remnant surviving from the wreck of ancient Israel. His invisible presence fills the ceremonial "Chair of Elijah" to preside over the rite of the covenant, or *berith,* performed upon every Jewish son at the eighth day; and again at the ceremonial feast he is the outstanding guest, represented by the "Cup of Elijah," with its libation of wine. And as a fitting crown to his legend is the mythic picture of his fiery ascent to heaven without passing through the gates of death (II Kings 2).

Elijah, indeed, stands at the psychological inauguration and fountainhead of that long, concrete religious development which more and more characterized Israel. This evolutionary process, "here a little, and there a little," "in divers portions and in divers manners," gradually carried the spiritual growth of the Hebrew people up to a point where the "remnant of Israel"—the Jews— finally passed out of polytheism into ethical monotheism. The dynamic impulses and motivating forces of this unique movement were generated within the depths of the peculiar socio-economic history (unlike any other) which brought face to face within a single political group the sophisticated cult of the *baalim* and the primitive, rustic, ultimately nomadic worship of Yahweh; the two religions being flung together in such a way that the problem inevitably arose, Which one shall prevail as the permanent, organizing force in the Hebrew community? The two cults were of such contrasted, antagonistic natures that neither of them could be indefinitely practiced within the limits of one and the same political organism. One or the other must perish! The practical result was that the cult of Yahweh—crude and primitive at first—refined itself slowly by reacting against ever-present, inescapable *baalism,* until at length it rose to victory. But the evolution was not impersonal or automatic. It found expression in the minds of successive prophetic personalities, beginning with Elijah, the prototype of Hebrew prophecy and the model on which the legend-building power created the figure known in Hebrew as "Mosheh."

Concrete expression of Israel's problem begins to crystallize

The primary, fundamental Hebrew prophet, then, is Elijah from the backwoods of Gilead. And while we have no writings from

him, his place in the series of situations which led slowly up to
Israel's eventual, post-exilic monotheism is clear: (1) The settlement of the house of Joseph in the central highlands brought the
practice of *mishpat* ideology into the vicinity of baalistic city-
states remaining in Canaan. (2) The contrast between Israel and
Canaan, moreover, was heightened and sharpened, midway of the
Judges period, when the Josephite clan of Manasseh destroyed
pre-Hebrew Shechem, whose *baalim* said of Israel, "Shall not
their cattle, and their substance, and their every beast be ours?"
(3) The abrupt emergence of the united monarchy raised the Canaanite city of Jerusalem to the point where it became allied with
Phoenician Tyre and enabled the Davidic dynasty to enslave the
house of Joseph. (4) The reorganization of the central hill country under the rule of the newly-built walled city of Samaria, in
alliance with baalistic Phoenicia, was a backward step toward pre-
Hebrew conditions.

All these definite historic situations acted with trip-hammer
force upon the mind of Israel, creating a widespread and powerful
public opinion against rule by city government on the Canaanite
pattern. The compiler of Kings, indeed, after quoting the earlier
source which tells about the Ahab-Naboth case, inserts a paren-
thesis of his own saying that Ahab did very abominably according
to all that the Amorites did (I Kings 21:25f.). The Naboth case
was, in fact, the match that set ablaze the combustible mentality
of Ephraim. The awful tragedy, like a flash of lightning, brought
suddenly into relief an appalling situation wherein the courts were
becoming instruments of the well-to-do; and in which debtors
who "feared Yahweh" were being enslaved by creditors.

Thus we see that by the time of Elijah the general condition of
Ephraim supplied an appropriate background against which looms
the tremendous figure of the Gileadite prophet, whose very name
—given to him perhaps on account of his work—signifies "Yahweh is Elohim!"

It has been characteristic of Jewish and Christian ecclesiasticism,
however, to misunderstand or to ignore the fundamental, economic
basis of Elijah's activity and to put stress upon the mythological

contest with Phoenician baalism at Mount Carmel, where Elijah is said to have destroyed the priests and prophets of the Tyrian god. This result, however, as we shall see presently, was achieved later in very secular fashion by forces traceable to Elijah, so that the legend of Carmel, if taken figuratively, is at least a useful and striking symbol of his work.

Economic conditions depressed further by warfare

Advancing from their capital at Damascus, the Syrians once more attacked the territory of Israel by seizing the city of Ramoth in the province of Gilead, across the Jordan. To assist in their expulsion, Ahab secured help from Judah, whose king Jehoshapat ("Yahweh has judged") came up with an army to join the forces of Ephraim (I Kings 22:2–40). The son of Jehoshaphat, the Judean crown prince Jehoram, had already married the princess Athaliah, daughter of Jezebel and Ahab (II Kings 8:16–18). The kingdom of Judah, indeed, had now become a kind of subsidiary, or feudal appanage, to the house of Joseph, which would be ample basis for that part of the Hebrew legend wherein Joseph is chief over the entire house of Israel:

And he said, Hear, I pray you, this dream which I have dreamed: For, behold, we were binding sheaves in the field; and, lo, my sheaf arose, and also stood upright; and, behold, your sheaves stood round about, and made obeisance to my sheaf. And his brethren said to him, Shalt thou indeed reign over us? or shalt thou indeed have dominion over us? . . . And he dreamed yet another dream, and told it to his brethren, and said, Behold, I have dreamed a dream more; and, behold, the sun and the moon and the eleven stars made obeisance to me. And he told it to his father and his brethren. And his father rebuked him, and said unto him, What is this dream that thou hast dreamed? Shall I and thy mother and thy brethren indeed come to bow down ourselves to thee to the earth? [Gen. 37:6f.].

This legendary fascicle, as it stands within the structure of Hebrew mythology, illustrates to good effect the "piece work" nature of the entire mythic cycle; for if the sources are examined closely, its present position is found to be out of place, because Jacob's question about himself and Rachel bowing down to Joseph assumes that the mother of Joseph is alive; whereas, Rachel, according to another phase of the legends, had passed away long before (Gen. 35:1f.).

In the conflict with Syria, King Ahab was compelled again to conscript a host of long-suffering Ephraimite *adonim* from their daily work in the fields. The gradual economic decline of these overtaxed landholders paved the way for the idealistic legend wherein Joseph, in contrast with actual history, preserves the lands of the people for their own use in a regime under which they retain what is (for the Orient) the enormous net produce of 80 percent "for seed of the field, and for your food, and for them of your households, and for food for your little ones" (Gen. 47:24).

Elijah finds active coöperation in Ephraim

Somewhere in the northeastern part of Ephraim was the village of Abel-meholah ("meadow of dancing"). In this place lived a prominent landholder by the name of Shaphat ("He has judged"). This man had large fields and used a team of twenty-four oxen (that is, "twelve yoke") for pulling his plow. The little community of Abel-meholah had no doubt contributed its quota to the army on various occasions; and all the happenings in the world of that day were canvassed by the talk of the people at their work in the fields and in the village at night. They had been startled by the horrible news about the judicial murder of Naboth and his sons and the seizure of his land by the king. But among all the villagers, none had been so stirred as one of the sons of Shaphat, a strong and wiry farm worker named Elisha. His pronounced opinions became known to the prophet Elijah, who decided to enlist him in the underground campaign against the house of Ahab. Reaching this decision one day at a place in the wilderness, Elijah "departed thence, and found Elisha the son of Shaphat, who was plowing with twelve yoke before him, and he with the twelfth. And Elijah passed by him, and cast his mantle upon him. And he left the oxen . . . and went after Elijah, and ministered unto him" (I

Kings 19:19f.). Leaving the conspiracy to develop, we turn to an event which complicated the general situation and had a serious effect upon the welfare of Ephraim.

Moab again rebels against Israel

The time is in the reign of Jehoram ("Yahweh is exalted"), whose father, King Ahab, lost his life in the battle of Ramoth-Gilead. The death of Ahab was followed by the refusal of Mesha, king of Moab, to pay the enormously valuable yearly tribute of "an hundred thousand lambs and an hundred thousand rams, with the wool" (II Kings 3:4, 5). The reduction of the annual revenue of Ephraim to such an extent would have calamitous repercussions throughout the whole country, among rich and poor alike; and hence the government was at once aroused by the Moabite rebellion. "And king Jehoram went out of Samaria . . . and numbered all Israel" (II Kings 3:6). In other words, the rural *adonim* were once more called away from their daily work into war service. The king also sent word to Jehoshaphat, who still reigned in Judah and again joined his army to that of Ephraim. These two kings led their forces down through Edom; and the king of Edom was compelled to become a part of the expedition, adding his army to those of the other two kings.

The combined host then moved around the southern end of the Dead Sea through the desert of Edom, and attacked the land of Moab, laying the country waste, but being unable to take the fortified capital city. The narrative goes on to say that the king of Moab, seeing his danger, decided suddenly to take his eldest son, the crown prince, and make a burnt offering of him upon the wall of the city to the god Chemosh in full view of the besieging armies. The shocking and horrid spectacle of human sacrifice had its effect: "And there was great wrath against Israel; and they departed from him, and returned to their own land" (II Kings 3:27). The Hebrew text shows considerable embarrassment at this point. Some explanation seemed necessary to account for the failure of the expedition and the loss of a tribute amounting to one hundred thousand lambs and one hundred thousand rams per year; but the narrative could hardly be brought up to its logical climax without apparently showing the power of the god Chemosh in opposition to Yahweh. That the actual situation was even worse than the text indicates is made clear by further quotations from the memorial stone of King Mesha:

And Chemosh said unto me, Go, take Nebo against Israel. And I went by night, and fought against it from the break of dawn until noon. And I took it, and slew the whole of it, 7,000 men and male strangers, and women, and female slaves. . . . And I took thence the vessels of Yahweh; and I dragged them before Chemosh. And the king of Israel had built Yahas, and abode in it while he fought against me. But Chemosh drave him out from before me [*supra*, p. 159].

Not only did the Moabite revolt deprive Ephraim of enormous annual revenue but also the drain which the war imposed upon the country, through death and wounds and interruption of work in the fields, augmented the economic forces already at work tending to submerge and ruin the bulk of Ephraimite landholders, pushing them down into slavery under the wealthier *adonim,* who prospered on the misfortunes of their poorer neighbors.

Religion in Moab compared with that in Israel

The Moabite stone is valuable not only with reference to Hebrew history as a process of secular events but also as a very interesting and instructive indication of the parallel religious atmospheres of Israel and Moab. Yahweh and Chemosh are both in the Bible and on the stone of King Mesha. Both were war gods, as well as deities presiding over the civil nonmilitary affairs of their communities. Both are described as having "spoken," that is, through the casting of lots or by the word of priests and prophets. Sacrifice was common to both religions. And, in fact, Yahweh and Chemosh, at this epoch, were on the same level.

The comparison is of special value because, although the two cults were psychologically identical, the religion of Yahweh was destined to soar into the realm of a universal faith, leaving Chemosh in obscurity. The "vessels of Yahweh" were dragged in the dust before the altar of Chemosh; but the god of Israel was to become known to all the earth, while his Moabite rival sank into pagan oblivion. And the forces producing this great contrast were even now coming into vigorous operation, symbolized by the figure of Elijah.

Israel was the only ancient people in which a god of clan ethics, or primitive *mishpat*, was abruptly enthroned (as at Jerusalem and Samaria) over a people increasingly exposed to legal usages identified with "other gods." That the moral and economic decline of Ephraim went along with Tyrian baalism at the capital city, was the primary assumption of Elijah; and whether or not the prophet's thesis was literally and absolutely true is a matter of small importance. He and the multitude of humble, inarticulate ones who believed as he did perceived that the tenets of clan brotherhood were being outraged by the social disintegration of Israel; and he felt that a start could be made in the right direction by casting out the Phoenician Baal together with everything symbolized by this obnoxious foreign god. Consequently, on the terms of primitive ethics, the cult of Baal should not be allowed to stand alongside the cult of Yahweh. "How long will ye try to walk upon two unequal legs? If Yahweh is *elohim*, follow the usages identified with him; but if Baal, then follow the system which he represents." (I Kings 18:21; interpreted rather than translated, but the rendering "opinions," in the older versions, does not do justice to the context.)

Revolution objectifies abhorrence of "other gods," 842 B. C.

The unsolved social-economic problem was the basic force behind the religious changes which began to take place in Israel during the Elijah period. That such a force has existed among all nations in some form is more or less true. But in Israel the peculiar organization of the kingdom at the point of new and unusual contacts between race and class interests created a channel through which economic and social forces produced unique results. The growing resentment among the masses of the people (to which Elijah gave the first effective utterance) was the foundation upon which was reared the basic dogma of the new Yahweh-cult—abhorrence of "other gods." This dogma took political form in a revolution which cast out the Tyrian Baal, destroyed the house of Ahab, and placed a new dynasty on the throne of Ephraim.

The revolution took place during, or soon after, another Syrian war. The Ephraimite king, Jehoram, son of the late Ahab, was in Gilead, "he and all Israel, because of Hazael king of Syria" (II Kings 9:14; the expression "all Israel" means that a host of poor farmers and shepherds was again under arms). Feeling that the time had at length come for a change, the prophet Elisha, successor to the great Elijah, entered into a conspiracy against the house of Ahab. His instrument was a member of a prominent landholding family, a man high on the official staff of the army—Jehu ben Jehoshaphat ben Nimshi. The narrative says that Elisha sent the following message to this military chief, doubtless amplified by the sources: "Thus saith Yahweh the god of Israel, I have anointed thee king over the people of Yahweh, even over Israel. And thou shalt smite the house of Ahab thy master, that I may avenge the blood of my servants the prophets, and the blood of all the servants of Yahweh at the hand of Jezebel. For the whole house of Ahab shall perish!" (II Kings 9:6f.).

The ghastly details of the program followed by Jehu, in wading through rivers of blood, are not worth reproducing here—the murder of the aged queen-mother, Jezebel and "the whole house of Ahab," and so forth (II Kings 9, 10). But reference must be made to the uprooting of Tyrian Baal worship. In this phase of the revolution Jehu had the assistance of a certain Jehonadab ben Rechab, head of primitive, tent-dwelling gypsies, who lived in the open country (II Kings 10:15; Jer. 35:1–10; I Chron. 2:55). These tent-dwellers were, not Israelites, but Kenites, like Heber the Kenite, whose wife, Jael, slew the Baal-worshiping Sisera at the battle of Esdraelon, in the Judges period (Judg. 5:24f.). Being fanatical devotees of Yahweh as a god of clan-brotherhood, the support of such an element was very valuable to candidate Jehu at this particular time. So the gypsy chief Jehonadab and the country landlord Jehu, combined their forces to slay all the priests and prophets of Baal and to destroy the image and temple of Baal in Samaria, the capital of Ephraim (II Kings 10:18–27). Thus, it was Jehu at Samaria, not Elijah at Mount Carmel, who actually put down Phoenician baalism in Israel.

Jehu complimented by heaven, according to compilers

It will prove worthwhile to notice that according to the compilers of Kings, Jehu was given direct personal sanction from heaven after completing his work of destruction: "And Yahweh said unto Jehu, Because thou hast done well in executing that which is right in mine eyes, and hast done unto the house of Ahab according to all that was in mine heart, thy children of the fourth generation shall sit on the throne of Israel" (II Kings 10:30). This, of course, means that some prophet may have made the statement in the name of Yahweh; or merely that the compiler imagined that some prophet said it. But in any case, it is entirely consistent with the fierce policy of Elijah (I Kings 21:19–22); and it accords, by implication, with the orders given to Jehu by the prophet Elisha in the name of Yahweh (II Kings 9:25, 26, 36). What we are actually considering, however, is the popular belief about the demands of Yahweh at that period of Hebrew history.

Jehu's dynasty endures about one hundred years, 842–745 B. C.

The dynasty founded by Jehu held the throne of Ephraim more than a century. During the first half of this long period further wars made exhausting demands on the resources of the country. Thus, in the reign of Jehu himself the terrible Assyrian power lunged westward again toward the Mediterranean coast, besieging Damascus, and collecting tribute from Phoenicia and from Jehu (Black Obelisk of Shalmaneser). This involved further taxation upon Israel; moreover, King Hazael, of Syria, took all the east-Jordan territory that had belonged to Israel for centuries (II Kings 10:32, 33). Furthermore, in the reign of Jehu's son, Jeho-ahaz, the country was at war with two successive kings of Syria, Hazael and his son Benhadad; after which, according to the ad-mission of the Biblical narrative, there were left "of the people to Jehoahaz only fifty horsemen, and ten chariots, and ten thousand footmen; for the king of Syria had destroyed them, and made them like the dust by threshing" (II Kings 13:3, 7). And as if these mis-fortunes were not enough, the sight of Israel's abasement led the Moabites to attack the country in revenge for past wrongs: "And the bands of the Moabites invaded the land at the coming in of the year" (II Kings 13:20).

It would be futile to enlarge upon such commonplace and sor-did events if they did not reveal, by implication, the social and economic processes which inevitably accompanied them in the ordinary life of the people. The domestic affairs of the smaller property owners were injured whether Ephraim was defeated or successful; and for this reason a more favorable turn in war, which came about in the following two reigns of the Jehu dynasty, could have had no influence toward arresting that internal decline of the kingdom which is clearly shown in the books of Amos and Hosea.

The Biblical narrative goes on to show that after the death of King Jehoahaz, the son of Jehu, he was followed on the throne by his son Jehoash, who was challenged to battle by Amaziah, king of Judah. This extraordinary defiance would hardly have been possible without the recent humiliation of Ephraim at the hands of Syria and the invasion of the land by the Moabites, which doubt-less made the king of Judah believe that he also could emancipate his little principality from its irksome dependence upon Israel. Ac-cordingly, the two Hebrew kingdoms went to war; "and Judah was put to the worse before Israel; and they fled every man to their tents [that is, the Judahite soldiers went home]; and Jehoash king of Israel . . . came to Jerusalem, and brake down the wall of Jerusalem . . . and he took all the gold and silver, and all the vessels that were found in the house of Yahweh, and in the treasures of the king's house, and hostages, and returned to Samaria" (II Kings 14:2–14).

Encouraged by success, the Ephraimite king declared war again upon Syria, with the object of recapturing the trans-Jordan territory: "And Jehoash the son of Jehoahaz took again out of the hand of Benhadad the son of Hazael the cities which he had taken out of the hand of Jehoahaz his father by war. Three times did Jehoash beat him, and recover the cities of Israel" (II Kings 13:25). The military fortunes of Ephraim were now temporarily on the upgrade. The next king, Jeroboam II, building on the victories of his father, "restored the frontier of Israel from the entering in of Hamath unto the sea of the Arabah," that is, from and including Syria, in the north, to the southern end of Jordan at the Dead Sea (II Kings 14:23–25).

This enormous widening of the Ephraimite frontiers, together with Judah's military subjection, restored Israel to something like the position reached in the times of the Davidic dynasty. But it brought no advantage to the mass of small farmers and shepherds who composed the bulk of the nation; and it merely increased the powers of a gangster-nobility which had been developing for generations in the capital city, Samaria. Jeroboam II, the great grandson of Jehu, reigned forty-one years; but the compiler and editor of Kings gives him only seven verses; and from the standpoint of moral desert, he may not have been worth even this.

Ephraimite monarchy terrorism

Four dynasties have now passed before us in rapid review; the end of the house of Joseph is already within sight, and a number of topics call for discussion before proceeding further. First, as to the nature of the government and the general atmosphere. We have seen that the house of Joseph broke away from the house of Judah because the Davidic dynasty hardened into a despotic totalitarianism. But the same tendency reasserted itself in Ephraim, where each royal house became absolutist and sought to retain power indefinitely. The first two dynasties, those of Jeroboam I and Baasha, lasted for about twenty years each; the house of Omri, in which Ahab was outstanding, maintained its hold longer, for almost half a century; while the dynasty of Jehu ruled a little more than one hundred years.

No other form of state was possible at that epoch in history, owing to frequent war and the general backwardness of the people. The whole force of the situation was toward a rigid form of government under which all freedom of public utterance was discouraged. This was the normal, ancient oriental pattern, and it was not peculiar to Israel. The only method of seeking relief was through assassination and the violent replacement of one dynasty by another. Under such conditions the mass of the people were always bound to be disappointed, because each new line of kings, whenever established, had no more economic and political wisdom than its predecessors in dealing with the social problems which demanded solution.

The absolute nature of the state in Ephraim is revealed clearly by the religious history of that kingdom. Politics and religion, "state and church," went hand in hand, here as elsewhere. All the kings, without any exception, acknowledged Yahweh as a conventional oriental deity. None of the prophets ever claimed that there was no recognition of the national god. What they opposed was the kind of worship conducted in the name of Yahweh, that is, the practices, or *mishpat*, recognized in daily life as having the sanction of the deity. Their opposition to "other gods" was not based on a metaphysical claim that such gods had no actual existence; it was always on the ground that the customs and practices identified with them were inimical to the general welfare and contrary to usages which the prophets identified with Yahweh. In other words, the prophets and their party opposed what they felt was the wrong kind of worship even if conducted in the name of Yahweh.

This made the prophetic doctrine quite complex at times. And such being the case, it is well to bear in mind that the higher form of Hebrew prophecy did not arise primarily in the heart of Ephraim, but found its impulse in the simpler and more primitive part of the country. Elijah, the founder of prophetism in this elevated sense, came, as we have seen, from the frontier province of Gilead; and his follower Elisha, although a member of a recognized Ephraimite landholding family, had to conduct an underground movement in order to expel Phoenician Baalism and place the dynasty of Jehu on the throne. Likewise, the prophet Amos, whose home was the village of Tekoa, in the wilder, eastern part of Judah, ventured north into Ephraim, raising his voice in the streets of Bethel, protesting against exploitation of the poor by the rich, and predicting divine punishment through exile. But Amos was at once driven away from Bethel by the priest Amaziah, who held office under Jeroboam II (Amos 7:10). There was never any freedom of speech in Ephraim; and men such as Elijah, and Elisha, and Amos were in peril of their lives. Hence, Amos declared, "The prudent shall keep silence in such a time; for it is an evil time" (Amos 5:13).

Bible begins to evolve secretly in Ephraim

But while there was no opportunity for freedom of speech in criticism of current official practices, there was for that very reason a tremendous amount of thought and debate and literary activity in the background of Ephraimite life; and this concealed movement was all the more vital and vigorous because of the very suppression and inhibition under which it was compelled to make its way. Its object was to explore the narratives and legends which had been growing up through hundreds of years in Ephraim and to select from them a certain amount of material which would be of use to the prophetic party in its campaign for a higher Yahwism. These writers and thinkers did not aim to produce a "Bible" in the same way as did their successors, the Jewish compilers after the Babylonian captivity; but their work, extending over many years, was nevertheless the foundation of the Hebrew Scriptures, or Old Testament, and indirectly of the New Testament. They began, therefore, with purely secular material and undertook to adapt, or to reshape, such matters to a new religious purpose.

A good example of such material is the story according to which Jacob gives his blessing to Ephraim, the younger son of Joseph, instead of to Manasseh the firstborn; which grew out of the historical fact that the older tribe, Manasseh, merged into the newer tribe Ephraim, which finally impressed its name on the whole of the central Canaanite hill country. This was a purely secular, historic fact, which took the form of a myth, or legend; and such facts, together with the legends growing out of them, constituted part of the material out of which the Bible was quarried.

House of Joseph the legend-building Hebrew "core"

Most of the legendary and narrative material used by the anonymous writers in Ephraim took form between the revolt headed by Jeroboam I (930 B. C.) and the death of Jeroboam II (745 B. C.)— the long and highly important stretch of time over which we have traveled since the downfall of the united monarchy founded by King David. In that period the foundations of the Pentateuch and Joshua were constructed, although a great deal of matter was added later, during the Babylonian exile.

Most modern critics, writing from literary and psychological standpoints, have held wrongly that there were two schools at work in this period; the earlier being in Judah and producing the J document of the Hexateuch; while the other worked a little later in Ephraim, producing the E document. The J source has been called "primitive" and older, because its idea of the deity is more simple; and Yahweh appears to the patriarchs in human form or talks with them through "angels"; whereas, in E, he merely speaks without appearing in personal guise.

This difference cannot be denied; but it is not a chronological criterion, as argued, for instance, by Cornill; [4] it is no sign of date, but arises from a contrast between the mental habits of Judah and

[4] *Einleitung*, "JE."

those of Ephraim, as manifested, for example, by Amos and Hosea. To the Judean prophet, Yahweh appears in person, standing upon a stone wall, holding a plumb line, and speaking; he shows Amos a basket of ripe fruit and some newly-created locusts; Amos "sees" the words of Yahweh. But on the other hand, the Ephraimite prophet Hosea sees neither words, things, nor the form of Yahweh; and he simply "hears" the word which comes to and through him. The Judean Isaiah, however, on the other hand, sees his prophecy as a vision; he beholds Yahweh sitting on a throne, wearing skirts and surrounded by seraphim (Isa. 6); and the same type of imagery reappears in the Judean book of Ezekiel, but complicated by the influence of Babylonian sculpture (Ezek. 1). Again, in contrast, the Benjaminite (that is, Josephite) Jeremiah, prophesies like Hosea: the word of Yahweh "comes" to him, and he "hears" the message. This particular difference, in relation to J and E, is merely a contrast of environments and habits of thought: Judah is more isolated and primitive. But on the other hand, although the inhabitants of the central hill country are backward enough, Ephraim is more in contact with the great outside world and more closely related to the commercial routes that run through the land. In other words, this part of the Hebrew people is more sophisticated than Judah. As Hosea, the Ephraimite prophet, declares, "Ephraim, he mixeth himself among the peoples; Ephraim is a cake not turned," that is, half-baked (Hos. 7:8).

But this difference between the two sections of the country gives an objective basis for only one phase of the contrast between J and E. Another consideration, equally important, is the fundamental fact that the Rachel element was always the primary, legend-building power in the Hebrew people. Here, in the central highlands, the main stock of Israel's tradition fixed itself with such hard, unyielding consistency that the later Judaic element could not venture to change essentials. No distortion of the legend was possible, for instance, which would place Leah, the mother of Judah, on a par with the Ephraimite mother, Rachel, in the affections of Jacob. Leah, like Judah, was forced upon Israel (that is, upon Jacob) and then put out of his tent, as Judah was rejected by the house of Joseph.

On the other hand, in the story of Joseph's betrayal by his brethren the original Ephraimite source makes the first-born son, Reuben, the leader who tries to save Joseph by inducing his brothers to hide him in a pit, intending himself to return secretly and carry the lad back to Jacob; but while the brethren are at their meal a company of Midianites pass by unobserved and kidnap Joseph, carrying him down to Egypt, where they sell him to Potiphar. Accordingly, at a later point in the Ephraimite narrative Joseph himself says in Egypt, "I was kidnapped out of the land of the Hebrews." But in the Judahite, or J, source the leader is Judah, who, seeing a company of Ishmaelites (not Midianites) coming, proposes to sell Joseph to these Ishmaelites, which is done forthwith. The purchasers afterwards sell him in Egypt, not to Potiphar, but to an Egyptian.[5] The Genesis narratives about Joseph in Egypt are put together likewise, partly from E, where Reuben, the eldest, is the spokesman (Gen. 42:22, 37), and partly from J, the lateness of which is revealed again by the fact that Judah has the spotlight instead of Reuben (Gen. 43:3, 8; 44:14, 16, 18; 46:28).

A still more important distinction is the difference between E and J in their treatment of the patriarchs with regard to sacrifice. Jacob in Ephraim, at Bethel, makes an offering of oil and promises to give a tenth of his goods, not to Yahweh, but to Elohim—the usual designation of deity in E (Gen. 28:18, 22). At the command of Elohim, he returns to Bethel, and according to the principles legalized in Ephraim by the revolution of Jehu, he tells his family to put away "strange gods"; after which he builds an altar to Elohim at Bethel and makes a drink offering and an offering of oil (Gen. 35:1–4, 7–8, 14). Again Jacob goes to Beersheba and offers sacrifices, not to Yahweh, but to Elohim (Gen. 46:1). Likewise, at the command of Elohim, Abraham goes to Moriah, where he offers up a ram as a sacrifice (Gen. 22:1, 13).

But in contrast (reflecting the late doctrine of one legitimate

[5] See analysis and explanation in *God and the Social Process*, pp. 323–25.

place of sacrifice in Canaan, established 621 B. C. by the Deutero-nomic reformation of Josiah) the J source makes the patriarchs merely build altars at various Canaanite localities without offering sacrifice. Abraham erects altars at Sichem, Bethel, and Hebron (Gen. 12:7, 8; 13:18); Isaac builds an altar at Beersheba (Gen. 26:25). Yet the same J source is very particular to say that sacrifices were actually offered by the pre-Hebrew patriarchs Cain, Abel, and Noah, who lived outside Canaan. Thus, Cain brings the fruit of the ground, not to Elohim, but to Yahweh—the usual designation of deity in the J document; while Abel brings the firstlings of the flock and the fat thereof, and Noah builds an altar and offers every clean beast and every clean fowl to Yahweh (Gen. 4:3, 4; 8:20).

"Baal-adon" distinction between E and J

The general relationship between E and J calls for special emphasis upon the use of two terms—*baal* and *adon*, as applied to human beings and gods. The term *adon* (owner, lord, master, proprietor) characterizes the J source in the Hexateuch, the historical narratives relating to both Judah and Ephraim in Judges, Samuel, and Kings, and the books of the Judean prophets Amos, Micah, and Isaiah. But on the other hand, although the term *adon* is found in the E document and in the narratives concerning Ephraim in Judges, Samuel, and Kings, nevertheless, the term *baal* is found in E as a characteristic, while it tends to occur in the Judges, Samuel, and Kings narratives about Ephraim, appears infrequently in Isaiah, whose home was in Amorite Jerusalem, and is often found in the Ephraimite prophet Hosea, as well as in the Benjaminite prophet Jeremiah.

The distribution of *adon* and *baal* in the sources follows a natural tendency, which is disclosed, not by grammatical and literary analysis, but by study of the objective historical circumstances amid which the documents evolved. We have several times observed that prior to the Josephite invasion pre-Hebrew Canaan as a whole was under the rule of walled cities, which were strongholds of human *baalim,* and of Baal cults which represented the social and economic regime. This condition, however, did not prevail so fully throughout the section of Canaan which afterward became Judah as it did in other parts of the land. Jebus (Jerusalem), had its *baalim* both before and after the Hebrew conquest. Uriah the Hittite, who owned a house in the city, is called by this term, as a matter of course: "When the wife of Uriah heard that her *ish* (man) was dead, she mourned for her *baal*" (II Sam. 11:26). The Jerusalem prophet Isaiah observes that the ass knows the stall of his *baal* (Isa. 1:3). The term is also used of the walled city of Keilah, which was not in the Judean highlands, but in the Shefelah, or low hills on the way down to the Mediterranean. David "goes down" to this place to fight the Philistines and is afraid to stay inside the walls, lest he be betrayed by the "*baalim* of Keilah" (I Sam. 23:4, 11, 12). But in the open country districts of what later became Judah, the landed proprietors and slaveowners are known by the more primitive term *adon.* Thus, the Calebite aristocrat Nabal is quoted as saying, "There be many slaves now a days that break away every man from his *adon*" (I Sam. 25:10). Some of these human chattels went to Nabal's wife and said, "David sent messengers out of the wilderness to salute our *adon;* and he railed on them" (I Sam. 25:14). The Levite of Ephraim, whose concubine was of Bethlehem, is called both her *ish* and her *adon* (Judg. 19:3, 11, 13, 26, 27). The owner of an Egyptian slave is called his *adon* (I Sam. 30:13). Boaz, the owner of land in Bethlehem, is *adon* (Ruth 2:13). Amos, the Judean prophet, calls the citizens of Samaria *adonim* (Amos 4:1).

Equally careful scrutiny is called for in relation to the hill country of Ephraim. In the very center of this area the walled city of Shechem, as we have already seen, remained "pre-Hebrew" for a long time after the invasion and settlement of the Joseph clans. Its leading citizens are called *baalim* fifteen times by the Hebrew text (Judg. 9:2, 3, 6 *et passim*). The narrative about Shechem is Ephraimite, not Judahite. The citizens of Jericho, in the lowlands of Ephraim by the Jordan, are referred to likewise by the E source in the book of Joshua: "The *baalim* of Jericho fought against you" (Josh. 24:11). But after the destruction of Shechem and its *baalim*, an Ephraimite aristocracy (whether of "pure Israelite" descent or not) was consolidated in the central highlands under the designation *adonim*. Thus, the owner of the hill Samaria is called "the *adon* of the hill" (I Kings 16:24). Nevertheless, a tendency is to be noticed for *baal* to creep into sources relating in any way to Ephraim. The late story in the appendix to Judges, narrating the outrage at the Benjaminite village of Gibeah, has been referred to several times. This material, which makes the Levite the *adon* of his concubine, refers to the old man from Ephraim, however, as *ha-ish, baal ha-bayith*, that is, the man, the owner (or master) of the house (Judg. 19:22, 23). In the chapter immediately following, the men of Israel are spoken of sixteen times as *ish*, while the men of Gibeah are called "the *baalim* of Gibeah" (Judg. 20:5). We have not yet arrived at the point of definite comparison between the J and E documents of the Hexateuch, but it will be useful here to observe that in the Judaic source the Sodom story, corresponding to the above tale, calls the men of that place *anshae ha-ir, anshae Sodom*, ("men of the city, men of Sodom"; Gen. 19:4). In the Elijah stories the prophet is entertained by a widow of Zarephath, who is called *baalath ha-bayith*, that is, the feminine owner of the house (I Kings 17:17). Zarephath, however, is not Ephraimite, but belongs to the Baal-worshiping city of Zidon (I Kings 17:9). Elijah is referred to by the Ephraimite text of Kings as *baal shaar* ("a hairy man"; II Kings 1:8). But in the J document Esau is a hairy man and is called, not *baal*, but *ish shaar* ("man of hair"; Gen. 27:11). In the story telling how Saul, the first king of Ephraim, consulted "the witch of Endor," the woman is called *baalath ob*, that is, feminine possessor of a spirit (I Sam. 28:7). Endor, however, is not in Ephraim proper, but in the plain of Esdraelon under direct Canaanite influence. One more illustration—this time from the city of Jabesh in the Ephraimite province of Gilead. Successive references to the men of that place in Judges, First Samuel, and Second Samuel use the term *ish* eight times

(Judg. 21:9; I Sam. 11:1, 5, 9, 10; I Sam. 31:12; II Sam. 2:4, 5).
But in the final reference the *ish* is displaced by *baal* (II Sam. 21:12).

Judahite and Ephraimite documents compared

In the Judahite, or J, source, Abraham is the *adon* of Sarah (Gen. 18:12). Yahweh is called by this term five times in the same chapter (Gen. 18:3, 27, 30, 31, 32), rendered in English by a large initial capital "L," followed by lower case, thus, "Lord." On the other hand, the proper name Yahweh occurs in this chapter ten times (Gen. 18:1, 13, 14, 17, 19 [twice], 20, 22, 26, 33), rendered in English by large initial capital "L," followed by small capitals and preceded by "the," thus, "the LORD." (Cf. Gen. 18:26 and 27.) Beyond these typographical distinctions, which ordinarily escape notice, the terms in question are completely hidden, appearing only in the Hebrew text. The J source in the twenty-fourth of Genesis refers to Abraham as the *adon* of a slave (*ebed*) twenty-one times (Gen. 24:9, 10, 12, 27, *et passim*, translated "master"). In the thirty-ninth of Genesis the Egyptian purchaser of Joseph is called *adon* seven times (Gen. 39:3, 7, 8, *et passim*, rendered "master" six times and "lord" once). The same term, again, is rendered "sir" (Gen. 43:20); and in the following chapter it is put into English exactly thirteen times as "lord" (Gen. 44:5, 7, 8, *et passim*). In chapter forty-seven it occurs four times, rendered "lord" (Gen. 47:18, 25). These examples are all from the J source.

But on the other hand, the Ephraimite, or E, document, introduces the term *baal*. The first appearance of this document in the Hexateuch is in the twentieth of Genesis, where Sarah is called *b'ulath baal* (Gen. 20:3, translated "a man's wife"). In other words, while Abraham in the J document was the *adon* of Sarah, the Ephraimite source transforms him into a *baal*. The same source makes Joseph a "baal of dreams" (Gen. 37:19, translated "dreamer"). Once more, the Ephraimite material assumes that any matter of legal dispute can be brought before judges only by a *baal* (Exod. 24:14, translated "man"). In the book of Numbers, E speaks of the "*baalim* of the high places of Arnon" (Numb. 21:28, translated this time "lords"). And in Joshua, as already cited, the same document speaks of the *baalim* of Jericho fighting against Israel (Josh. 24:11, translated simply "men"). The Ephraimite source not only calls Abraham a *baal*, as above, but also speaks of him as a *nabi*, or "prophet" (Gen. 20:7). The same document gives further evidence of its affinity with prophetism in the passage expressing the wish that all the people of Yahweh might be prophets (*nebiim*) and that Yahweh would put his spirit upon the entire nation (Numb. 11:29).[6]

Ephraimite source original prophetic document; Judahite source avoids baal as Ephraimite

In considering the significance of the contrast between E and J with reference to the terms under discussion, a number of important facts must be held in mind: (1) The prophetic movement against Baalism, led by Elijah and his followers, began in Ephraim, not in Judah. The kings of Judah were "doing evil in the eyes of Yahweh," and the common people of that more primitive part of the land were following their flocks and herds; while the forces behind prophetism gathered strength in Ephraim and finally, under the house of Jehu, committed the religion of Yahweh to official antagonism against Baal. (2) Along with other phenomena showing that the Ephraimite source in the Hexateuch is earlier and that J is a modification of it, the absence of "*baal*" from the Judahite source gives added proof that material common to both documents has undergone manipulation by the J school of writers. (3) That the practice of calling Yahweh a *baal* began comparatively early has been shown. But this usage was roundly condemned by the Ephraimite prophet Hosea: "Saith Yahweh . . . Thou shalt call me no more 'My Baal' " (Hosea 2:16). Jeremiah, who is Benjaminite, not Judaic, denounces Baal worship as *bosheth*, or shame (Jer.

---

[6] On the ostraca dug up from Ahab's time by the Harvard archaeologists, *eleven* of the royal officials bear names compounded with "Yahweh," while six have names compounded with "Baal." Cf. *Harvard Excavations at Samaria* (Cambridge, 1924), I, 277f., and J. W. Jack, *Samaria in Ahab's Time* (Edinburgh, 1939), p. 157.

11:13). Accordingly, we have seen that the Judaic redactors, following this hint from the Josephite prophets, began to change *baal* names in the older historical documents to *bosheth* names: Jerubbaal (Judg. 7:1) becomes Jerrubbesheth (II Sam. 11:21). Ish-baal, the son of King Saul, becomes Ish-bosheth (II Sam. 2:8). But the fact that so many *baal* names of persons are left standing in the Hebrew text proves two things: first, that the changes actually made were part of an anti-baal movement which began comparatively late in the history and, second, that there never was any supreme, central authority among the Judaic redactors by which the process of manipulating the documents could be finally carried through in a wholly consistent way. For instance, a soldier in David's army had the name "Yahweh is Baal" (I Chron. 12:5, *B'aliah*); but before any pragmatic editorial hand could undertake to dispose of this pagan item, the text of the Old Testament had crystallized into unchangeable sanctity. To transform it into "Boshethiah" would be very embarrassing, because that would mean "Yahweh is shame." Nor could it be thrown out entirely, because it had slowly acquired protection under the dogma that every word and letter of the Hebrew text was given by the Holy Spirit. Thus it remains in the Bible today—the symbol of a problem too complicated for antiquity and a little-regarded portent of warning to the modern Church and Synagogue.

Wealthier landed proprietors transformed into baalim

The work of Elijah was not lost. It remained as an abiding triumph in the realm of spirit. The religion of Yahweh was now, for the first time, committed officially to opposition against Baal. Yet, in spite of the bitter campaign into which Elijah had thrown all the weight of his tremendous personality, in spite of the political and cultic revolution which carried the house of Jehu to the seat of power, nevertheless, impersonal economic forces continued inexorably to operate, and an invisible wedge was driven into the class of Ephraimite landholders and slaveowners. The poorer *adonim* lost their lands and slaves to the richer; and these unfortunate freemen themselves became slaves under the yoke of their wealthier neighbors and "brothers" in the house of Israel. The situation thus emerging in the period of the Jehu dynasty must be clearly envisaged if the problem of Bible history is to be understood; because these very circumstances contain the force which created the Biblical dogma of One God.

Like the development of monotheism itself, the ethical reaction of the prophets to the economic and social problem did not originate on the plane of abstract ideology, but always arose out of concrete situations involving the economic plight of the poorer landholders and slaveowners. Thus, human slavery in the abstract is not condemned anywhere in the Old Testament—or in the New, for that matter. Instead, it is taken for granted, as follows:

In regard to thy male slave (*ebed*), and thy female slave (*amah*), whom thou shalt have: From the nations that are round about you, of them shall ye buy *ebed* and *amah*. . . . Of them shall ye take your bondmen *forever*. But over your brethren, the children of Israel, ye shall not rule, one over another with rigor [Levit. 25:42–46].

These facts, however, should not prejudice the subject in modern eyes: on the contrary, the Hebrew religious evolution works out the same as any other line of human progress—beginning concretely and moving toward more general conceptions as it goes along. In other words, we have no right to demand that the Bible shall forthwith display abstract ethical perfection and yield infallible programs of reform. The problem which weighed upon Ephraim under the dynasty of Jehu was desperate. The country had gone through many and frequent wars; its territory was not large; no opening for national relief was possible. In the midst of such conditions it was natural that impoverished members of the proprietary classes should borrow from the more fortunate, with the inevitable result that when interest or principal was not liquidated they lost their lands and slaves and fell into bondage to the wealthier section of the aristocracy.

This process was not peculiar to Israel; it worked throughout the ancient eastern world, and it reappeared in the history of Greece and Rome. The problem was too complicated to be handled successfully in those ages by any government or public authority anywhere. But thinkers in Ephraim undertook to compile a series of ordinances, or *mishpatim,* which might be available in case opportunity offered to put them into effect. The lesson of the revolution which replaced the house of Ahab by the house of Jehu had never been lost; and since this upheaval had committed Ephraim officially to the proscription of Tyrian Baalism, some new revolution might happen at any time by which a further objective advance could be made if an appropriate plan were formulated beforehand.

Idealistic proposals of Ephraimite document

Proposals looking toward reform are embodied in the E document, composed in the "time of silence" under the dynasty of Jehu, when free speech was not permitted. The growing intrusion of the term *baal* will be noticed, as compared with the older term *adon,* which is dropping slowly out of use. The compilation begins at Exodus 21:1, and concludes with 23:19. Part of this material may be taken from an earlier, pre-Hebrew code. While there is a clear logic underlying it, the various items are thrown together in disorderly array. But the salient preoccupation of the "Code," as it may be called, is with the unfortunate "poor"—what may be described as the "left wing" of the Hebrew upper class. This is revealed by the opening *mishpat,* which will be considered first; after which other items will be rearranged in logical relation to it.

NOW THESE ARE THE MISHPATIM WHICH THOU SHALT SET BEFORE THEM:
Thus saith Yahweh:
"If thou buy a Hebrew slave (*ebed*) he shall serve six years; and in the seventh, he shall go out free for nothing" [Exod. 21:2].

Observe that this proposed rule contemplates an economic regime wherein free Hebrews are already in a desperate condition and that it seeks a compromise between (1) the idea that an Israelite should never be the slave of another Israelite and (2) the claims of the Israelite creditor, or purchaser, who would otherwise hold the unfortunate man in bondage indefinitely. But no evidence exists indicating that any such "ideal" was ever enacted into law; save one case (Jer. 34), in which Hebrew slaves were hypocritically set free to gain the favor of Yahweh, and then almost immediately reënslaved; on the contrary, the prophetic books (Amos, Hosea, and so forth) presuppose the existence of oppressive economic and social conditions which had once flourished under the rule of pre-Hebrew Amorite Baal worshipers (Cf. II Kings 17:9f.).

The Code then goes on to say:

If he [the erstwhile Hebrew freeman] came in [to slavery] by himself, he shall go out [of slavery] by himself. And if he were *baal* of a wife (*ishshah*, woman), then his wife shall go free with him. But if his *adon* has given him a woman, and she has borne him sons or daughters, then he shall go free himself; and the woman and her children shall belong to her *adon* [Exod. 21:3, 4].

A further attempt at compromise in favor of wealthy proprietors is made evident by the following: "He that smiteth a man (*ish*) so that he die, shall be surely put to death" (Exod. 21:12).

If a man (*ish*) smite his male slave (*ebed*), or his female slave (*amah*) with a rod, and he die under his hand, he shall surely be punished. Notwithstanding, if he [the slave] continue a day or two, he [the owner] shall not be punished; for he is his money [Exod. 21:20, 21].

"If thou lend money to any of my people that is poor, thou shalt not be to him as a creditor (*nosheh*, one who oppresses); neither shalt thou lay upon him interest" (Exod. 22:25). In other words, the poor *adon* shall get loans from the wealthy *baal* without charge. This idea, if put into operation, would have drafted the economic surplus of the wealthier freemen as an endowment for supporting the poorer freemen in a state of pauperized aristocracy.

In its impractical utopianism, the foregoing proposal resembles the following:

Six years shalt thou sow thy land, and shalt gather the fruits thereof. . . . In like manner shalt thou deal with thy vineyard and with thy oliveyard. But the seventh year thou shalt let it rest and lie still, that the poor of thy people may eat [Exod. 23:10, 11].

Thou shalt not pervert the *mishpat* of the poor [that is, the unfortunate freeman] in his law-case. . . . Put not thine hand with the wicked to be an unrighteous witness. . . . Keep thee far from a false matter; and the innocent and righteous slay thou not; for I will not justify the wicked [Exod. 23:1, 6, 7].

In the background of such precepts we hear the resounding echoes of perverted justice and judicial murder which characterized the historic Naboth case.

The prophetic origin of all these *mishpatim* is attested by their identification with Yahweh, who says,

In all the things that I have said unto you be circumspect: and make no mention of the name of other gods; neither let it be heard out of thy mouth. . . . He that sacrificeth unto any god, save unto Yahweh only, he shall be utterly destroyed [Exod. 23:13; 22:20].

As a platform of social-religious progress the Code is relatively advanced as compared with current economic and legal usages which it condemns. But even so, the foregoing demand that worshipers of other gods be destroyed reminds us that we are in the wake of Elijah and the murderous destruction of Baal worshipers by Jehu in the name of Yahweh.

The death penalty for worshiping other gods is in the same category with several other injunctions of the Code; for instance, "Thou shalt not suffer a witch to live" (Exod. 22:18). This raises many problems, instead of solving one. What is witchcraft? How is witchcraft to be proved legally as a fact? Who is competent to try, and to condemn, and to execute "witches"? Taking the injunction as literally passed down from heaven, many clergymen and laymen of Salem, Mass., in the seventeenth century, felt themselves to be fully equipped for answering all these questions.

The relative occurrence of *adon* and *baal* in the Ephraimite Code is very striking when considered from the standpoint of the textual phenomena already cited. Thus, the older *adon*, common to both J and E, is used only seven times (Exod. 21:4 [twice], 5, 6 [twice], 8, 32). In these cases it denotes ownership of erstwhile free Hebrews, their wives, or daughters. But the Ephraimite term *baal* is used twelve times (Exod. 21:3, 22, 29 [twice], 34, 36; 22:8, 11, 12, 14, 15). Moreover, it is employed in these cases with reference to ownership of women, oxen, asses, houses, and land.

The Code, standing thus in the Ephraimite document of the Hexateuch, is a product of the struggle against the growing prevalence of usages and customs derived from pre-Hebrew Canaan. These usages were gradually overwhelming the ancient *mishpat* once followed in the central highlands of Ephraim. The transfer of land from inalienable, family tenure to a liquid, commercialistic tenure brought with it a tendency for displacement of the term *adon* by the Canaanite term *baal*. Of no effect in itself, this linguistic change was the symbol of an objective, social transformation which marked the slow economic death of the Hebrew people. "When Ephraim . . . offended in Baal, he died. . . . The iniquity of Ephraim is bound up in store" (Hos. 13:1, 12).

Books of Amos and Hosea, 785–745 B. C.

The little books of Amos and Hosea cannot, of course, be considered here in detail. They deal with social, economic, and religious conditions under Jeroboam II, whose reign almost completed the period of the Jehu dynasty (Amos 1:1; Hos. 1:1). Amos, who was a shepherd from the village of Tekoa in Judah, uses the name Joseph as the equivalent of Israel: "Seek Yahweh, and ye shall live; lest he break out like fire in the house of Joseph" (Amos 5:6). He denounces the wealthy, who live in the walled city of Samaria, the Josephite capital: "Woe . . . to them that are secure in the hill of Samaria." Especially does he arraign their wives, whom he calls "cows," in derisive contempt: "Hear this word, ye cows that are in the hill of Samaria; that oppress the poor; that crush the needy; that say unto their lords (*adonim*), 'Bring, and let us drink.'" Denunciation rises to climax when he declares, "They are not grieved for the affliction of Joseph" (Amos 4:1; 6:1, 6). Again, he uses the name of another patriarch, the father of the nation, calling down the wrath of Yahweh upon the people collectively: "The Adon Yahweh hath sworn. . . . 'I abhor the pride of Jacob, and hate his palaces! Therefore will I deliver up the city with all that is therein' " (Amos 6:8). Like the Davidic dynasty of the united kingdom, with its hired strong men (*gibborim*), the rulers of Samaria had the same kind of tools to enforce policies that oppressed the rustic freemen. These instruments of tyranny are specially denounced by the shepherd-prophet, who declares that they shall be ruined in the downfall of the kingdom: "Flight shall perish from the swift; . . . neither shall the *gibbor* deliver himself."—"The *gibborim* shall flee away naked in that day, saith Yahweh" (Amos 2:14, 15). Here, then, is revealed, in clearest words, the protest of small property holders in country villages against wealthy exploiters who live secure in walled cities. It is not remarkable that Amos was driven from the streets of Bethel by the priest Amaziah (Amos 7:10).

In view of the emphasis which Amos puts upon the term Joseph, his reference to the conquest of Canaan is very significant, as bringing into relief the total destruction of the Amorites in the central highlands, the proper "house of Joseph." Accordingly, Amos declares: "Thus saith Yahweh. . . . I destroyed the Amorite before them, whose height was like the height of the cedars; and he was strong as the oaks. Yet I destroyed his fruit from above and his roots from beneath" (Amos 2:9). This "root and branch" extermination of the pre-Hebrew, Amorite aristocracy, in the central highlands of Canaan, reached its climax, as we saw, in the downfall of the fortified city of Shechem and the massacre of its burgesses, or human *baalim;* followed by the rise of a new Hebrew aristocracy of *adonim,* worshiping Yahweh instead of Baal. These two movements of conquest and reconstruction were the essence of "enclave" history in the house of Joseph during the Judges period. Looking at Israel as Amos did, from the standpoint of Judah, all that one could see was precisely "the house of Joseph." Hence he was accurate in speaking of the conquest as a "root and branch" destruction of Amorite society.

This fact, however, is not a mere *datum* isolated from the problem of Hebrew history and religion. It pertains to the essence of the situation. And when the sanctuary of Shiloh emerges into view in the latter part of the Judges period, the house of Joseph is worshiping Yahweh, not only as a war god, but as a "god of the land" who fertilizes the soil and gives the fruits of the earth to his devotees. Moreover, so far as the central highlands are concerned, Yahweh does not acquire the qualities of a nature-fertility god from the defeated Canaanite Baalim through some secret, bootlegging absorption of their powers at second-hand from the deities of the Amorites, as claimed by critics from Wellhausen on.

Consistently with his idea of a thorough conquest, Amos regards Israel as a "line-bred" nation, unmixed with alien stock. Accordingly, he condemns Israel as a community which has perversely broken away from its ancient moral moorings. The city rulers repudiate the old social usages of the primitive rural clan, substituting customs and usages which bear hard upon poor freemen: They "turn *mishpat* to wormwood" (Amos 5:7). Hence, Amos demands reversion to the ideals and practices of the clan brotherhood: "Let *mishpat* roll down like waters" (Amos 5:24).

Hosea, like Amos, takes his stand on the immemorial customs of the villagers against the city nobles and merchants who lead Ephraim into paths that were followed by Canaan before the coming of Israel from the desert: "Ephraim is oppressed; he is crushed in *mishpat*" (Hos. 5:11). "Thou didst trust in thy way, in the multitude of thy *gibborim*. Therefore shall . . . all thy fortresses be destroyed" (Hos. 10:13, 14).

Amos, coming north out of Judah, seems not to have penetrated beyond Bethel, which lay only ten miles above the frontier (Amos 7:10, 13). It was therefore easy and natural that he should think of Israel as a "line-bred," undiluted community, whose sin consisted in deserting its ancient moral principles. But on the other hand, Hosea, as already noticed, looks upon the shortcomings of Ephraim in relation to its mixture with non-Hebrew, Canaanite elements. The walled cities Taanach, Megiddo, and Bethshan, in the plain of Esdraelon, had never been destroyed like Shechem and Bethel in Ephraim; because the Davidic dynasty had introduced a considerate policy toward these and other pre-Hebrew centers of Amorite life. Such places, while included in "Israel," had always retained an Amorite, or Canaanite, quality. They acknowledged Yahweh as the general deity of Israel; but at the same time there was no reason why they should not continue to worship their ancient Baalim and to follow the baalistic laws of landholding. The social, economic, and religious outlook of these alien cities on the plain became increasingly attractive to the ruling classes in Ephraim as the old clan life and *mishpat* of the central highlands broke down and were liquidated under the Jehu dynasty. Thus, Amorite customs and Baal-worship spread through the upper classes of Ephraim—especially in Samaria the capital. Hence, Hosea says, "Ephraim, he mixeth himself among the peoples. Ephraim is a cake not turned [half-baked]. Strangers have devoured his strength, and he knoweth it not." (Hos. 7:8, 9). "Canaan, the balances of deceit are in his hand. He loveth to defraud. Ephraim said, Surely I am become rich; I have found me wealth" (Hos. 12:7, 8).

Where Amos refers to Israel as "Joseph," Hosea speaks of Ephraim, using this term thirty-seven times; while the term "Baal," which does not occur in Amos, is found seven times in Hosea. We do not know where Hosea was born or where he lived; but he is preëminently the prophet of Ephraim. His whole outlook is Ephraimitic. His denunciation of Baal worship is part of his polemic against the anti-*mishpat* regime. But Wellhausen and his followers have isolated Hosea's anti-Baalism from the context of his book and have made it a norm, or test, for interpreting the entire Baal problem in such a way as to sidetrack scholarship and obscure the sociological and economic background of Biblical history. This point, therefore, must be cleared up.

Hosea's oft-quoted complaint, "She [Israel] did not know that I [Yahweh] gave her the grain, and the new wine, and the oil" (Hos. 2:8)—this is, to most critics, the crux of the situation. Ephraim, according to Harper, is guilty

not of worshipping the Baalim as gods who existed in opposition to, or alongside of, Yahweh, as the givers of the blessings of field and flock; but rather of having retained, as an essential element of the worship of

Yahweh, the rites formerly carried on as a part of the cultus of the Baalim. They do worship Yahweh as the source of these material blessings, but they have corrupted his worship with so much that pertains in reality to the cultus of the Baalim, that they might as well be worshipping the latter.[7]

Hosea is here supposed to be giving an authoritative exposition of the religious psychology of "all Israel" with reference to Yahweh, who is imagined, by Hosea and his modern critical disciples, to have absorbed into himself all the biological, nature-functions of the Canaanite Baalim, and is himself called "My *Baal*" (*Baali*, Hos. 2:16); the result being that Ephraim really worships the Amorite gods without knowing it.

But if Hosea does actually assume that so far as "all Israel" is concerned, Yahweh has, in effect, swallowed the Baal gods and assimilated them into himself—one might ask in the first place: By what right has Hosea generalized the entire situation in this categorical and sweeping way? Is Hosea's generalization equally true for the hill country of Judah, of Ephraim, and of Galilee? Does it apply equally well to the people of the fertile plain of Esdraelon and to the masses of plain people in the Ephraimite hills? Does it refer with the same force to the upper classes in the city of Samaria and to the poor farmers and shepherds in the country outside the capital? Does it include the people of the walled cities Taanach, Megiddo, Bethshan, and others, with dwellers in the hills of Gilead, east of Jordan, whence came Elijah the great *nabi*, representing thousands "who had not bowed unto Baal"? (I Kings 19:18).

Merely to put these questions ought to suggest that not only Hosea but also his critical expositors go too far in dealing so generally and summarily with a broad and complex problem. Hosea's term "she," as equivalent of "all Israel," or Harper's "they," as covering the entire nation, or the references of various critics to "the people"—all such use of language oversimplifies the problem too easily.

Take the statement of Hosea, "She [Israel] did not know that I

[7] Harper, *Amos and Hosea*, p. 228.

gave her the grain," and so forth. This proposition assumes that in the mind of Israel there was no distinction between Yahweh and the Canaanite Baalim. But it also assumes that the distinction simply existed in the mind of Hosea, who, as the only instructed person in Israel, knew that the entire nation was wrong in treating Yahweh as if he had actually swallowed the Baalim and absorbed their fertility functions. But if the distinction did actually exist in Hosea's mind, what right had he to assume that it did not exist in the minds of at least some other Hebrews? The critics take his words uncritically as applying to the entire Hebrew people; but if they do, what right has Hosea or the critics to assume so easily that everyone (except the prophet himself) had bowed the knee to Yahweh as a deity having the same character as the Canaanite Baalim? If Hosea's language does, indeed, bear the interpretation which modern critics put on it, are not both Hosea and the critics making the mistake that Elijah is said to have made when he declared in general terms, "The children of Israel have forsaken thy covenant; and I, even I only, am left"? (I Kings 19:14). May not Hosea and his modern disciples be as far from the real situation as Elijah is said to have been when he was informed that there were seven thousand in Israel which had not bowed the knee to Baal? (I Kings 19:18). The observation may be interposed that Hosea spoke hyperbolically—in other words, that the prophet was consciously or unconsciously exaggerating. But if so, what becomes of the passage in question as a norm, or test, for interpreting the entire Baal issue in Bible history?

Is it not more reasonable to assume that Hosea himself resided in a neighborhood where the Yahweh cultus approximated the usages of the old, Canaanite Baal shrines; that his home, for instance, was in the fertile plain of Esdraelon, in some village overshadowed by one of the walled cities which had come down intact from pre-Hebrew times? Or, that he had in mind the cult practices of the corrupt Ephraimite ruling class, and ignored the more old-fashioned customs of the austere country folk in the central highlands? As a matter of fact, his use of the simple term "Ephraim" shows that his point of view varies from passage to passage: Ephraim is oppressed and crushed in *mishpat* and is the innocent victim of wealthy exploiters; "Ephraim" is here identical with the "righteous" who, in Amos, are sold for silver (Hos. 5:11; cf. Amos 2:6). But on the other hand, Ephraim is the oppressor himself, who loves to defraud, and who has become wealthy by his corrupt ways (Hos. 12:7). If Hosea can vary his point of view with such ease in reference to "Ephraim," he may do likewise when speaking of the current attitudes toward the Baal cult. Moreover, if his experience with the woman Gomer was real, not assumed in imagination for didactic or symbolic purposes, his thought may have been distorted by grief when she went away to play the harlot at a Baal shrine in some neighboring walled city; which would justify Robertson Smith's remark that Hosea's prophecy " is an argument of the heart, not of the head."

Without depreciating the great moral and spiritual importance of Hosea, it is well to observe that so far as the general historical significance of Baalism is concerned, modern scholars have taken this prophet with entirely too much seriousness. Hosea's disciple Jeremiah is just as much interested in the Baal question; but Jeremiah does not complicate the issue by discussing the relative powers of Yahweh and Baal with reference to the production of grain, wine, and oil. Assuming that Yahweh sends the rain and fertilizes the soil, Jeremiah denounces Baal worship as a phase of the regime which perverts *mishpat* and oppresses the smaller property holders. In the eyes of Jeremiah social injustice and Baal worship are, not two separate phenomena, but aspects of the same problem. And it is only in this way that Hosea can be understood, no matter how vague his language: he approaches Ephraim from the northern, more Baalized section of Palestine; while Amos comes up from the south, and looks at the problem in the light of simpler antitheses.

Definite moral advance registered by Hosea

We noticed that in the struggle between Yahweh and Baal which took place under the dynasty of Ahab, the campaign of the prophets was motivated by the purpose of assassination. Yahweh himself is represented as commissioning Elijah at Mt. Horeb, instructing him that whoever escapes the sword of Jehu shall be slain by Elisha (I Kings 19:17); and accordingly Elisha, in the name of Yahweh, directs Jehu to smite and destroy the whole house of Ahab (II Kings 9:6–9). The great anti-Baal campaign under the house of Ahab took place more than a century before the time of Hosea; and whether he ever saw any of the old narratives about Elijah and Jehu we do not know. But in any case, Hosea, speaking in the name of Yahweh, condemns the bloody program by which the house of Ahab was destroyed and the reigning dynasty of Jehu came to the throne. The murders took place at Jezreel, the eastern part of the Esdraelon plain; and they are categorically denounced in terms which are contrary to the commands of Yahweh as given in the books of Kings, thus:

When Yahweh spake at the first by Hosea, Yahweh said unto Hosea, Go, take unto thee a wife of whoredom. . . . So he went and took Gomer the daughter of Diblaim; and she conceived, and bare him a son. And Yahweh said unto him, Call his name Jezreel; for yet a little while, and I will avenge the blood of Jezreel upon the house of Jehu, and I will cause the kingdom of the house of Israel to cease [Hos. 1:2–4].

Hosea's view of Yahweh stands out in startling contrast with doctrines which obtained a hundred years earlier in the time of Elijah. The slow process of secular history was needed in order that religious ideas be carried gradually upward to higher levels. Yet it must be emphasized that Hosea's theology was only a matter of private opinion in his own day; it was not in any way a part of the official Hebrew religion. Just as the anti-Baalism of Elijah and his disciples was at first a matter of private conviction, becoming official doctrine only through the revolution of Jehu, so the little book of Hosea took its place among the manuscripts of the antiquarians and waited longer than the work of Elijah before becoming an official part of Israel's culture. Even Hosea himself could scarcely have made any impression upon the future if the ground had not been cleared for him by the social forces which came to an effective climax around the personality and memory of Elijah, the first great Hebrew prophet.

Jehu's dynasty destroyed, 745 B. C.

When Jeroboam II died, a son succeeded him, only to be assassinated within a few months by a man who reigned but a single month and was in turn slain by still another aspirant, Menahem ben Gadi; this politician, however, managed to keep his footing on the unsteady throne of Ephraim for ten years (II Kings 14:28, 29; 15:8–14). Only three verses are given to the reign of Menahem, who tried to extend the frontier of Ephraim northward, so as to obtain more territory (II Kings 14:16). The most dramatic event of his time was another lunge of the huge Assyrian empire toward the Mediterranean:

Pul the king of Assyria came against the land; and Menahem gave Pul a thousand talents of silver. . . . And Menahem exacted the money of Israel, from every *gibbor hayil,*—from each man fifty shekels of silver. . . . So the king of Assyria turned back, and stayed not there in the land [II Kings 15:19–20].

The *gibbor hayil,* we have learned, was not the same as the professional *gibbor,* the hired strong man or thug. He was the individual, private holder of land, who paid regular taxes and was liable to be conscripted in time of war. The Assyrian tax of 1,000 talents (at 3,000 shekels to the talent, of which every property holder paid 50 shekels) would give a taxable population of 60,000, over and above women, children, and slaves. This, in turn, would mean a census totaling, perhaps, from 350,000 to 1,000,000. The Assyrian tax was unjust because it fell equally upon rich and poor. A given tax, which a wealthy man pays without feeling it, may strike a poor man at the margin of his resources, compelling him to borrow from his more fortunate neighbor or from some moneylender in a city; such an occasion may be the means of plunging thousands into unpayable debt, eventuating in bondage. Taxation was thus among the economic forces in Ephraim tending to make the poor poorer and the rich richer—a condition which also prevailed in ancient Greece and Rome.

Territory north of Esdraelon seized by Assyrians, 732 B. C.

After the death of Menahem a son succeeded to the throne, but he was presently murdered by a new adventurer, Pekah, who ruled Ephraim for twenty years (II Kings 15:21f.). Several noteworthy events marked the downward course of Israel in this reign. The Assyrians under Tiglath-pileser, suddenly took the entire district north of Esdraelon and carried the inhabitants away into captivity—an ominous portent of Ephraim's end. Then the new king, Pekah, tried to blockade further advance of the Mesopotamian colossus by attempting a military coalition between Ephraim, Syria, and Judah. But when Judah refused to enter into such an alliance, the armies of Ephraim and Syria coöperated in besieging Jerusalem for the purpose of compelling Judah to enter the anti-Assyrian league.

Ephraim swept into captivity, 722 B. C.

During the siege the king of Judah sent messengers with tribute to Tiglath-pileser, asking help; whereupon the Assyrians at once attacked Damascus, the capital of Syria, and carried many of the Syrian people into captivity. This prompt action raised the siege of Jerusalem (II Kings 16:5–9). Meanwhile Pekah, who had thus failed in his plans, was murdered by still another political upstart. This man, Hoshea ben Elah, became the last king of Ephraim, as a tributary of the Mesopotamian power. In other words, both Israel and Judah were now reckoned as parts of the Assyrian empire. While Judah remained quiet and sent regular payments to the suzerain, the course of events was not smooth in Ephraim, where King Hoshea began to default on his obligations.

And the king of Assyria found conspiracy in Hoshea; for he [Hoshea] had sent messengers to So, king of Egypt, and brought no tribute to the king of Assyria, as he had done year by year. . . . Then the king of Assyria came up throughout all the land, and went up to Samaria, and besieged it three years. In the ninth year of Hoshea, the king of Assyria took Samaria, and carried Israel away into Assyria, and placed them in Halah, and in Habor by the river of Gozan, and in the cities of the Medes. . . . And the king of Assyria brought men from Babylon, and from Cuthah, and from Ava, and from Hamath, and from Sephar-vaim, and placed them in the cities of Samaria instead of the children of Israel; and they possessed Samaria, and dwelt in the cities thereof [II Kings 17:3–6, 24].

Thus Ephraim vanished from world history.

IX. JUDAH AND EXILE

B Y THE TIME Ephraim vanished from the stage of history,
Judah had already begun to suffer from the concentration of
landed property in the grip of a small class; and the prophet
Isaiah, of Jerusalem, was denouncing woe unto those who added
house to house and field to field (Isa. 5:8).

Historical matter about Judah is very scanty in the books of Kings
between the time when the house of David lost control of Ephraim
and the point where Ephraim disappeared. The kings of Judah are
described as "doing evil," permitting sacrifice to go on at the "high
places," or *bamoth*, all over the country, instead of at the one place,
Jerusalem, which the editorial compilers believe to have been designated by supernatural revelation as the only legal sanctuary. They
are so interested in the question of the place where Yahweh ought
to be worshiped that they deliberately distort the records by omit-
ting and cutting down much that would be of the highest importance
to a comprehension of the history as a secular process; instead, they
give us mere scraps from the ancient written sources, referring us
constantly to "The Book of the Doings of the Kings of Judah" if we
want more information.

On the other hand, as is pointed out elsewhere, the compilers give
us large quantities of their own, *post eventum* interpretations and
comments, written from the standpoint of Deuteronomy, which,
for a brief time during Josiah's reign, shortly before the Babylonian
exile, became the official ordinance of Judaic religion, politics, and
economics. This method, however, defaces and obscures the real,
objective course of events, and if our information about the history
of Judah were to be found only in the books of Kings, we should
be like mariners afloat on a trackless ocean without chart or compass.
Our only real guidance is the prophetic books of Micah, Isaiah,

Zephaniah, Jeremiah, and Ezekiel; and not until a recent period have these writings themselves begun to be understood as material for *history*, instead of as mere "prophecies," or predictions about the future.

Judah more pastoral and primitive than Ephraim

Rural property holders composed the bulk of Judah's population, the same as in Ephraim, but with an important difference. The community was of a simpler character—less agricultural and more pastoral. This contrast with Ephraim originated in the physical circumstances of the country; for Judah lay higher than Ephraim, and its hills were stonier. It was avoided by the important commercial highways, which passed beyond the frontiers, leaving Judah in a peculiar isolation. Its primitive social character was also emphasized by another physical contrast: Ephraim was barred from the desert by the river Jordan; but Judah's hills led slowly down southward into the wilderness without natural obstruction, so that the semi-nomad clans of Judah linked the country with desert usages and ways of thought more directly than in the case of Ephraim, which was always tending toward commercial, sophisticated "civilization." Thus Judah inclined more effectively to the original *mishpat* which lay at the basis of prophetic thought, and its population was more uniformly consolidated as a group of *adonim* following the cult of Yahweh. That Ephraim was aroused against Baal, not by one of its own people, but by the fiery prophet Elijah from the hills of Gilead, east of Jordan, must always be remembered.

Judah duplicates social problem of Ephraim

Taxation and military service were factors tending toward social and economic problems in Judah, as in Ephraim, but on a smaller scale and more gradually. The texture of *mishpat* usage was tougher and more obstinate in giving way to the advance of "civilized" methods. But the trend of history was inexorable. A heavier burden of taxation was thrown upon Judah by the revolt of Edom, which, as in the parallel case of Moab and Ephraim, deprived the country of a rich annual tribute and reduced the national income (II Kings 8:20–22).

The rebellion of Edom occurred in the reign of Jehoram 850–843 B. C. This king married the Ephraimite princess Athaliah, daughter of King Ahab and Queen Jezebel. After the death of Jehoram, his son Ahaziah succeeded him. The new king, on a royal visit to Ephraim, became involved in the furious events attending the downfall of the house of Ahab and was murdered by the partisans of Jehu. Thereupon a conspiracy took place in Judah by which all but one of the descendants of David were slain, and the dowager queen, Athaliah, seized the throne. She remained in power as head of a usurping government for six years 843–837 B. C. During this reign of terror a temple was built in Jerusalem for the Baal of Tyre, and a priest, Mattan, was appointed to officiate in the new sanctuary. Thus the social and religious condition of Judah took on a resemblance to that which prevailed in Ephraim under the house of Ahab, marked by growing economic unrest and Baal worship (II Kings 11:1–2).

Popular and priestly revolution in Judah

The reaction against Baal worship in Judah gathered force more quickly than the corresponding movement in Ephraim; and it differed in another way also, since there were no prophets to lead the uprising. The downfall of Athaliah and her party was effected by coöperation between three elements—the priests of Yahweh, the temple police, and the country people (called in Hebrew the *am ha'arets*). The sole survivor of the house of David, a little boy of seven, was brought suddenly out of hiding and proclaimed king; the usurping queen, Athaliah, was murdered; while the *am ha'arets* wrecked the temple of Baal and slew the priest Mattan before the altar of Baal (II Kings 11:4f.).

Tendency toward monotheism and ethical progress

An anti-Baal revolution had now occurred in each of the Hebrew kingdoms; and although Israel was even yet a long distance from the monotheistic doctrine and practice of post-exilic Judaism and Christianity, the religion was thus on the highway toward the lordship of one deity, Yahweh, not by means of an abstract revelation given on some flaming mountain in the desert, but as expressed concretely in uprisings of the people against wickedness enthroned in the walled cities of Samaria and Jerusalem. Backslidings there might be in the future; but the tendency toward monotheism was at work in the minds of the people at large.

Moreover, the tendency toward One God, along with antipathy against "other gods," was only a phase of this evolution; which was also toward economic justice and against economic injustice, toward purity and against impurity.

Judah grows more violent and subversive, 837–798 B. C.

The boy king who emerged from the anti-Baal revolution in Judah is called Joash in the early source, but Jehoash by the Deuteronomic interpolator (II Kings 11:2; cf. 12:1). He is said to have "done right in the eyes of Yahweh"; but at the same time the compiler is forced to admit that the mass of the people continued to worship on the "high places," or *bamoth*, everywhere in the country; or, as we might say, in the village churches throughout the land instead of the temple at Jerusalem; thus proving again that the religion did not yet officially approximate the so-called "Mosaic" ideal of sacrifice at one, legitimate, central altar.

After a reign of more than thirty-five years King Joash met a violent death at the hands of conspirators, who placed his son Amaziah on the throne (II Kings 12:20, 21). The murder of a king in Ephraim presaged the rise of a new royal family; but in Judah the conspirators usually employed some descendant of David as their tool, in order to utilize the prestige attaching to the ancient dynasty. No reason is given for the slaughter of Joash by the group, or faction, which deposed him; but the general drift of Judah, like Ephraim, is toward increasing violence and unrest.

New king wars against Edom and Ephraim, 798–790 B. C.

Like his father Joash, the new king, Amaziah, is said by the compiler to have done right in the eyes of Yahweh; "howbeit the high places were not taken away: the people did as yet sacrifice and burn incense on the high places" (II Kings 14:4).

Ever since the revolt of Edom and the consequent stoppage of its annual tribute, the loss had rankled in Judah. But the new king determined that the imperial "rights" of his people should be re-established. So he mobilized an army and set out against the Edom-ites. The text says "He slew of Edom ten thousand in the valley of salt, and took Sela [the rock stronghold] by war" (II Kings 14:7). Elated by his victory, Amaziah, as already noticed (*supra*, p. 175), challenged the power of Ephraim, but he quickly had occasion to regret his foolhardiness. A furious encounter took place near the city of Beth-shemesh, the results of which are described as follows: "And Judah was put to the worse before Israel; and they fled every man to their tents" (II Kings 14:12). The Ephraimite king, as we have seen, took the king of Judah and brought him to Jerusalem, where he broke down a long stretch of the city wall. Then he seized all the gold and silver, and all the valuable vessels in the temple, and all the treasures of the royal palace; and taking with him hostages to assure the good behavior of Amaziah, he returned to Samaria (II Kings 14:13, 14).

After these events the humiliated king of Judah lived on for fif-teen years of shame, in the midst of a situation which must have been very depressing. The reconquest of Edom and the unsuccessful battle with Ephraim were a drain upon the strength of the common people, many families being broken up through the death or crip-pling of the men in war. That a conspiracy was made which re-sulted in the murder of this king is understandable (II Kings 14:17–19).

Azariah made king by people of country districts, 790–738 B. C.

That the king's violent death was popular may be inferred from the statement that "all the people of Judah took Azariah, who was sixteen years old, and made him king instead of his father Amaziah" (II Kings 14:21). The new king is referred to as Uzziah in the Deuteronomic matter (II Kings 15:32, 34), and is also spoken of by that name in the book of Isaiah, whose author began to prophesy in this reign (Isa. 1:1; 6:1). The compiler of Kings mentions the fact that Uzziah reigned more than half a century; but he does not allow any important material about this ruler to reach us; likewise with regard to Jotham, who reigned sixteen years. The book of Isaiah, however, shows that a process of economic deterioration was going on all this time, by which the class of *adonim*, who owned slaves and held the soil of Judah, was growing smaller; the poorer members of the aristocracy, like the same element in Ephraim, becoming slaves to the wealthier, who more and more took the form of a corrupt ring of Tammany politicians with headquarters in Jerusalem, where they dominated the government.

King Ahaz pays tribute to Assyria

We have seen that in the reign of the next king, Ahaz, an attack was made upon Jerusalem by an allied army of Ephraimites and Syrians and that Ahaz, in order to save himself, sent word to the king of Assyria, who dispatched an army, which took Damascus, the capital of Syria, and presently destroyed Ephraim. In return for this deliverance, however, a huge tribute had to be paid: "And Ahaz took the silver and gold that was found in the house of Yahweh, and in the treasures of the king's house, and sent it for tribute to the king of Assyria" (II Kings 16:8). But Judah was now the only remnant of the once united Hebrew nation; and for the next hundred years, the little kingdom in the southern hills of Canaan could secure its own safety only by paying burdensome taxes to the robber empire enthroned in Mesopotamia.

Heavier tribute in reign of Hezekiah, son of Ahaz, 735–720 B. C.

Regular tribute meant that over and above the ordinary taxes paid by the *adonim* of Judah, an additional levy was imposed for the purpose of making up the yearly budget. The aggregate tax burden became so heavy that the next king, Hezekiah ben Ahaz, was driven into rebellion (II Kings 18:7). This imprudent action was very likely caused by the shepherds and farmers in the country districts, who had but little conception of the terrific forces at work on the field of international politics, and it could have only one result: the Assyrian army was once more put into motion, and upon reaching Palestine, it overswept a large part of the rural districts, carrying destruction everywhere save in the capital city. The situation is described so clearly and unequivocally in the text that it is worth reading:

Now in the fourteenth year of king Hezekiah [721 B. C.] did Sennacherib king of Assyria come up against all the fenced cities of Judah, and took them. And Hezekiah king of Judah sent to the king of Assyria to Lachish, saying, I have offended; return from me; that which thou puttest on me will I bear. And the king of Assyria appointed unto Hezekiah king of Judah three hundred talents of silver and thirty talents of gold. And Hezekiah gave him all the silver that was found in the house of Yahweh, and in the treasures of the king's house. At that time did Hezekiah cut off the gold from the doors of the temple of Yahweh, and from the pillars which Hezekiah king of Judah had overlaid, and gave it to the king of Assyria [II Kings 18:13-16].

The walls of the smaller fortified cities outside the capital were thus reduced by the invaders; while Jerusalem itself was left standing, so that the city of David should continue to pile taxes upon the *am ha'arets*, and send caravans, loaded with tribute, across the desert into the great metropolis of *Nineveh*, capital of the Assyrian empire.

Extremes of poverty and wealth

Inevitably these conditions drove a wedge into the Judean proprietary class. Its poorer members, who possessed only a few acres and a small number of slaves, were increasingly compelled to obtain tax money by borrowing on landed security from the wealthier *adonim*, who had larger properties and more slaves. And if the principal or interest of such loans were not paid at the stipulated time, the creditor came to take the land, or he invoked the aid of hired strong men (*gibborim*), sent out from the law courts at Jerusalem to facilitate legal processes. Deprived thus of land, slaves, houses, and movable goods, the poorer countrymen either fell into the lower enslaved class, or, if the creditor were willing, remained on the ancestral soil as rent payers. At the same time, the wealthier section of the Jewish upper class became virtual agents of the absentee imperial power; so that while the country as a whole was impoverished through the draining away of its products into a foreign country, and while the poorer shepherds and farmers were enslaved, nevertheless, the wealthy few became still richer, profiting from the misfortunes of the many.

Prophet Isaiah active, 745–700 B. C

When the book of Isaiah is taken out of its context in the Old Testament and read by itself, it is unintelligible. But when studied as a product of the secular history unrolling before us, it is charged with deep significance. The book is not to be reviewed in detail here, but certain observations must be made with reference to it.

Isaiah was greatly impressed by the circumstance that when the country districts of Judah were occupied by the Assyrian army the city of Jerusalem was left standing. And in his book the fact is erected into the doctrine that Jerusalem could not be destroyed because Yahweh needed it as the visible earthly seat of his rule and power (Isa. 29:7, 8). This idea was very acceptable to the wealthy exploiters and oppressors, who sheltered themselves in palaces behind the stout walls of the Judaic city; and in time it became a regularly accepted theological dogma, which, as we shall see, made a great deal of difficulty later for the prophet Jeremiah, who took a different view of Jerusalem's fate. Isaiah, being himself a citizen of Jerusalem, was no doubt insensibly prejudiced in its favor. Indeed, if the city had been demolished in the days of Isaiah, the religious development of Judah might not have been coherent and powerful enough at that time to evolve any further.

Nevertheless, Isaiah's doctrine about Jerusalem was not endorsed by his contemporary the prophet Micah, who lived in the country village of Moresheth and spoke in the name of Yahweh as follows:

Hear this, I pray you, ye heads of the house of Jacob, and rulers of the house of Israel, who abhor *mishpat*, and pervert all equity. They build Zion with blood, and Jerusalem with iniquity. The heads thereof judge for reward, and the priests thereof teach for hire, and the prophets thereof divine for money. Yet they lean upon Yahweh, and say, Is not Yahweh in the midst of us? No evil shall come upon us! Therefore shall Zion for your sake be plowed as a field, and Jerusalem shall become heaps, and the mountain of the house as the high places of a forest [Mic. 3:9–12].

This passage gives a countryman's reaction against the capital; and although Micah and Isaiah agree in their diagnosis of social conditions, they differ on the fate of Jerusalem.

Isaiah, like Micah, sees the entire economic and moral problem centered upon the question of law, justice, or *mishpat:*

Yahweh will enter into *mishpat* with the elders of his people and the princes thereof: It is ye that have eaten up the vineyard; the spoil of the poor is in your houses! What mean ye that ye crush my people, and grind the face of the poor? saith the adon Yahweh of hosts [Isa. 3:13].

Micah, like Isaiah, emphasizes the question of the land: "They covet fields and seize them; and houses, and take them away; and they oppress a man and his house, even a man and his heritage" (Mic. 2:1, 2).

Both Isaiah and Micah condemn the perversion of *mishpat;* they identify Yahweh with their demand for "righteous" *mishpat;* and they both denounce the worship of other gods; but they do not succeed in definitely identifying these "other gods" with "perverted" *mishpat.* And for this final achievement, we must await conditions which produced the prophet Jeremiah.

Problem of Judah moves toward climax

The exhortations of Isaiah and Micah had no effect in holding back the foreclosure of mortgages by the wealthy and the toppling of poorer *adonim* into the lower, enslaved class. Inexorable economic forces removed land from the status of inalienability into the status of liquidity, making the soil a mere item of commerce, to be bought and sold, rented and mortgaged, like movable goods. This process brought into play the pre-Hebrew, "baalistic" regime of property which prevailed in Canaan before the Israelite invasion and had never been wholly eradicated from all parts of the land.

That two different legal systems were in conflict, was not clearly understood by the prophets; and this important circumstance, while fundamentally simple, was historically complex and confusing. The traditions of Israel, as we have seen, tell how the *baalim* of pre-Hebrew Shechem sold land to Jacob (Gen. 33:18, 19). But the prophets looked upon that system of private, alienable titles to land as morally wrong; in their eyes the methods of mortgage foreclosure took on the character of perverted *mishpat*, bribery, and corruption. When denouncing the concentration of land in the grasp of the few, the prophets were not merely expressing their individual, personal opinions: they spoke for the great mass of impoverished *adonim* who constituted what might be called "the left wing" of the propri-etary class.

The solicitude of the prophets and of the Old Testament in general for the "poor" (*ebyon*, or *dal*) has therefore no reference to poverty in the abstract, but always refers to these left-wing un-fortunates who have lost their land in their own lifetime or to those whose fathers lost the lands which might otherwise have been the children's endowment. To dispose of the question as Professor Kirk-patrick, of Cambridge University, seeks to do, by suggesting that the foreclosure of a mortgage was "unbrotherly" does not in the least reckon with the realities of the case.[1] Yet many sincere theo-logians have sought to handle the subject in precisely this easy, "individualistic" way. Hence the translations which make the proph-ets demand "justice" (*mishpat*), as if a mere word settled the matter —all these passages, instead of solving the fundamental problem of ethics, merely side-step the entire question. The fact is that the in-alienable family heritage, which the Josephite clans established when taking over the soil of central Canaan, was no longer possible in the days of the prophets. And equally impossible, on the other hand, was the reëstablishment of the Amorite regime of liquid, alienable, private land ownership under the aegis of Baal, with its inexorable concentration of property in the grasp of the wealthy few (cf. chap. iii, *supra*).

---

[1] *Doctrine of the Prophets*, pp. 225–26.

But if both regimes were impossible, where then do we find any solid ground in the midst of the historical process unrolling before us? The answers to this question are (1) that no nation save Israel ever before brought the Yahwistic and Baalistic regimes face to face within the limits of the same social group and (2) that these incompatible and impossible regimes, when brought into contact, generated the social force which impelled the Yahweh-religion upward through higher and higher ethical stages, leaving Baalism behind as a mere pagan cult—but without solving the fundamental moral and economic issues.

Evil reign of Manasseh ben Hezekiah, 696–641 B. C.

So far as the book of Kings is concerned, the reign of Manasseh, son of Hezekiah, is described only in a late passage, by the Deuteronomic editor, expressed in abstract form, lacking the concrete details without which no definite picture could be made of this long, fifty-five year, tragic, evil reign (II Kings 21). But when the editorial matter is placed alongside the testimony of Isaiah, who came before Manasseh, and of Jeremiah, who came afterward, the situation breaks into startling relief. Since Manasseh was only twelve years old at the beginning of his reign, it is evident that the policies impressed upon the government of Judah at that time were the work of "Tammany" grafters, using the boy as a figurehead behind which they operated. These politicians were, in brief, agents of the comparatively small "right-wing" element in the Jewish proprietary class. This element stood between the Assyrian imperial robbers, on the one side, and the bulk of the poor Judean *adonim*, on the other; and each year they had to wring enough taxes out of the country not only to pay the foreign tribute but also to cover the expenses of the Jewish national administration, as well as to give themselves a good private profit as middlemen.

Under the circumstances, the only possible result was the concentration of the soil and the national resources in the grasp of the little, wealthy group centering in Jerusalem. The pressure of taxation was inescapable and implacable, bearing down like an impersonal force upon the entire property of the country, both movable and immovable. To administer the inexorable demands of the revenue, an army of assessors and collectors was needed; and there had to be legal authorities—judges, courts, bailiffs, recorders, and also police, or "strong men" (*gibborim*)—to accelerate the processes of law when the *am ha 'arets*, or "people of the land," resisted what they felt was wrong.

Baalization of religion the result of economic changes

Since religion and the state were absolutely identified, the break-up of inalienable titles to land, formerly guaranteed by Yahweh, required a corresponding change in the structure of the state and the government. The liquidation of land titles into private, commercial ownership, therefore, involved a reversion toward pre-Hebrew, Canaanite, or Amorite, baalistic legality. The wealthier *adon*, who had money to lend, was formerly spoken of as *nosheh* in the Ephraimite code (Exod. 22:25; II Kings 4:1); but eventually, he began to be called, in Amorite fashion, a *baal* (Deut. 15:2.— "Every *baal* that lendeth unto his neighbor"). And now, for the first time, the official religion was deliberately transformed so as to introduce Baal worship in validation of the changing social and economic regime. Hence, we read that Manasseh "reared up altars for Baal," and that "he did wickedly, above all that the Amorites did" (II Kings 21:3, 11).

And after the fashion of the Assyrian emperor, "he built altars for all the host of heaven in the two courts of the house of Yahweh," "and worshiped all the host of heaven, and served them," that is, he followed the star worship of the East (II Kings 21:5, 3). Prophets of Yahweh who protested against the Baal regime were slain: "Your sword hath devoured your prophets like a destroying lion" (Jer. 2:30). Poor freemen, outraged by the new laws, were treated without mercy: "Manasseh shed innocent blood very much, till he had filled Jerusalem from one end to another" (II Kings 21:16).

These vivid words, quoted from the Deuteronomic editors of the Hebrew Bible and from Isaiah and Jeremiah, imply that the problem of the day was very simple—with all the right on one side, and all the wrong on the other. But such is by no means the case; and there will be no real progress in understanding the Old Testament or the New, which evolved from the Old, until the cult battle between Yahwism and Baalism is envisaged in its true perspective as warfare between two ideologies, both of which had merits, while both were impossible as programs for lasting social adjustment.

Reign of terror stimulates prophetic literary zeal

The reign of Manasseh (or rather of the gangsters using his prestige as a descendant of David) was a reign of terror, like that of the Jehu dynasty, when the prophet Amos, driven out of Bethel, declared that it was an evil time, wherein to keep silence. And in the same way that the corresponding period in Ephraim led to secret literary activity, so in the days of Manasseh the prophetic party was driven "underground." The result, first of all, was the preparation of a remarkable new roll, or "book," influenced by the work of the prophets Elijah, Hosea, Amos, Micah, and Isaiah and based more specifically upon the Ephraimite Mishpat Code of Exodus, chaps. 21–23. Who wrote this book and where it was kept after being composed cannot now be known; but under circumstances presently to be noticed it comes into view as the official beginning of the Hebrew Scriptures, or Old Testament.

The long and horrible administration of Manasseh was followed by the brief reign of his son Amon, which lasted only two years and continued the policy of his father; so that the Baal regime of the dark, Manasseh period adds up to fifty-seven years. But finally a dispute arose in higher governmental circles, and another conspiracy took place, resulting in the murder of Amon. This king's name, by the way, seems to be the same as that of the Egyptian god Amon. Cf. Amon-Ra and Tutankh-Amen.

Josiah enthroned by "people of the land," 639–608 B. C.

The history now moves into a revolt against Baalism, which proves to be not simply an internal affair of Judah, but which also comes into relation with events on the international field. The Assyrian empire was in a state of collapse and unable to enforce its rule on the Mediterranean littoral. Its conquests had included the once-potent kingdom of Egypt; but Assyria was unable to hold the Nile valley in permanent subjection. The recovery of Egyptian independence during the latter part of Manasseh's reign may indeed have had something to do with the name borne by his son Amon. But in any case, the movement of international politics had reached a point where the kingdom of Judah found itself in temporary isolation, of which the masses of the people were quick to take advantage. And since the weight of Assyrian tribute was now lifted from the annual tax budget, the "people of the land " (*am ha 'arets*) perceived that a readjustment of society was in order: "And the *am ha 'arets* slew all them that had conspired against King Amon; and the *am ha 'arets* made Josiah his son king in his stead" (II Kings 21: 24). In other words, the mob massacred the Baal politicians at the capital, placed their own candidate on the throne, and cleared the way for a different regime.

Reign of Josiah puts mishpat in foreground

The compiler of Kings, being a "Deuteronomist" and an academic religious writer looking back from the times of the Babylonian exile of Judah, treats the reign of Josiah as if it revolved entirely around the little book of Deuteronomic law brought forward from the temple by the priest Hilkiah. And modern historians of Israel, following the Scriptural compiler, have also put the scroll at the center of the Josian picture. For instance, the *Old Testament History* of H. P. Smith (a scholar who performed great service on behalf of Biblical criticism in America) presents the reign of this king as centered in a literary event. The importance of the literary event cannot be denied; but it has been viewed out of its true focus by historians. Everybody admits that the scroll in question was not put into effect until the eighteenth year of Josiah's reign (II Kings 22:3). But this leaves an immense chronological blank which is characteristically ignored by the ancient Biblical compiler and his modern followers.

If the book of Kings were our only source for the Josian period, we should be confronted by the picture of a cultic revolution in which emphasis was upon the matter of worship, that is, abolition of sacrifice in the name of Baal, and concentration of sacrifice at one place in the name of Yahweh; together with suppression of temple prostitutes (*kedeshoth*) and male sex perverts (*kedeshim*). All of which was, of course, to the good and furnishes excellent material for "safe" Sunday School pedagogy, as well as for sermonic effort in line with conventional religious exhortation avoiding all reference to economic problems.

But at this point we are once more saved by definitive prophetic testimony, which comes to the rescue of Bible history at so many decisive epochs. The prophet Jeremiah characterizes Josiah in a few vivid strokes linking his reign logically with the entire secular process, and throwing a flood of light upon the eighteen-year period following the revolution by which the people of the country districts murdered the Baal politicians of Jerusalem. Jeremiah, speaking to the son of Josiah, who succeeded his father on the throne, says, "Did not thy father [that is, Josiah] do justice and righteousness (*mishpat* and *zedakah*)? Then it was well with him. He judged the law cases of the poor and needy! Then it was well! Was not this to know me, saith Yahweh" (Jer. 22:15, 16).

This tremendous passage is full of importance for Bible history viewed as a secular process and for the prophetic doctrine of Divinity in relation to the process. It means that under the impulse of the popular uprising which destroyed the Baal politicians and enthroned a boy of eight the law courts underwent reform so as to bring back the "*mishpat* of Yahweh" in opposition to the reviving baalistic, Amorite legality. The need for such reform is implied by Zephaniah, who prophesied apparently in the early part of Josiah's reign, before the revolution came into full swing. Speaking of Jerusalem as an "oppressive city," he says, "Her princes in the midst of her are roaring lions! Her judges are evening wolves!" (Zeph. 3:1–3). With the appointment of new judges and court officials, however, the little *adon*, or landholder on the "left" of the proprietary class ("the poor and needy"), could no longer be dominated and overridden by the wealthy *baal* on the "right." There were so many possible ways of restoring the bulk of enslaved *adonim* to their old status that in the absence of more definitive data it is useless to speculate on the subject. A family which had been dispossessed at any time within the memory of living witnesses had only to establish the truth in court and, *ipso facto,* the present holders of title were outlawed. Or, as in many historical crises, popular action may have come first, followed by acquiescence of the courts. On this principle, farmers in western Massachusetts, after the Revolution, prevented the local courts from sitting for seven years; and their conduct was afterward overlooked by the General Court, or legislature, through an "act of oblivion." Likewise, the peasantry throughout a large part of France, at the time of the Revolution, destroyed the châteaux of the landed aristocracy and burned the records of debt; all of which was legalized afterward by the reconstructed government at Paris.

Religious life defined by Jeremiah

The other point in connection with Jeremiah's verdict on Josiah's reign is the fact that this volcanic prophet, whose book eventually became Holy Scripture, declares that the doing of *mishpat* is to "know Yahweh." He denounces other kinds of secular conduct as proving that one fails to know Yahweh and is acquainted with "other gods." He does not, therefore, say that all secularity is what we call "religious"; he merely asserts, in effect, that religion springs out of and is identical with a large part of what we call the purely secular phase of life. This is, indeed, the position of all the great prophetic leaders; but Jeremiah, who lived in the final age of Judah and witnessed the death of the ancient Hebrew remnant, brings out with special clarity many of his predecessors' doctrines.

Deuteronomy legalizes anti-baalistic revolution

The "discovery" and adoption of the booklet in the eighteenth year of Josiah's reign was followed by reforms in the cultus corresponding very closely with the demands of the book of Deuteronomy in the Old Testament. Described with emphasis, the outstanding feature of Josiah's reform is the suppression of Baal worship which would naturally crown the revival of Yahweh *mishpat* (II Kings 23:4, 5). Other details mentioned went along with reaction against cultic Baalism (II Kings 23:6ff.). Moreover, the country "high places" (or *bamoth*)—always the special aversion of the Old Testament compilers—were now demolished; and the temple at Jerusalem was made the only legal sanctuary of Yahweh. These changes in the cultus agree with the book of Deuteronomy so closely that the "scroll" produced from the depths of the temple by Hilkiah the priest and Shaphan the scribe, was either Deuteronomy as it now stands in the Bible or, more likely, a shorter form of it.

Deuteronomy, in fact, is the official beginning of the Bible. All previous Hebrew literature—such as the "Ephraimite" document and the books of the prophets—had no standing at this time as "Holy Scripture"; and such writings became Bible only at later periods when they were formally adopted by various Jewish governments which continued the validating process begun by Josiah and his cabinet. Based primarily on Hebrew prophecy, the book of Deuteronomy and the rest of the Hebrew Scriptures at length had the effect of doing away with prophecy itself, because the assumption more and more came into vogue that the word of Yahweh could be now ascertained in official, written form. This book (brought into notice by a priest and a scribe) was the beginning of Judaism, which necessarily exalted a priesthood and a literature as the outstanding factors in religious life.

Idealistic four-point emphasis upon land mishpat

Turning to the book of Deuteronomy, we find that the question of land receives a new and idealistic emphasis. Very few readers of the Bible are aware that the book of Deuteronomy attempted unsuccessfully to put into general use a revised version of the "ten commandments" whose earlier form is in the "Ephraimite Code" of Exodus. The subject of land is implicit in the original tenth commandment, thus, "Thou shalt not covet thy neighbor's house" (Exod. 20:17). Now, a house, of course, rests on land; but the land may be only a small plot, whereas the farmer must also possess a field out of which he makes his living. So the prophets of Judah, who lived long after the Ephraimite document was written, were careful to stress the field. Thus, as we have seen, Isaiah pronounces woe upon those who add field to field; while Micah says, "They covet fields, and seize them" (Isa. 5:8; Mic. 2:2). Accordingly, the Deuteronomic version of the tenth commandment not merely reproduces the older injunction, "Thou shalt not covet thy neighbor's house," but also adds the words "*his field*" (Deut. 5:21), bringing the land problem into more explicit notice.

In addition to the reconstruction of this commandment, the removal of landmarks is forbidden, since this procedure was involved in the foreclosure of mortgages on real estate (Deut. 19:14; 27:17). Moreover, the fortunate property holder with surplus money or goods must make loans to the less fortunate members of the Jewish upper class without charging interest, and at the end of seven years the wealthier *baal* must "write off" the loan entirely (Deut. 23:19–20; 15:1–2). In this way (according to the idealistic program of Deuteronomy), the financial and legal process culminating in foreclosure upon land belonging to "the poor and needy" will be arrested.[2]

The Deuteronomic program, therefore, contemplates the well-to-do *baal* as accumulating an economic surplus, only to pass it over freely to the less fortunate property-holders. The more wealthy would thus work and save and continually deprive themselves of goods and money in order to stabilize the *mishpat* of Yahweh by maintaining the upper class of landowners and slaveowners intact

[2] It is instructive to notice how in Deuteronomy, as in the Ephraimite Code of Exod. 21 and 22, the term *adon*, designating the landed proprietor, tends to be replaced by the Amorite, or Canaanite, or pre-Hebrew term *baal*. The possessor of an economic surplus which can be loaned is called *baal* (Deut. 15:1–2). A woman's husband, instead of being her *ish* (man), is now referred to as her *baal* (Deut. 21:13). In older times, he is described simply as "taking" the woman (e. g., I Sam. 25:39, David-J source; Gen. 6:2,J and 11:29,J). Whereas, in Deuteronomy, he not only "takes" but also *baals* her (Deut. 24:1). Accordingly, the Hebrew expression translated into English "a woman married to an husband" is in the text of Deuteronomy *b'ulath baal* (Deut. 22:22). But along with later usages, older terms persist; for example the slave (*ebed*) who escapes must not be assisted to return to his owner (*adon*) (Deut. 23:15).

as a definite social body in contrast with the lower, alien class of gentile bond servants. The Deuteronomic center of gravity goes back to the psychology of the wilderness from which the clans of early Israel emerged. The nomad clansmen share everything. This was naturally the philosophy of an environment such as that of "Kadesh," or "En-Mishpat," in the desert (Judg. 11:16; cf. Gen. 14:7). But in a settled social economy, with a large lower class of slaves, a regular burden of taxation, and frequent wars, it was against human nature and therefore utopian.

Hence, a difference appears between the Deuteronomic redactor of Kings and the book of Deuteronomy itself. The redactor avoids the term *mishpat* and uses instead the more abstract word *yashar*, translated "right." Thus, Josiah does *yashar* in the eyes of Yahweh (II Kings 22:2; cf. I Kings 14:8; 15:11; II Kings 10:30; 12:2; 14:3; 15:3, 34, *et passim*). The term here has a ritualistic, not an economic, meaning: Josiah follows the worship of Yahweh and suppresses the worship of Baal, and so forth. Accordingly, the book of Kings gives no such picture of Josiah as we find in Jeremiah, who says that the king did *mishpat*, judging the law-cases of "the poor and needy" *adonim*. The contrast between *yashar* and *mishpat*, indeed, is the line of distinction at which the redactor begins (no doubt unwittingly) to desecularize the history of Israel and obscure the religious evolution.

Josiah meets tragic death

The book of Deuteronomy promises that if one does *yashar*, he shall go out against his enemies and put them to flight, even if their forces are greater than his own army (Deut. 20:1; 28:7). The history of Judah now emerges again from isolation and becomes involved once more in world affairs. The decline of the Assyrian empire had arrived at a point where the Egyptian king Necho felt that he should support Assyria against the rising power of Babylon by sending an army across Palestine into Mesopotamia.[3] When his huge

[3] That the Pharaoh did not fight Assyria, but helped Assyria in opposition to the rising might of Babylon, is maintained by C. J. Gadd, *The Fall of Nineveh* (1923).

force came up along the Mediterranean coast into the plain of Esdraelon, it suddenly encountered the little army of Judah under command of Josiah. The inevitable tragedy is told in the laconic narrative which the compiler excerpts from an old chronicle: "And king Josiah went against him. And he [Necho] slew him at Megiddo when he had seen him. And his servants carried him in a chariot dead from Megiddo, and brought him to Jerusalem, and buried him in his own sepulchre" (II Kings 23:29–30). Thus ended the thirty-one-year reign of Josiah who did *yashar*, according to the Book of Kings.

Judah in bondage to Egypt, 607 B. C.

Aghast at the sudden turn of world events by which their champion had been slain, the people of the country districts again invaded the capital and sought to assure continuity to the *mishpat* policy by enthroning the late king's younger son, the prince Jehoahaz: "And the *am ha'arets* took Jehoahaz the son of Josiah, and anointed him, and made him king in his father's stead" (II Kings 23:30). This was a democratic, secular process, independent alike of the priesthood and the political gangster forces which had controlled Manasseh. Yet the show of popular authority was without avail; because the Pharaoh, returning from Mesopotamia through Palestine, assumed imperial sway over Judah, dethroned the people's choice, and put Eliakim, another son of Josiah, into power, changing his name from Eliakim to *Jehoiakim*. But this high-handed procedure was only a beginning. The Egyptian despot now laid upon Judah the enormous tribute of one hundred talents in silver and one talent in gold: "And Jehoiakim exacted the silver and the gold from the *am ha'arets*, from every man according to his taxation, to give it unto Pharaoh Necho" (II Kings 23:33–35).

Baalism again triumphant

The Baal party, which had been so long terrorized by the sanguinary *am ha'arets*, were now able to lift their heads and ridicule their opponents about the disaster suffered by the good King Josiah. If nothing succeeds like success, nothing fails like failure; and this was an occasion upon which the enemies of Yahweh could blaspheme without fear. All the conditions which under the oppressive rule of Assyria had raised up a gang of wealthy Jewish exploiters were now reproduced under the tyranny of Egypt. This was the real Egyptian bondage. The tribute must be raised at once and paid year by year with regularity. The country people were in the same plight as their descendants, under the Persian king many years later, whose condition is described in the following passage:

Then there arose a great cry of the people and of their wives against their brethren the Jews. For there were those that said, We, our sons and our daughters, are many! Let us get grain, that we may eat and live. Some also there were that said, We are mortgaging our fields, and our vineyards, and our houses. Let us get grain, because of the dearth. There were also those that said, We have borrowed money for the king's tribute upon our fields and our vineyards. Yet now our flesh is as the flesh of our brethren,—our children as their children. But, behold, we bring into bondage our sons and our daughters to be slaves (*abadim*); and some of our daughters are brought into bondage already; neither is it in our power to help it, for other men have our fields and our vineyards [Nehemiah 5:1–5].

This passage brings into sharp relief the economic and political machinery at work transforming land titles from rigid inalienability into liquid, commercial assets which come into the hands of a small wealthy group; while the remainder of the proprietary class falls into slavery. Carrying the illustration back into the period immediately after the death of Josiah, it is easy to observe the working of economic forces which defeated the reforms of that king. A powerful reaction set in toward pre-Hebrew, Amorite conditions, which tended to give the term *baal* greater vogue with reference to men of property; displacing the rural and more archaic term *adon*, while at the same time fostering a recurrence to ritual Baalism as validating the economic and social reaction. Baal worship, in fact, was again triumphant at the capital. The new king, Jehoiakim, elder son of Josiah, was nothing but an Egyptian tool, placed on the throne of Judah by Pharaoh Necho in preference to Josiah's younger son, the people's choice. In the reign of this king the new Deuteronomic law of the "central sanctuary" (adopted under Josiah) was perverted from its original intention of keeping the worship of Yahweh pure by abolishing the country shrines; while its requirement upon the *am ha'arets* to attend worship in Jerusalem now became a factor in exalting the power of centralized monarchy, subjugating the people to the rule of tyrannical judges, priests, and *baalim*, who grew rich by exploiting the small property holders.

Jehoiakim denounced by Jeremiah

In the riot of oppression which followed the change of government, Jehoiakim, the Egyptian figurehead, set the example by laying heavy burdens upon the poor. He built an expensive and gorgeous palace from the unpaid work of labor gangs, after the manner of king Sh'lomoh many centuries before. For this he was denounced by the prophet Jeremiah:

Woe unto him that buildeth his house by unrighteousness, and his chambers by injustice; that useth his neighbor's service without wages, and giveth him not his hire; that saith, I will build me a wide house and spacious chambers, and cutteth him out windows; and it is ceiled with cedar, and painted with vermillion. Shalt thou reign because thou strivest to excel in cedar? . . . Therefore thus saith Yahweh concerning Jehoiakim the son of Josiah, king of Judah, They shall not lament him, saying, Ah my brother! . . . He shall be buried with the burial of an ass, drawn forth and cast beyond the gates of Jerusalem! [Jer. 22:13-15, 18, 19].

Baalism again controls courts and priesthood

Speaking in the name of Yahweh, Jeremiah said, "Run ye to and fro through the streets of Jerusalem, and see now, and know, and seek in the broad places thereof, if ye can find a man, if there be any, that doeth *mishpat*, that seeketh faithfulness; and I will pardon her" (Jer. 5:1). Rejection of *mishpat* is correlated with Baalism:

Thus saith Yahweh against all mine evil neighbors, that touch the inheritance which I have caused my people Israel to inherit, Behold I will pluck them up from off their land, and will pluck up the house of Judah from among them. . . . And it shall come to pass, if they will diligently learn the ways of my people, to swear by my name, "As Yahweh liveth," even as they taught my people to swear by Baal, then shall they be built up in the midst of my people. But if they will not hear, then will I pluck up that nation, plucking up and destroying it, saith Yahweh [Jer. 12:14f.].

Speaking of the evil times in the horrible reign of Manasseh, when Baalism held the center of public attention, Jeremiah speaks in the name of Yahweh, saying, "Their fathers forgat my name in Baal" (Jer. 23:27).

Baalism more than worship of gods who give soil fertility

While Jeremiah was influenced by Hosea in denouncing Baal, he was never misled into identifying the Baal cult with mere deification and worship of the fertilizing power. Certain expressions in Hosea's book, as already remarked, have been misinterpreted by critics who do not perceive the sociological and economic phases of Hebrew history. No one who reads the book of Jeremiah and relates it intelligently to secular history can mistake the sense in which this prophet condemns the Baal cult. He does, indeed, put emphasis upon sexual sin:

They committed adultery, and assembled themselves in troops at the harlots' houses. . . . Neither say they in their heart, Let us now fear Yahweh our god, that giveth rain, both the former and the latter in its season; that preserveth unto us the appointed weeks of the harvest [Jer. 5:7, 24].

This passage, however, does not mean that Jeremiah isolates Baal worship as a thing by itself, relating only to the fertilizing functions of nature and putting the rejection of *mishpat* in still another category, as pertaining to a wholly different phase of life, standing out of relation to the Baal problem. Baalism is regarded by Jeremiah in its true and broader sense as parallel exploitation of the poor through economic bondage and of women through ritual harlotry: "According to the number of the streets of Jerusalem have ye set up altars to shame (*bosheth*),—even altars to burn incense to Baal." "The *bosheth* hath devoured the labor of our fathers from our youth; their flocks and their herds; their sons and their daughters" (Jer. 11:13; 3:24). These passages must, of course, be taken in connection with others already cited from Jeremiah and should also be considered with relation to the Deuteronomic statement that worshiping "other gods" is the precise opposite of observing the commandments, and statutes, and *mishpatim* of Yahweh (Deut. 30:16, 17).

So far as present-day scholars are concerned, the fountainhead of erroneous Baalistic interpretation is Wellhausen's *Geschichte*, which was followed monotonously by German, British, and American critical scholars for two generations. The writings of these earlier critics are still used and still have influence upon opinion; but they are based upon a nonsociological, noneconomic sense of history, which has become too narrow for scientific Biblical interpretation.

Judah becomes tributary to Babylon, 605 B. C.

One of the most important events in ancient history was the battle of Carchemish, on the Euphrates river, in 605 B. C., when the Egyptian army, under Pharaoh Necho, was disastrously beaten by the forces of the newly-rising Babylonian power under Nebuchadnezzar. "And the king of Egypt came not any more again out of his land; for the king of Babylon had taken from the river of Egypt unto the river Euphrates all that pertained to the king of Egypt." (II Kings 24:7). This new development on the stage of world affairs meant the forcible transfer of Judah's allegiance from Pharaoh Necho to Nebuchadnezzar; so that the annual tribute which King Jehoiakim had been sending into Egypt was now to be forwarded in the opposite direction, to Babylon: "Nebuchadnezzar king of Babylon came up [to Jerusalem], and Jehoiakim became his servant three years. Then he turned and rebelled against him" (II Kings 24:1).

Judah given ten years of grace, 597 B. C.

The revolt was caused by the burden of yearly tribute and was a rash choice between two evils, because it led up directly to what is known as "the first Babylonian deportation." King Jehoiakim, meanwhile, passed away, and his son Jehoiachin had reigned three months before the arrival of the punitive expedition. Without destroying the city or disrupting the political structure of the country, Nebuchadnezzar appointed as king still another son of Josiah, whose name was Mattaniah, which he changed to Zedekiah. This was similar to the procedure followed by Pharaoh Necho when he made Eliakim king and changed his name to Jehoiakim. It showed the power of the conqueror and made the Jews feel humiliated. This is how the event is described in the words of the Deuteronomic editor:

And Nebuchadnezzar king of Babylon came against the city; and his servants did besiege it. And Jehoiachin king of Judah went out to the king of Babylon, he, and his mother, and his servants, and his princes, and his officers; and the king of Babylon took him. . . . And he carried out thence all the treasures of the house of Yahweh, and the treasures of the king's house, and cut in pieces all the vessels of gold. . . . And he carried away all Jerusalem, and all the *gibborae ha 'hayil* [that is, men of property],—even ten thousand, and all the craftsmen and smiths. And he carried away Jehoiachin to Babylon, and the king's mother, and the king's wives, and his officers, and the mighty of the land, carried he into captivity from Jerusalem to Babylon. And all the men of might, seven thousand, and craftsmen and smiths, a thousand, and all *gibborim* [that is, hired strong men] . . . even them the king of Babylon brought captive to Babylon. And the king of Babylon made Mattaniah, his father's brother, king in his stead, and changed his name to Zedekiah. None remained, save the poorest sort of the *am ha'arets* [II Kings 24: 11–17].

Destruction of ancient Judaic state, 586 B. C.

Around the new king gathered a new ruling group which the prophet Jeremiah called "bad figs" (Jer. 24). Instead of being chastened by the terrific experience through which the country had passed, these upstarts were inflated with pride, saying, "Unto us is the land given as a possession" (Ezekiel 11:15). Zedekiah and his princes had ruled nine years when they reached the preposterous decision to renounce allegiance to Babylon, just as Jehoiakim had done. But this time vengeance took a more terrible form. The im-

perial overlord had lost all patience and was now determined upon
destruction of Jerusalem and annihilation of the kingdom of Judah.
"Nebuchadnezzar king of Babylon came, he and all his host, against
Jerusalem, and pitched against it; and they built forts against it
round about" (II Kings 25:1, 2).

A characteristic incident occurred in connection with the siege
of Jerusalem, which throws a brilliant light on the entire economic
process in the Hebrew nation. The old Ephraimite Code in Exodus
contains a *mishpat* ordinance, repeated in Deuteronomy, commanding in the name of Yahweh that poor Hebrew freemen who have
been unfortunate enough to fall into slavery to their brethren of the
house of Israel shall be released after a six-year period of bondage
(Exod. 21:2; Deut. 15:12). Recollecting this ordinance during the
Babylonian siege of the capital, the princes liberated their Hebrew
slaves by a solemn oath in the temple of Yahweh: "Every man let
his man-slave (*ebed*) and his woman-slave (*shifkah*), that is a Hebrew or a Hebrewess, go free; that none should make slaves of them,
—of a Jew his brother" (Jer. 34:9). The injunction was put into
effect for the purpose of influencing, or compelling, Yahweh to take
supernatural action and raise the siege!

Immediately after the great humanitarian measure was adopted,
the besieging army of Babylon disappeared from its positions around
the walls of Jerusalem and vanished away into space. Great was the
rejoicing among the princely oppressors, who had now discovered
a magic method for shaping history by employing the deity as an
instrument for their own selfish ends. And what should they now
do but incontinently reverse their action and subjugate their Hebrew slaves afresh! As Jeremiah declares, with great indignation,
"Afterwards they turned and caused the men-slaves and the women-
slaves, whom they had let go free, to return, and brought them into
subjection for men-slaves and for women-slaves" (Jer. 34:11).

But they had acted too soon. For in a few days the reason for
the sudden disappearance of the Babylonians became clear. The
Egyptian Pharaoh, making a final desperate move to reassert his
power, had mobilized an army and was coming up against Nebu-

chadnezzar to overwhelm him while he was preoccupied with the siege of Jerusalem. So the Babylonians had been compelled precipitately to withdraw from the city walls in order to readjust their forces on a more favorable terrain. It was during this time that the arrogant and foolish oppressors within the city walls had been congratulating themselves on the discovery of a method for manipulating the magic, supernatural forces of the universe. Nebuchadnezzar's army, meanwhile, had utterly defeated the Egyptians and was now returning to Jerusalem.

At this juncture the denunciations uttered by Jeremiah in the name of Yahweh took on a terrible quality:

The word of Yahweh came to Jeremiah from Yahweh, saying . . . Ye turned and profaned my name, and caused every man his man-slave and every man his woman-slave, whom ye let go free at their pleasure, to return; and ye brought them into subjection, to be unto you for slaves. Therefore, thus saith Yahweh, Ye have not hearkened unto me to proclaim liberty, every man to his brother and every man to his neighbor! Behold, I proclaim unto you a liberty, saith Yahweh, to the sword, to the pestilence, and to the famine; and I will make you to be tossed to and fro among all the kingdoms of the earth. . . . And Zedekiah king of Judah and his princes will I give into the hand of their enemies, and into the hand of them that seek their life, and into the hand of the king of Babylon's army that are gone away from you [Jer. 34:12–21, *passim*].

This prophecy was made in the continued absence of the enemy. But presently the returning host emerged into view and resumed operations. "And the city was besieged unto the eleventh year of King Zedekiah. And . . . the famine prevailed in the city; and there was no bread for the people of the land. And . . . all the men of war fled by night by way of the gate between two walls, which is by the king's garden. . . . And the king went the way toward the plain. But the army of the Chaldees [that is, Babylonians] pursued after the king, and overtook him in the plain of Jericho. . . . So they took the king, and brought him up to the king of Babylon. . . . And they slew the sons of Zedekiah before his eyes, and put out the eyes of Zedekiah, and bound him with fetters of brass, and carried him to Babylon. And . . . the captain of the guard . . . burnt the house of Yahweh, and the king's house, and all the houses of Jerusalem, and every great house burnt he with fire. And all the army . . . brake down the walls of Jerusalem round about. And the rest of the people that were left in the city . . . with the remnant of the multitude, did the captain of the guard carry away. . . . So Judah was carried away out of their land" (II Kings 25:2–21, *passim*).

The end came suddenly. Ephraim had vanished into the void long ago. And now Judah became an exiled remnant by the waters of Babylon.

X. SIGNIFICANCE OF BIBLE HISTORY

LIQUIDATION of Ephraim in 721 B. C., followed by the captivity, or *galuth*, of Judah in 586 B. C., brought to an end the history of ancient Israel. This was the termination of what is properly called "Hebrew history," which had a peculiar logic of its own, as being identified with the struggle between Yahweh and Baal. But that struggle ceased when Judah left Palestine; and it was followed by a new succession of events, the history of the Jews, which took on a different logic, separated sharply from everything that had gone before. More than five hundred years elapsed between the exile of Judah and the times of the New Testament. During that immense period a number of important developments occurred in the evolution of Jewish religion, as distinguished from the prior, Yahweh-Baal process.

Exile shocks Jews into monotheism

The physical shock attending the destruction of Jerusalem and the misery of exile converted the remnant of Israel to monotheism without regard to the actual merits of the struggle between Yahweh and Baal which had convulsed Israel in the land of Canaan. After the exile the Jews not only began to believe exclusively in the name of Yahweh but also, in course of time, they feared even to pronounce the name Yahweh itself. The monotheistic formula, which was made official by the adoption of Deuteronomy as Scripture in the reign of Josiah, reads as follows in the Hebrew: *"Shema Israel! Yahweh elohenu, Yahweh echodh"* (Hear Israel! Yahweh our God, Yahweh is One! Deut. 6:4). But in repeating this declaration, the post-exilic Jews made still another of those changes which have marked the course of their cultic evolution. Without actually altering the text of Deuteronomy, a verbal change was instituted which has been heard for thousands of years in Jewish synagogues and religious gatherings, as follows: "*Shema Israel! Adonai elohenu, Adonai echodh!*" In other words, having turned from Baal to the exclusive worship of Yahweh, the Jews went even beyond the prophet Hosea, who said, "Ye shall no more call me 'My Baal' " (Hos. 2:16); and in the practice of the cult, the ancient common noun *adon* replaced not only *baal* but also the name Yahweh itself. The exhortation is rendered in English, "Hear Israel! The Lord our God is one Lord!" This was, in effect, a spiritual climax to the long-continued struggle of the *am ha'arets*, or poor and needy *adonim* of the country districts, against the wealthy oppressors, or *baalim*, who lived in the security of walled cities.

Nevertheless, while the Jewish masses in and after the exile took possession of the objective practices and verbal symbols of religion, it now becomes a matter of primary importance to emphasize that the central problem of *mishpat*, or social justice, was not solved by the arithmetical victory of monotheism.

Interruption of Josianic reform broadens mishpat

We saw that the *mishpat* revolution of Josiah was violently checked by Egypt and Babylon, which put the reactionaries Jehoiakim and Zedekiah on the throne against the wishes of the *am ha'arets*. This tremendous fact of recent history in the homeland was another force working upon the Jewish imagination in exile. The gentiles, or *goyim*, had obviously halted the progress of Judah toward *mishpat*. Moreover, being now engulfed within a gentile empire, Judah was completely stripped of governmental and legislative power to modify the social and economic structure. Under such inhibitive conditions the truth slowly became clear to Jewish thinkers that social justice would be futile if established only in the one little country of Israel, or Judah, and that in the long run the gentiles at large must move in the direction of social justice if the world were to be made safe for *mishpat*.

Accordingly there grew up in captivity a new sense of Israel as being the mystic "Servant of Yahweh," whose destiny was to spread the reign of *mishpat* throughout the earth. Many passages depicting the "Servant" are found in the exilic portions of Isaiah (that is, the "Second" Isaiah). The captivity impressed upon succeeding generations of exiles the sense of Israel as bearing the guilt of transgressors—being despised and rejected of men, a man of sorrows, acquainted with grief, who is figuratively "dead" in a strange land, but who should see the travail of his soul and be satisfied (Isa. 53:1f.). The doctrine of the "Servant" becomes a lofty symbolism which elevates the relation of Israel to Yahweh above the mere tie of a pagan people with its god and makes it an incident in the redemption of humanity:

Behold my Servant, whom I sustain,—my chosen, in whom my soul delighteth. I have put my spirit upon him. He shall bring forth *mishpat* to the *goyim* (gentiles). . . . He shall faithfully bring forth *mishpat*. He shall not fail nor be discouraged until he have set *mishpat* in the earth; and distant countries shall wait for his teaching [Isa. 42:1–4].

To this broader ethical end, the Jewish wise men and scribes in and after exile created the Hebrew Bible, which is built of source-materials, piled upon each other like geologic strata. The primary layer is Ephraimite, or E, originating in Ephraim, where the prophetic movement started. Thus, E begins at Genesis 20, where Abraham is a prophet, or *nabi* (Gen. 20:7). This term, *nabi*, is characteristic of E. Nevertheless, the Judaic, or J, source, using a different phraseology, is centered also in the prophetic ideal.

Thus, the J document reveals the Jews living under the shadow of the great city of Babylon (that is, *Babel*), where they develop an international sense of sin, according to which all cities, everywhere, are viewed as being strongholds of corruption. The very first city in the prehistoric world is built by the first murderer, Cain, after he "goes out from the presence of Yahweh" (Gen. 4:16, 17). If he had but remained "in the presence of Yahweh," he would have continued with his parents, Adam and Eve, in the garden of Eden. Following the establishment of city life by Cain, Yahweh beholds the wickedness of man and sees that every imagination of his heart is evil continually. Yahweh then destroys the human race by a great flood, from which only one righteous man emerges—Noah (Gen. 6:5, 7, 8f.).

But in spite of the water cure, the same evil of city life reappears in the descendants of Noah. And when the flood is ended, the "reconstruction era" is characterized by the building of great cities all over the oriental world—the culmination being the city of Babel, with a huge tower, in the land of Mesopotamia, where the Jews are captive. "But Yahweh came down to see the city and the tower; and . . . Yahweh scattered them abroad from thence upon the face of all the earth; and they left off to build the city" (Gen. 11:1–9).

The news about Babel reaches the great Chaldean municipality of Ur, where one of the citizens, a gentile, or *goy*, named Terach, decides that metropolitan life is not desirable; so he leaves the city and goes into the rural environment of Aramea, or Syria. With him are two sons, Nahor and Abram, and a grandson, Lot; all become shepherds and tillers of the soil (Gen. 11:28f.).

The picture of an entire family leaving a walled city for the purpose of starting life in the open country symbolizes a new scheme of salvation: Yahweh chooses one man out of this promising household, Abram, telling him to go forth into the land of Canaan. (Gen. 12:1f.; Abraham, Gen. 17:5; 18:18, 19; 20:7). He is to do righteousness and *mishpat* (justice). And now the sense of world-wide sin evokes an international moral ideal: "In thee shall all the families of the earth be blessed" (Gen. 12:1–3). Having found that wickedness could not be destroyed by washing it away in a flood of water, Yahweh prepares to save the world through individual and social reformation.

Finally, in order to concentrate the faith of the Jewish people upon the religion expounded by the prophets, a great system of priestly worship was compiled. The priestly element, P, is the latest part of the Pentateuch, or Torah. It is the "framework" upon which are built the books of Genesis, Exodus, Leviticus, Numbers, and Joshua. The priestly writings bulk larger than all the other material in the Pentateuch; they are wholly Jewish, and they give the tribe of Judah an importance in the early history which it never had, but which corresponds to the importance thrust upon the Jews by the fall of Ephraim and the exile of Judah, when the mission of Israel was laid upon the Jew alone (cf. Appendix: "The Pentateuch a Judaic Work").

Doctrine of immortality takes form

But the evolution of religious ideas did not culminate in the doctrine of the "Servant of Yahweh" giving *mishpat* to the gentiles. The new idea of world-wide social salvation brought another problem in its train. *Mishpat* could not, by any stretch of the imagination, be established immediately. Its achievement was necessarily gradual; so that even if history be conceived as moving in the direction of social readjustment, countless millions of human beings must perish in darkness along the upward path before the goal of universal justice could be reached. What, then, is the meaning of the individual in the purpose of God? This question did not quickly find clear utterance in the five-hundred-year epoch lying between the captivity of Judah and the New Testament period; but it was dealt with slowly—here a little, and there a little—during the exile and after the return of the Jews to Palestine. And while the hope of *mishpat* was never abandoned, the general conclusion was reached that the mere attainment of social salvation could not be the ultimate, or sole, purpose of creation, since countless numbers were continually passing away, while the world was even yet ruled by injustice.

Crude ideas began to take form concerning bodily resurrection. But here, again, the omnipresent *mishpat* theme cuts across the growing hope of immortality, consigning wealthy oppressors to punishment or destruction, while the "poor and needy" enjoy unending bliss. The book of Psalms (*T'hillim*) is a post-exilic collection of songs, based in part upon pre-exilic material, and written mostly from the standpoint of the "poor," who believe, or hope, that Yahweh will break in pieces the proud and wealthy oppressor. The *mishpat* theme underlies the Psalms; but the process of translation into other tongues modifies it insensibly, so that the prophetic background is obscured. The tardiness of justice in the real, actual, objective world leads to spiritualization of thought:

I saw the prosperity of the wicked. . . . They have more than heart could wish. . . . Surely thou settest them in slippery places; thou castest them down to destruction. . . . Nevertheless, I am continually with thee. . . . Thou wilt guide me with thy counsel, and afterward receive me to glory. . . . God is the strength of my heart, and my portion forever [Ps. 73, *passim*].[1]

While this is not an outright doctrine of personal immortality, it moves toward the hope of a life beyond the present; and the anticipation takes more definite form in the book of Daniel, dated long after the return from exile: "Many of them that sleep in the dust of the earth shall awake—some to everlasting life, and some to shame and everlasting contempt" (Dan. 12:2).

Mishpat and immortality in New Testament period

By the time Jewish thought had arrived at the New Testament period, the sense of immortality had become stronger and more definite. The idea of "Abraham's Bosom" as a place, or condition, of the departed, was now a common tradition; although we do not know how it arose. The parable of the beggar Lazarus and the rich man in the book of Luke takes for granted that the Jewish listeners to whom it was addressed were already equipped with certain views about life beyond the grave: The poor man dies and is carried away by the angels into "Abraham's Bosom." But the rich man dies without benefit of celestial transportation. He is "buried" and finds himselfs in the torments of Hades (Luke 16:19f.). It is declared that the wealthy shall find it very difficult to obtain entrance into "the kingdom of God"—harder than for a camel to go through the eye of a needle (Luke 18:24f.). But even so, the doctrines of the Jews about the future life were conflicting and unofficial. The wealthy faction, led by the priests, or Sadducees, were appropriately anti-resurrectionists; while on the other hand, the Pharisees, representing the middle classes, believed strongly in resurrection from death.

---

[1] Speaking of Ps. 9:18, Professor Oesterley observes that "the usage in general of these terms shows them to refer to the humbler classes; and this applies as a rule to their use in the Psalms." Oesterley, *The Psalms* (London, 1939), I, 59.

Theological veil tends to obscure mishpat

Further complications of theological doctrine began to grow up around the idea of *mishpat* and obscure it still more, as Biblical monotheism spread from Palestine into the Roman empire at large. It is well known that Christianity was at first mainly a lower-class movement and that the middle and upper classes were gradually absorbed into the Church later. Prevailing conditions made impossible any religious propaganda whose object was the immediate establishment of social justice. Such a movement would have been broken up at once by the imperial police. The enormous difference between the psychological background of Christian missionaries among the Gentiles and that of Jesus himself in Palestine, is made clear by comparison between the emphasis on "rich and poor" in the Synoptic gospels and the lack of such economic stress in the Pauline epistles. It is impossible to imagine Christians in the Roman Empire proclaiming the difficulties of a wealthy person at heaven's gate. Instead of circulating the parable of Lazarus and the rich man, the Christian propaganda instinctively revolved about Jesus as intermediary between the human race and the God of Israel. Even so, the Christian message was in danger of becoming too philosophical. If the narrative in the book of Acts is to be trusted, Paul at Athens preached an abstract unitarianism, but he met with such an experience that upon going to Corinth, he "determined not to know anything . . . save Christ, and him crucified" (I Cor. 2:2; cf. Acts 17:16f.).

Pagan audiences did not have the presuppositions necessary to an understanding of the Yahweh-Baal struggle in Hebrew history, which, when emphasized by the Exile, evolved into Jewish monotheism. There was no printed Old Testament; and the mere process of making a new manuscript copy involved so much expense that Christian converts could not afford one. The Christian missionaries themselves had neither scientific knowledge of the Jewish Bible nor any accurate comprehension of Hebrew history.

Hence it is natural that when spreading from Palestine into the Roman empire at large the Biblical doctrine of *mishpat* monotheism underwent modifications of considerable importance. A thousand years of education had enabled the Jew, looking back over the historic past of Israel, to carry in his own mind some of the generalizations evolved in the national experiences of the Hebrew people. But in the eyes of the Greek and Italian communities where the Biblical faith took root, an abstract God of *mishpat,* or social justice, could only be meaningless. The Christian missionaries, then, were not simply preoccupied with watching the imperial police; they worked in a social environment very unlike that of Palestine.

As a political structure the Roman empire was based upon brutally holding down most of its inhabitants in serfdom or actual slavery; while at the same time its religious cults condoned sexual corruption and embodied no protest against economic injustice. From the standpoint of these appalling conditions, it is easy to see that the worship of Jesus in the Roman empire was an upward step so vast that it was immeasurable. Never before had human beings in the mass taken a step of such tremendous moment.[2]

Social justice temporarily submerged in Rome and Europe

Submergence of the *mishpat* theme under a gospel of individualistic appeal was therefore inevitable and natural. The Roman empire was gradually declining through the operation of economic forces which no one at that period of history could understand. The Church could only emphasize personal righteousness, promote civil order, and proclaim the doctrine of immortality as compensation for the trials of an evil world: "For we know that if the earthly house of our bodily frame be dissolved, we have a building from God, a house not made with hands, eternal in the heavens" (II Cor. 5:1).

In a world where the ruling authorities did not want a religion which put stress on social justice, the Church had scarcely completed the task of organizing itself and formulating its official theology, when the Roman empire began to dissolve under pressure from

[2] Cf. Wallis, *Sociological Study of the Bible,* 1912, pp. 229f.; *God and the Social Process,* 1935, pp. 308f.

barbarian tribes which, in course of time, developed into the nations of medieval Europe. The governments of all these nations were founded by conquerors who seized the soil of each country as the basis of landed aristocracies which became the ruling element everywhere. In medieval Europe, as in the Roman empire, Christianity was an upward step from paganism.

New problem caused by dogmatic theological individualism

Organized Christianity was thus placed in a position fated to be more and more difficult. By repudiating the Gnostic, Marcionite heresy (pp. 10, 11, *supra*), the Church admitted that the religion which revolved around the person of Jesus was in some way linked with Hebrew history and the Hebrew Bible. But the connection remained obscure; and the prevailing emphasis continued to be placed upon official individualistic theology. The difficulty lay in the implicit antagonism between "orthodox" dogma and the social emphasis which the Yahweh-Baal struggle had wrought into the very fiber of Biblical monotheism, both Jewish and Christian. This fact was brought out by St. Francis of Italy and the Catholic Bishop Grostete of England in the thirteenth century, and by Savonarola in the fifteenth.

Nor did Protestantism change the situation as radically as many have supposed, even though it registered certain gains. In order to exist, the Church had been compelled for a thousand years to make terms with ferocious landed aristocracies. But the Reformation, on the whole, voiced the interests of the rising commercial and industrial classes. Various Protestant dogmatisms gradually took form which obscured the ancient *mishpat* theme.

Religion of Bible imperiled in Europe

Under the Czars the official Christianity of Russia completely buried the vital impulse of prophetic passion and became the unhallowed handmaid of an oppressive aristocracy. Its repudiation was only natural. But in Germany the pattern of events has been more complicated. Almost half the population of that country was destroyed in "religious" wars, ending in 1648 with the Peace of Westphalia, which compelled the inhabitants of any given state (either Protestant or Catholic) to follow the religion of the local reigning sovereign. The country as a whole, however, fell more and more under the Lutheran Hohenzollern monarchy, whose official Church developed an elaborate system of dogma, which transformed the religion of the Bible into an absolute individualism, oriented entirely toward "the other world" and lacking all social vision.

Universities were set up in the German Protestant states, where eventually the practice of Biblical higher criticism achieved a left-handed recognition, the Protestant clergy being forbidden to dispense the results of scholarship in their pulpits. The boasted "academic freedom" of Germany, even in her best days, was merely freedom quarantined in an intellectual vacuum. Not only did German Protestantism lack social vision but also the breach between scientific scholarship and orthodox religion was an official hypocrisy which caught the notice of rising generations and quickened the drift of German youth away from the churches. Thus a fund of animosity against institutional religion was accumulated which in due time furnished part of the driving power behind Naziism.

In the Anglo-Saxon world, on the contrary, Biblical criticism has fused with social conscience to such good purpose that British and American scholarship finds itself more and more at the service of democracy. This difference between Germany and the English-speaking peoples has not been stressed as it should be. For the democratic and social significance of Bible history has found no appreciation among German scholars, except in the case of a tiny minority, headed by such men as Troeltsch and Weber. Theological professors in that country have taken the standpoint of the aristocracy and have been satisfied to be let alone in the enjoyment of their stipends while carrying on the minute analysis of Biblical documents in cloistered isolation from the problems of life. The failure of German theological science to make terms with objective reality is brought into sharp relief by the almost sarcastic statement of Wellhausen that we cannot tell why Yahweh of Israel, rather than Chemosh the god of Moab, became the patron of righteousness and the creator of the universe.[3]

Religious evolution in Anglo-American churches

While the principle of scientific freedom in theological interpretation has been fully and irrevocably established in the great democratic nations, its progress among the churches in general has been slow; and much work remains to be done. A striking illustration is the formal way in which the Hebrew Bible has been adopted as the Christian Old Testament and then parted from the New Testament by a high wall of dogma. The artificial contrast set up between the two divisions of the Bible is then surreptitiously ignored in practice by the general use of ancient Hebrew Psalms as Christian responsive readings. So long as the wall of dogma is allowed to stand, the churches are literally in the position of bootlegging the Psalms. The Christian world indeed has never been fully extricated from the toils of the Gnostic controversy.

Historical process explains Biblical religion

It is natural that the development of religion in Hebrew life should have been centered at first in the struggle for *mishpat*, or social justice. "It is not the spiritual that comes first, but the physical, and then the spiritual" (I Cor. 15:46, Goodspeed). The artificial wall between the Old and New Testaments, however, cannot be maintained as a line of demarcation between material and spiritual, since the evolution toward spirituality began far back in the Old Testament period. The saying "man shall not live by bread alone," which appears in the New Testament, originated in the book of Deuteronomy (Deut. 8:3; cf. Luke 4:4). The Christian idea of "spiritual" circumcision, as contrasted with physical circumcision, took its rise in Hebrew prophetic thought (cf. Jer. 4:4; Deut. 30:6; 10:16, and Rom. 2:29; Col. 2:11). We have already observed the upward course of evolution in the contrast between Elijah and

---

[3] *Kultur der Gegenwart*, 1909, I, 15.

Hosea, who were separated by a century; the former declaring that Yahweh commanded the slaughter of Ahab's house; whereas the latter, speaking likewise in the name of Yahweh, denounced the assassinations. The prophets of Israel were always in the attitude of proclaiming, "It hath been said by them of old time; but I say unto you." And when Jesus took this attitude, he was applying an established principle. The religion of the Bible as a whole (New Testament as well as Old) is an evolution of ethical insight reacting to the secular pressure of history. To the degree that this truth is absorbed into the world's culture, Jesus becomes more authoritative, not only for Gentiles but also among the Jews themselves. And the Cross becomes the symbol of a spiritual process which welds the conception of God into the heart of the struggle for a better world, whose broadening perspective includes the regeneration of the individual, the salvation of society, and a faith in Eternity which gives worth to the problems of Time.

APPENDIXES

SOURCE VIEW FOLLOWED
IN THIS BOOK

1. E (Ephraimite) Material: Judges Epoch to 750 B.C.

At first oral, then written. Deborah song; narratives relating to Ephraimite heroes within "framework" of deuteronomic editorial comments in Judges, Samuel, Kings. E document proper begins at Genesis 20:1. Scattered through Genesis, Exodus (not Leviticus), Numbers, Deuteronomy, Joshua. Uses term "baal" to indicate proprietary class, but also uses "adon." Prophets Ahijah of Shiloh, Elijah, Micaiah ben Imlah, Hosea, Jeremiah were Ephraimite.

Prophets Amos, Micah, Isaiah were Judaic. Their influence, and that of Ephraimite Hosea, led to deuteronomic reformation which was contemporary with prophet Jeremiah's early life.

2. D (Deuteronomic) Material: 650 B.C. into Exile

Evolves on basis of Ephraimite matter in Exodus 20–23. Constitutes book of Deuteronomy nearly entire; also the deuteronomic editorial comment on Hebrew history interpolated in Judges, Samuel, Kings. Uses both "baal" and "adon." It is the earliest Judaic source in Pentateuch, midway between Ephraimite material and so called "J" (Yahwistic) source. Deuteronomic program is an ethico-ritualistic technique for controlling the fertility power of Yahweh (Deut. 28:4, 5), conditioned upon adherence to primitive mishpat. Earlier Judaic matter in Samuel, Kings, Prophets.

3. J (Yahwistic) Material: Exilic

J document proper begins at Genesis 2:4b. Seeks to manipulate basic Ephraimite legends of Israel to favor Judah. Makes patriarchs offer sacrifice outside Canaan, but avoid ritual in Canaan owing to lack of central, deuteronomic sanctuary at Jerusalem. Puts ritualistic code of Exodus 34 in place of Ephraimite "Commandments" of Exodus 20–23. Disrupts deuteronomic recension of Judges, Samuel, Kings by manipulating history in favor of Davidic dynasty. Avoids term "baal" as designation of proprietary class, substituting "adon," "ish," etc. Judaic anti-baal reaction priestly (II Kings 11). J document reveals phase of evolution toward final Judaic source, or priestly document.

4. P (Priestly) Material: Late Exilic, 570 to 400 B.C.

P source proper begins with Genesis 1:1. Alternates with E, D, and J in Genesis, Exodus. Constitutes most of Leviticus, Numbers. Appears a little in Joshua. Priestly system of Pentateuch projected back into prehistoric times where it could not be checked up. Aims to improve upon Deuteronomy as technique for controlling fertility power of Yahweh (Levit. 26:20). Elaborate priestly system also devised in Babylonia by prophet-priest Ezekiel, and projected into future, but never observed. Books of "Chronicles" based upon assumption that P was given before Israel entered Canaan.

NOTE ON THE NAME YAHWEH
AS USED IN THIS BOOK

THE EXPRESSION "his name is Yah" occurs in Psalm 68:4; and the well-known term "hallelujah" is a Hebrew exhortation to praise Yah. The syllable is an abbreviated form of the name Yahweh; while the more familiar "Jehovah" is an impossible combination of consonants and vowels which never occurs in the Hebrew text and was introduced without warrant in Gentile translations of the Bible in modern times. The actual significance of the name is purely conjectural and unknown; it was originally used in the sense of a local deity, either of Palestine or Sinai, but the word later passed through a process of historical evolution and its original meaning is therefore of little importance.

REMARKABLE FILIATION OF
SUPERIORITY IN BOOK
OF GENESIS

UPON FIRST INSPECTION, the genealogical scheme in the book of Genesis appears to be a simple, disinterested compilation of objective history. In reality, it represents a manipulation of myth and legend for a deliberate purpose. The nature of the purpose becomes clear as the genealogy is drawn out.

In the epoch before the Flood, the posterity of "Adam" becomes wholly corrupt, with the exception of one man, Enoch, who "walked with God." His line of descendants gave rise to Noah, "a righteous man, perfect in his generations, who walked with God" (Gen. 6:9). Noah survives the Flood and lives on into post-diluvian times.

The purpose of the schematic filiation begins to be evident when the sons of Noah come upon the scene. These sons are called Shem, Japheth, and Ham. A story is told which reflects great credit upon Japheth and Shem, the elder brothers, while holding up to shame the younger son, Ham, the father of the Canaanites (Gen. 9:18f.). According to the story (which is in the J document), Ham was a man of such bad character that his father Noah condemned Ham's descendants to slavery: "Cursed be Canaan! A slave of slaves shall he be" (Gen. 9:25). Thus, the Canaanites, who in pre-Hebrew times possessed "the land flowing with milk and honey," incurred the penalty of bondage. Noah's curse, then, furnishes the excuse which later on justifies Israel in conquering Canaan and subjugating the inhabitants of the land.

Honorable prehistoric pedigree for Israel

The Israelites, meanwhile, are provided with a pedigree running through the honorable Shem and a succession of first-born sons to another patriarch of righteousness, Abram (or Abraham). This genealogy comes from the Priestly document; and it stands between two sections of the J source (Gen. 11:10–27 inclusive). Abram journeys from Mesopotamia to Canaan with his nephew Lot, in relation to whom a discreditable story is told about the origin of Israel's neighbors, Moab and Ammon. These two nations, located on the border of the desert, east of Israel, are said to have come from incest between Lot and his two daughters (Gen. 19:30–38).

Now the motives underlying the alleged filiation emerge even more clearly into relief. Abraham's first-born son, Isaac, becomes the father of Esau and Jacob. From these two brothers come the nations of Edom and Israel; and since in the actual history Israel subjugated and enslaved Edom, a story is told to the effect that Esau, the ancestor of the Edomites, was a foolish man who despised his "birthright" and sold it to Jacob for a mess of pottage, and whose descendants, therefore, deserved to be enslaved by Israel (Gen. 25:23, 27–34).

House of Joseph preferred

The genealogical development now goes on to accomplish within Israel what it has already performed with reference to Israel versus outside nations. In the same way that Israel as a whole is depicted in a character of superiority to gentile nations, the various tribal, or clan, elements which make up Israel are disposed in relationships of superiority and lesser merit. The center and core of the nation is derived from Joseph and Benjamin, the only sons of Jacob and his favorite wife Rachel. The ascendency of Joseph's younger son, Ephraim, over his elder son, Manasseh, is explained by a story which makes Jacob give the blessing of birthright to Ephraim, whose name overspreads the bulk of the nation lying north of Jerusalem (cf. chap. iv, *supra*). The bitter hatred between the Ephraimites, or Josephites, and the tribe of Judah is explained by a tale which derives Judah from a hated wife, Leah, who was foisted upon Jacob by deceit on the night of his wedding to Rachel. The remaining tribes of Israel are derived, as we have seen, from slave girls or from the hated Leah.

Final redaction favors Judah

Very clearly, then, the house of Joseph monopolized the legend-building power in Israel. But the fact remained, nevertheless, that after the Joseph-tribes were disorganized by the Assyrians and lost in captivity, the tribe of Judah survived in a pagan world, giving witness to the One God. And thus the Jewish writers, unable to reconcile the high attainment of their tribe with its actual position in the secular history, produced the desecularized Hebrew Bible, putting in the forefront the Priestly document which confers upon Judah in early times an importance achieved only after the downfall of the house of Joseph.

In its genealogical aspect, therefore, the book of Genesis illustrates the manipulation of history and mythology in the interest of preconception. And only as this fact is clearly perceived are we able to make historical use of the sources which compose the book.

THE KENITES IN BIBLE HISTORY

SCARCELY PRESENT in the consciousness of Christians and Jews, the people or tribe known as Kenites bore an important relation to the roots of Hebrew religion. A foreign people, and yet worshipers of Yahweh; coöperating with Israel in the Deborah-battle against the army of the Baal-worshiping Sisera; honored by Saul, the first king of Israel because they befriended Israel in the desert before the invasion of Canaan; appearing from time to time in Hebrew history, from the days of the wilderness-wandering to the Babylonian exile; these people are nevertheless "blacked out" and covered with opprobrium by the compilers and editors of the Pentateuch, or books of Moses. The story is a strange one; but its inner meaning becomes clear when the evidence is carefully examined.

Kenites pictured as allies in Judges and other books

According to the book of Judges, "Mosheh" took a wife from this people in the wilderness: "And the children of the Kenite, Moses' father in law, went up . . . with the children of Judah into the wilderness of Judah" (Judg. 1:16). Later a portion of this tribe went north across the hill country of Ephraim and settled in the plain of Esdraelon: "Now Heber the Kenite, of the children of Hobab the father in law of Moses, had severed himself from the Kenites, and pitched his tent unto the plain of Zaanaim, which is by Kedesh" (Judg. 4:11). The Deborah Battle Song praises Jael, the wife of Heber the Kenite, for slaying Sisera, the general commanding the enemies of Israel: "Blessed above women shall Jael the wife of Heber the Kenite be; blessed shall she be above women in the tent" (Judg. 5:24). They were, then, a primitive tent-dwelling folk, whose manner of life was the same as that of Israel in the desert before the invasion of Canaan. In that earlier period they are said to have shown some great and special kindness to Israel, which is described by the term *hesed*. Thus, when King Saul was pursuing the Amalekites, he found certain Kenites in their company: "And Saul said unto the Kenites, Go, depart, get you down from among the Amalekites, lest I destroy you with them; for ye showed *hesed* to all the children of Israel when they came up out of Egypt" (I Sam. 15:6). The Kenite Jehonadab, the son of Rechab, supported Jehu and Yahweh against Baal (II Kings 10:15f.; cf. I Chron. 2:55). Bearing Yahweh names, the Kenites were called upon by the prophet Jeremiah as faithful witnesses to ancient ways (Jer. 35). Who and what, then, were these Kenites of the wilderness, who showed *hesed* to Israel when Israel and they alike were tent-dwelling nomads of the desert?

"Hesed" a special, divine quality

Independent of reference to the Kenites, the quality, or attribute, known as *hesed* is related, in its higher manifestation, to deity, or *elohim* (God). Thus, David asks, "Is there not yet any of the house of Saul, that I may show the *hesed* of God (*elohim*) unto him?" (II Sam. 9:3). The angels of Yahweh showed *hesed* to Lot (Gen. 19:1-19). "I delight in *hesed*, saith Yahweh" (Hos. 6:6; cf. Micah 7:18). "The eye of Yahweh is upon them that hope in his *hesed*" (Ps. 33:18; 147:11). "Yahweh was with Joseph and showed him *hesed*" (Gen. 39:21). It was this divine force, or quality, that Israel experienced through the Kenite people in the wilderness; and so strong was the tradition, or memory of it, that even when King Saul was about to destroy Israel's most hated enemies, the Amalekites, he stayed his hand so that the Kenites could separate themselves from the foe.

Early Israel pagan (E document)

That the ancestors of Israel in Mesopotamia and in Egypt were not worshipers of Yahweh is recalled by the Ephraimite document, E, wherein Joshua says, "Put away the gods which your fathers served on the other side of the [Euphrates] river and in Egypt"

(Josh. 24:14, E). In other words, the Ephraimite source recalls that Israel was heathen, or pagan, until after the exodus from Egypt.

This Ephraimite form of the Hebrew tradition is far simpler than the "orthodox" one, which makes Israel observe an elaborate sacrificial worship in the wilderness. That no system of burnt offering and sacrifice was given during the pre-Canaanite history is declared in the name of Yahweh by Jeremiah, the Ephraimite prophet (Jer. 7:21, 22f.). Moreover, it was in the wilderness that Israel and Yahweh were "married," as people and deity: "Thus saith Yahweh, I remember concerning thee the *hesed* of thy youth, the love of thine espousals—how thou wentest after me in the wilderness,—in a land that was not sown. Israel was set apart unto Yahweh,—the first fruits of his [Yahweh's] increase" (Jer. 2:1–3). "Yahweh's portion is his people. Jacob is the lot of his inheritance. He found him in a desert land,—in the waste and howling wilderness" (Deut. 32:9, 10).

Israel experiences "hesed" at hand of Kenites

What, then, is the historical reality, or circumstance, in the background of this impressive tradition? If Israel followed other gods "beyond the Euphrates river and in Egypt"; if Israel, upon coming out of Egypt, experienced *hesed* through the Kenites; and if the Kenites already worshiped Yahweh independently of Israel; then Israel acquired its first, or primary, sense of Yahweh through this foreign people who, in fact, remained friendly with Israel in subsequent history up to the Babylonian exile. And as time evolved its lengthening perspective, Yahweh, not the Kenites, naturally stood out as the dramatic force, or Power, which befriended Israel, and to which Israel turned in time of need. This is not to say that the Hebrew prophetic religion, as evolved in Canaan, was derived from the Kenites; but the suggestion is that Israel began to find God in a special way through an act of kindness, or *hesed*, shown by an alien people.

Nor can the view of Budde, Harper, Paton, and others be accepted—that "the religion of Israel became ethical because it was a religion of choice," which caused the masses to inquire, in times of misfortune, how the nation had offended Yahweh; for no such inquiry was needed to show that the *mishpat* of the clan brotherhood was in collision with the usages of baalistic legality. What Israel's contact with the Kenites did was to bring their own immemorial sense of *mishpat* into relation with what was (to them) a new divinity, who showed *hesed* to Israel, and who symbolized these ancient customs prevailing in the locality of "Kadesh" (holy place) to the south of Canaan. That the exodus brought Israel to this place by a briefer itinerary than the tortuous journeys indicated by the Priestly document, is made clear by the E material in Judges: "Israel came up from Egypt, and walked through the wilderness unto the Red Sea, and came to Kadesh. . . . And Israel abode in Kadesh" (Judg. 11:16; cf. E material crowded between sections of P in Numb. 14:25; 20; 14f.). The oasis of Kadesh, which thus became a temporary home for the small clan or tribe of Israel, was a kind of headquarters for primitive judicial decisions; its other name being "En-mishpat," or "Fountain of Justice." The terms are interchangeable in the Ephraimitic source composing the fourteenth of Genesis: "En-mishpat, which is Kadesh" (Gen. 14:7). Abram appears in this document as "baal of a covenant," in league with pre-Hebrew inhabitants of Canaan (Gen. 14:13).

Pentateuch blacks out Kenites

In view of the significant and long continued contact between Israel and the Kenites, as depicted in the non-Pentateuchal books of the Hebrew Bible, one would seem justified in expecting that the so-called "books of Moses" would put them in the honored forefront of Israel's life just prior to the invasion of Canaan. But by the time the Pentateuch was compiled, the triangle "Israel-Kenites-Yahweh" was no longer understood as a piece of anthropological experience. Also, the Jewish scribes (as if they suspected some dim heretical possibility in the relationship) canceled the Kenites completely out of the wilderness period by means of a device which, for want of a better term, we shall call "the Midianite cycle," as described in the following note.

THE MIDIANITE CYCLE

IN THE LEGENDS of Genesis the Midianites are sinners who kidnap the boy Joseph and sell him into Egyptian slavery: "Then there passed by Midianites, merchantmen; and they drew and lifted Joseph out of the pit . . . and the Midianites sold him into Egypt unto Potiphar an officer of Pharaoh's" (Gen. 37:28, 36). As if by way of expiation for the bondage of Joseph, the J document makes the Midianites assist Israel after leaving Egypt; the Midianite (not Kenite) priest gives his daughter to Moses (Exod. 2:16f.); but presently Moses divorces his Midianite wife, sending her back, with his two sons, Gershom and Eliezer, to her father (Exod. 18:1–4). Meanwhile, he marries another woman—an Ethiopian—against the protest of his relatives (Numb. 12:1–2).

After this, Moses's father-in-law, Jethro (E source) comes to Moses in the wilderness with Moses' wife and his two sons; but the Midianite goes away again into his own country (Exod. 18). The separation is enlarged upon by the J source, which still knows the father-in-law under other names and puts emphasis upon his refusal to accompany Israel into Canaan: "And Moses said unto Hobab, the son of Raguel the Midianite, Moses' father-in-law, We are journeying unto the place of which Yahweh said, I will give it you. Come thou with us, and we will do thee good. . . . And he said unto him, I will not go; but I will depart to mine own land, and to my kindred" (Numb. 10:29f.).

Midianites hire Balaam to curse Israel

Next, the elders of Midian join with elders of Moab in hiring a pagan prophet, "Balaam," to curse Israel (Numb. 22:2f.). But Balaam, instead of calling down woe upon Israel, curses the Kenites, who now strangely appear for the first time as an independent tribe who have had no previous relation to Israel and are fated to be driven into captivity (Numb. 24:21f.). The Pentateuch then proceeds, in the "Priestly" source, to make a final disposition of the Midianites as an evil influence in the life of Israel. The daughter of a Midianite chief is taken by an Israelite into his tent in the camp of Israel: "And when Phineas, the son of Eleazer, the son of Aaron the priest, saw it, he rose up from among the congregation, and took a javelin in his hand; and he went after the man of Israel into the tent, and thrust both of them through, the man of Israel, and the woman through her belly" (Numb. 25:6–15, P).

Yahweh now commands Moses to wage war against the Midianites (Numb. 25:16–18). The divine decree is carried into effect: "And they warred against the Midianites, as Yahweh commanded Moses; and they slew all the males" (Numb. 31:7). According to the Priestly document the Midianites are thus completely exterminated just prior to the Israelite invasion of Canaan. Yet when we step out of the fantastic P document into the actual settlement of Israel in the land of Canaan, the Midianites rise from the dead and attack the Josephites, being driven away by Gideon, of the tribe of Manasseh, the elder "son" of Joseph (Judg. 6 and 7).

Thus we reach the point where we started—the Midianites again hostile to "Joseph"; the Kenites completely erased from the pre-Canaanite experience of Israel; all reference to hesed eliminated; while the Kenites themselves are incidentally cursed by the magician Balaam. In other words, the Pentateuch successfully washes out of the picture these nomadic, tent-dwelling folk, who served Yahweh before Israel and came into friendly touch with Israel during the primitive, wilderness period.

THE PENTATEUCH A JUDAIC WORK

THE FACILITY with which the Kenites and their *hesed* are blacked out behind the shadow of Midian is equaled by the success with which the entire movement of pre-Canaanite religion is desecularized by the scribes in Babylonia and carried over into the realm of miracle by the Judaic documents—especially the P source, which gives form to the Pentateuch, or Torah. There is no evolution. The cult is decreed upon Mount Sinai. The cult originates outside human life and is abruptly thrust into the stream of history as a divine totalitarianism, to be kept intact by a blood purge (Gen. 17:14, P). There is thus no causal connection between the supernaturally revealed cult and the secular forces manifest in the development of society. The religion is not a product of Israel's experience in Canaan; its germ is not found in the kindness of an alien people; it is already decreed as an abstraction before Israel enters Canaan.

Ephraimite-Horeb version of pre-history

While the Priestly source composes by far the larger part of the Pentateuch and is intended by its authors to be normative, the presence of other documents, included by the final compilers, reveals that more than one version of the pre-history took form. This fact is brought out by fascicles of the E, or Ephraimite, non-Jewish document. While both E and P are hundreds of years later than the events which they allege as having occurred prior to the settlement in Canaan, the important consideration is, not whether one is truer than the other, but the mere fact that they differ drastically. The point of emphasis in E is the customary place of the Yahweh shrine outside, not inside, the camp of Israel in the desert.

According to E, then, Moses took the Tent of Yahweh and set it up outside the camp of Israel far away from the camp; and every-

one who inquired of Yahweh went out to this tent, which lay beyond the camp. And when Moses went out unto the Tent, all the
people rose up and stood every man at the door of his tent and
looked after Moses; and when Moses entered the Tabernacle, the
pillar of cloud descended, and stood at the door; and Yahweh spoke
to Moses. Moses would then return into the camp. But his minister,
Joshua, departed not out of the Tent (Exod. 33:7–11, E). "And
Yahweh said to Moses, Gather me seventy men, and bring them
unto the Tent; and Yahweh came down, and gave the spirit unto
the seventy; and they prophesied. But there stayed two men in the
camp, and the spirit rested upon them; and they were of those that
were called, but went not out unto the Tent; and they prophesied
in the camp. And a young man went and told Moses, and said, El-
dad and Medad do prophesy in the camp. And Moses said unto him,
Would that all the people of Yahweh were prophets! And Moses
withdrew into the camp" (Numb. 11:16–17, 25–30, E). "And Yahweh spake unto Moses, Aaron, and Miriam, Come out, ye three,
unto the Tent; and they three came out; and Miriam was shut out
from the camp seven days" (Numb. 12:4, 15, E). In E the place of
the ark of Yahweh on the march was in advance of the moving host:
"And they departed from the mount of Yahweh three days' journey; and the ark of the covenant of Yahweh went before them in
the three days' journey, to search out a resting place for them"
(Numb. 10:33 E).

The Ephraimite picture of Israel in the desert has obvious affinity
with the actual, historic ark and temple at Shiloh in the hill country
of Ephraim as it appears in First Samuel. This ark does not accompany Israel in the original attack upon the land of Canaan (Judg. 1).
It does not figure at the great Deborah battle in the plain of Esdraelon (Judg. 4, 5). It does not go with Ehud in the attack upon
Moab, or with Gideon when going forth against Midian, or Jephthah when warring against Ammon (Judg. 3:28f.; chaps, 7, 8, 11).
It is a later Ephraimite development, in the times of Eli and Samuel.

The authentic Shiloh ark was attended, not by an official of
priestly descent, but by an Ephraimite, Samuel, who was conse-

crated to Yahweh by his mother's vow. In the same way, the imaginary ark of E is attended by Joshua, of the tribe of Ephraim; while Yahweh is revealed, not privately to ecclesiastical monopolists, but publicly, at the door of the tent, in a pillar of cloud. The emphasis of the Ephraimite tradition is not upon priesthood and ritual, but upon prophecy, as befits a corpus of ideas originating in the section of the country where Hebrew prophecy arose. In the E document, again, priestly functions are discharged by "young men of Israel"; while Moses himself acts as priest, sprinkling the blood of sacrifices on the altar (Exod. 24:5-8, E). In E the sons of Moses are Gershom and Eliezer (Exod. 18:2-4). This document is directly related to the embarrassing Ephraimite story of the Judges period about "Jonathan the son of Gershom the son of Moses," who acts as priest (Judg. 18:30).

Priestly document gives monopoly to line of "Aaron"

Turning now to P, the main document of the Law, a wholly different picture comes into view. A rigid ecclesiastical monopoly is given by the Priestly source to "Aaron" and his sons. They alone may be the priests of Yahweh, offering the stated sacrifices; and they alone may enter the holy place where the ark rests (Numb. 4:5-15; 18:1-7, P). Neither Moses nor any son of his nor any Levite outside of "Aaron" and his descendants may exercise priestly functions. Aaron the Levite and the sons of Aaron are the only legitimate priests, or *kohanim*. All non-Aaronic Levites are mere church porters, or ecclesiastical janitors, who shall perform the menial work of the sanctuary—not as assistant-priests, but as humble helpers of the priests; and if they dare approach the altar of Yahweh, they will be instantly struck dead (Numb. 3:21-26, 27-31, 33-37; 4:15, P).

The Priestly document is anti-Ephraimite and pro-Judaic

Contrasted with E, the Priestly document locates the sanctuary of Yahweh continuously within and at the very center of the camp of Israel in the desert. The place of honor, on the east side of the holy Tent, facing the sunrise, is reserved for Moses, Aaron, and the sons of Aaron (Numb. 3:38, P). The sanctuary is then protected by a cordon of plain Levitical janitors all the way around on the four sides (Numb. 1:53). Beyond this cordon the tribes of Israel are disposed on every side—east, west, north, and south—in a very significant order: the house of Joseph, consisting of Manasseh, Ephraim, and Benjamin (the "Rachel" tribes), is located on the west or rear of the camp, in the least honorable position; and the combined encampment of these three tribes is called "the camp of Ephraim," which is one indication that the Priestly document was prepared after the tribe of Ephraim had risen to primacy over the elder tribe of Manasseh in Canaan (Numb. 2:18–24). On the north side of the camp are located the tribes of Dan, Asher, and Naphtali; while on the south come Reuben, Simeon, and Gad (Numb. 2:10–16, 25–31, P). But standing out in distinction from these nine tribes, and located on the honorable side of the camp with Moses, Aaron, and the sons of Aaron, is the "Leah" tribe of Judah with two other Leah tribes, Issachar and Zebulun (Numb. 2:3–9, P). Such was the order of the tribes when the camp was at rest in the wilderness.

When the camp was broken and the order of march taken up, the procession is led by the Leah tribe, Judah, with the Leah tribes Issachar and Zebulun, under whose standard are 186,400 fighting men (Numb. 2:9). Next are the two Leah tribes Reuben and Simeon, with Gad, born of Leah's maid Zilpah, under whose combined standard are 151,450 (Numb. 2:16). After them, in third place, is the house of Joseph, under the standard of Ephraim, with 108,000 (Numb. 2:24). And finally, at the hindmost of the line are three slave-girl tribes, Dan, Asher, and Naphtali, under whose standard are counted 157,600 (Numb. 2:31). Thus, not only does the standard of Judah go foremost; but it is given the highest number of armed men (186,400); while the camp of Ephraim is given the smallest number (108,100). Moreover, the marching arrangement provides that all the Leah tribes go ahead of all the Rachel tribes.

Continuing the same idea of precedence, the Priestly document says that the chief architect of the Tabernacle itself was Bezaleel, of the tribe of Judah, who, with Aholiab, of the tribe of Dan, has charge over all the workmen from the various tribes (Exod. 31:1-6). The mention of these two names, from the tribes respectively southernmost and northernmost in Canaan, reflects the customary saying "From Dan to Beersheba," which came into use only after the tribe of Dan had moved from its first position southwest of Ephraim and settled permanently in the far north of Israel.

The P source then goes on to relate that when the Tabernacle was completed the princes of the twelve tribes were called upon to make offerings for the equipment and service of the sanctuary: "And he that offered his offering the first day was Nahshon . . . of the tribe of Judah" (Numb. 7:12, P). Next, on the second and third days, came the princes of Issachar and Zebulun; so that, beginning with Judah, three Leah tribes were ahead of all Israel in zeal for the Tabernacle (Numb. 7:18-29). Not until the seventh, eighth, and ninth days do the princes of Ephraim, Manasseh, and Benjamin, the Rachel tribes, bring their offerings. Here, again, the historically significant allusion to Ephraim the younger brother comes before mention of Manasseh the elder (Numb. 7:48-65). Finally, as in the marching order, the princes of the slave-girl and least-honored tribes, Dan, Asher, and Naphtali, bring their gifts (Numb. 7:66-83). A background for the priority of Judah is thus furnished.

Priestly document seeks to overcome priority of Joseph

The order of precedence in P seeks to compensate Judah and the other Leah tribes for the consideration which the Ephraimite legend shows in general to Rachel and her sons, who in the "core" of tradition are the proper family of Jacob. A specific instance is found in the story about the patriarch's conduct when his offended brother Esau was approaching with four hundred men: "Then Jacob was greatly afraid and distressed. . . . And he divided the children unto Leah, and unto Rachel, and unto the two slave-women; and he put the slave-women and their children first [that is, in the most hazardous position]; and Leah and her children [next] after; and Rachel and Joseph hindermost [that is, in the safest place; Benjamin was not yet born]" (Gen. 32:6-7; 33:1-2; J document, under stress of E tradition—another item showing posteriority of J to E).

The outstandingly favorable treatment given to Judah by P and the dominant position of P in the "books of Moses" are conclusive evidence that the Pentateuch in its final form is a Jewish product. The exilic authors, compilers, and redactors did their work in full view of the striking and inescapable fact that ever since the destruction of Ephraim by Assyria, Judah had carried on alone. The new importance thus conferred upon the Judean remnant of Israel is naturally projected into the dim past, affording another example of literary form as molded upon the pattern of objective history.

But over and above the foregoing considerations, the P element is loaded with miracles far in excess of the other documents; this feature of supernaturalism is joined with special emphasis upon revelation of the Yahweh-cult as a monotheistic religion, wholly independent of history and given at Sinai prior to the long national experience in Canaan (cf. chap. i). This fact alone—that is, considered apart from the manifestly Judaic, anti-Ephraimite tendency of P—is enough to show the real nature of the Pentateuch as a work issuing from scribes whose approach to the problem of religious origins proves that they are out of touch with objective reality.

MITSRAIM AND MOSHEH

THAT THE pasture land of Goshen, on the northwestern frontier of *Mitsraim* (Egypt), may have been inhabited for a time by a small clan called "Joseph," or at least by a kindred group whose descendants, after penetrating the central Canaanite range, became known as "the house of Joseph," is a possibility. Even the orthodox tradition itself sends Joseph into *Mitsraim* first and brings in the other "sons," or "tribes," of Jacob later. But the conventional tradition concerning a twelve-tribe community, with 600,000 fighting men and a total population of millions, enslaved in *Mitsraim* proper and going thence into the desert, is involved in too many inconsistencies and too complicated, formidable and fantastic to be actual history (cf. Exod. 12:37; Numb. 1:46; 11:21; 26:51).

Assuming, on the other hand, that a Joseph element of some description was in Goshen (not in *Mitsraim* proper) and that when seeking to leave the country it was hindered by an Egyptian frontier guard—a circumstance of this kind might remain as a tradition and impress itself upon the Hebrew people as a whole in Canaan. That a very large element of the composite "Israel" in Canaan was derived from earlier stock, native to the country, is definitely stated by a number of Biblical documents; and since, at one period prior to the settlement of "Joseph" in Canaan, the Pharaoh of *Mitsraim* actually ruled over Canaan, a tradition of slavery under Egyptian masters could have entered the Hebrew consciousness from this direction also. The historic overthrow of Sisera's army and chariots in the river Kishon (Judg. 5) might contribute an important strand of tradition, reappearing in documents E, J, and P, as the overthrow of Egyptian chariots in "Yam Suph" (the Red Sea).

Kenite black out conceals fundamental facts

The anxiety of the Pentateuchal compilers to obscure the relation of Kenites and Israelites under the "Midianite cycle" evidently conceals a key circumstance in the wilderness experience of the "Joseph," or "Ephraim," clan. The figure of *Mosheh* (Moses) is primarily involved with the Ephraimite tradition; and the story of his descendant, the Levite Jonathan, acting as *kohen* to the Danites, is very embarrassing to the orthodox view, which denies priestly character to *Mosheh* and contemplates legitimate *kohanim* as descended only from Aaron. But Aaron himself is elusive in the Pentateuch. The traditional Aaronic priesthood may be only "sons of the ark (*aron*);" and the evanescent figure of Aaron himself may be the ark (*aron*) personalized (*God and the Social Process*, pp. 218f.).

Again, there is a possibility that the "Joseph" element was never in any part of *Mitsraim*, but was actually oppressed by some tribe in the desert far south of Canaan. The *hesed* shown by the Kenites (which the Pentateuch so ungallantly obliterates) may, in that case, have been incidental to the alliance of the Kenite clan with the proto-Josephite Israel; the intermediary being an obscure individual who supplied a concrete starting point for the figure which eventually became the orthodox *Mosheh*.

Prophet Elijah prototype of Moses

In any case, *Mosheh* is built up on the sanguinary prophetic figure of the actual, historic, Ephraimite *nabi* (prophet) Elijah, who in ritual practice means more to the Jewish tradition than Moses himself. And Moses is called a *nabi* in the book of Deuteronomy, which links with Ephraimite Horeb tradition, rather than with the priestly Sinai cycle. Deuteronomy, in fact, stands between E and P, and recognizes all the Levites as *kohanim* rather than as mere porters of the sanctuary, calling them repeatedly "the priests the Levites" (Deut. 17:9; 24:8; 21:5, *et passim*). This breach between "D" and the rigid, high-church "P" with regard to priesthood is too serious and comprehensive to be ignored as it is by the later, orthodox tradition.

That any system of sacrifice was given to Israel in the exodus period is flatly denied, in the name of Yahweh, by the prophet Jeremiah, who, as an Ephraimite of Benjamin, was on the watch against the advent of ritualism and priestcraft in Judah: "Thus saith Yahweh . . . I spake not unto your fathers, nor commanded them, in the day [that is, the period, or epoch] that I brought them out of the land of *Mitsraim,* concerning burnt offerings or sacrifices. But this thing I commanded them, saying, Harken unto my voice" (Jer. 7:22–23). "How do ye say, We are wise; and the law (*torah*) of Yahweh is with us? But, behold, the false pen of the scribes hath wrought falsely" (Jer. 8:8). In the times of Jeremiah, just before the Babylonian exile, the forces which produced the book of Deuteronomy, and were already reducing Hebrew religion to book form, were ascending upon the horizon of the Judaic mind; they were eventually to supersede the free voice of prophecy. But the reign of the ecclesiastical *Mosheh* had not yet begun; and the great non-Judaic prophet Jeremiah was on guard against the rising priestly tide. That both prophecy and priesthood were needed in the evolution of religion was not realized by Jeremiah.

If there was in the pre-Canaanite period of Israel some inconspicuous person to whom the impressive priestly tradition of *Mosheh* ultimately attached itself, we have no means of rescuing such a figure from under the superincumbent mass of conflicting data in the Hebrew Bible. It should be emphasized that this question is not central to the problem of religion, even though it be a matter of historical interest. The priestly tradition of *Mosheh,* and of *Mitsraim* and of an abstract, supernatural revelation independent of history, are intimately connected; and they stand or fall together. They refuse to be settled offhand, because they involve so many collateral questions (such as the Kenites) which must be kept in mind while final conclusions are in process of being reached.

ISRAEL, MOAB, AND YAHWEH-BAAL STRUGGLE

A CORRESPONDENT wishes further light on Israel's religious development along socio-economic lines, raising the question why the same kind of evolution did not occur in the little neighboring country of Moab, across the Dead Sea. This recalls Wellhausen's observation that we cannot tell why Yahweh of Israel, rather than Chemosh of Moab, should have become the righteous God of the universe.

The situation and histories of these two peoples were superficially alike, but fundamentally different. Moab was on the edge of the desert and was uniformly pastoral; the king himself was a great sheepmaster; and the social group known as "Moab" integrated uniformly, without the complication of descent from two general parent stems represented by contrasting cults like those of Yahweh and Baal. Chemosh was presumably "Baal-Peor," taking on whatever fertility-function attached to the Canaanite gods, while at the same time preserving the clan-*mishpat* emphasis of the nomadic world from which Moab sprang.

West of Jordan the development of the national organism was far more complex. The *mishpat* of the desert clan, affirming the right of all individuals within the group to the resources of the land over which it roamed, was thrown into the melting pot alongside the commercial, baalistic rule that land could rightfully be alienated by sale or foreclosure and could thus ethically accumulate in the grasp of a small *baal* class. These opposing ideas, or usages, represented by the terms "Yahweh" and "Baal," were violently flung together within the limits of the same group mechanism; and their partisans were therefore precipitated into a struggle for control of the government which determined the rules or laws of the State. No other State in human history evolved precisely as Israel did in

Canaan; and in correspondence with this distinctive evolution the ethical development of Israel was therefore unlike that of Moab or any other nation.

Further treatment of land-factor necessary

It has been argued also that the problem of *mishpat* as between Baal and Yahweh has no special reference to land; that it simply denotes the idea of just and fair dealing and has only a secondary reference to landholding. If this view is well founded, the interpretation cannot, of course, be maintained that land *mishpat* entered into the very substance of the Yahweh-Baal antithesis which differentiates the history of Israel from that of all other nations. This phase of the problem is enlarged upon in the main text; but a few paragraphs now follow in further treatment of the subject.

LAND AND MISHPAT

THE OLD, conventional objection that Bible history and the religion of Israel had nothing to do with economics reappears more subtly in the claim that the chief sense of *mishpat* is independent of connection with land. The clan groups which attacked Canaan in the Judges period sought possession of "a land flowing with milk and honey." This land-economic fact is outstanding and fundamental in Bible history. All tribal and racial migrations, from the cave man to Hitler, have been motivated by a desire for land and "living room." Any argument which undertakes to isolate ancient Israel from this universal human motive goes contrary to general experience as well as to the essential facts of Hebrew history itself.

In the nomad stage the clan group feels that the area (that is, land) in which they wander is divinely guaranteed as a means of life open to the entire group. In the same way, the "land flowing with milk and honey" was regarded as "given" by Yahweh to Israel collectively, after which it was supposed, in later times, to have been divided by casting the sacred "lot" (*goral*); the term being used in P not only for the process of casting lots but also to indicate the landed property resulting from that process (Josh. 14:2 and 15:1, P). That any widespread, systematic assignment of land among twelve tribes actually took place in the fashion P supposes was, of course, impossible in view of the real, objective history. But our concern here is with the belief which crystallized after the nation took form in Palestine. The Priestly injunctions about land were based upon earlier ideas expressed, for instance, in the Ephraimite source, where Naboth refuses in the name of Yahweh, to sell his ancestral inheritance to King Ahab (I Kings 21:2, 3, E). Accordingly the priestly "Holiness Code," speaking in the name of Yahweh, prohibits the alienation of land (Levit. 25:23).

Canaanite view of landed property

In contrast, under a different regime, the Amorite *baalim* of Shechem are pictured as readily selling land to Jacob; while Hamor urges Jacob to remain peacefully in Canaan so as to acquire still more land (Gen. 33:19; cf. 34:10). Hamor was not only the chief *baal* of Shechem but also "prince of the land," that is, having power to levy taxes and control the law courts. He cast covetous eyes upon Jacob, who had "increased exceedingly, and had much cattle, and women-slaves, and men-slaves, and camels, and asses" (Gen. 30:43). Hamor knows that if the Israelite settlers will only remain peacefully in Canaan, respecting the "rights of property," these crude cattlemen can be insidiously subjugated by the *baalim* of Shechem. In a private conference with the "leading citizens" he says, "Shall not their cattle, and their substance, and every beast of their's be our's?" (Gen. 34:20–23). The whole economic problem of Hebrew history is reflected here in miniature, with its enslavement of the rural *adonim* to the baalistic, propertied element in the walled cities.

The Genesis tale about Shechem, as pointed out elsewhere, is a distorted reflex of the more literal narrative in Judges. The legal status of the metropolitan proprietary, which gives them control of the taxing power and the courts, is threatened by the growth of Gideon's government. Alarmed by the shifting of political power into the open country, the *baalim* send out and slay all the sons of Gideon (Judg. 9). But the country people, in a revolutionary uprising, destroy the city (Judg. 9:46f.); whereupon the land in the open territory around Shechem accrues to the "sons of Israel," who, reversing Hamor's plan, take all the cattle and wealth of the Shechemite *baalim* (Gen. 34:25f.).

Landed property and political power

In the case of Naboth's land, Queen Jezebel asks Ahab if he "governs" Israel (I Kings 21:7). This woman's idea of property was derived from the commercial, baalistic usages of her native home in Phoenicia, where the idea of "government" was bound up with legal practices contrary to those of the rural Israelite clans in Ephraim. Hence, the Israelite courts had to be invoked and corrupted in the king's name before Naboth's land could be seized (I Kings 21:8–13).

Only when these considerations are borne carefully in mind can we realize the economic significance and implications of *mishpat* as this term appears, for instance, in Isaiah: "Yahweh will enter into *mishpat* with the elders of his people and the princes thereof. It is ye that have eaten up the vineyard" (Isa. 3:13). He looked for *mishpat;* but, behold, oppression. . . . Woe to them that lay field to field" (Isa. 5:7, 8). Likewise, in Micah: "They covet fields and seize them. . . . Ye heads of Jacob and rulers of the house of Israel, is it not for you to know *mishpat?*" (Mic. 2:2; 3:1).

Mishpat, then, is deeply involved in the land question; it is always the rulers, princes, government, and legality which appear in the forefront of the problem. So the prophet Ezekiel, as he looks back over the course of Hebrew history and onward into the future: "My princes shall no more oppress my people. But they shall give the land to the house of Israel according to their tribes. . . . Thus saith the *adon* Yahweh. Let it suffice you, O princes of Israel; remove violence and spoil, and execute *mishpat.* . . . The prince shall not take of the people's inheritance, to thrust them out of their possession" (Ezek. 45:8, 9; 46:18).

The book of Nehemiah declares that the house of Israel did not keep the *mishpat* of Yahweh in the olden time (Neh. 1:7). A concrete example from Nehemiah's own day is found in current mortgage foreclosure with seizure of land (5:1). This practice is bitterly censured by Nehemiah as "not good" and as contrary to "the fear of our God"; whereupon he exhorts the foreclosers to restore the lands (5:6f.).

To say that *mishpat* has no bearing on the land problem, then, is almost as far from the truth as to say that no economic forces entered into the history and religious life of Israel. Not only was Hebrew history economic in the same sense as the histories of other nations but also the meaning of the Hebrew word *mishpat* is intimately bound up with land questions. The original emphasis of

Yahwism was toward fixed, inalienable titles to the soil; while Baalism was, in the contrary, commercialistic and went along with liquidity of land ownership and concentration of land in the power of a small group.

HISTORY AND THE
COMMANDMENTS

THAT THE "ten commandments" are evolutionary and that three different editions are found in various literary strata of the Pentateuch
is well known to scholars, but not to the lay world. The form of the
commandments which is best known to Christians and Jews occurs
in the E (or Ephraimite) document at Exodus 20 and is the earliest.
A Judaic improvement upon this E version appears in the Deuteronomic document at Deut. 5:6f. And midway in time between the
two is another Judaic set of commandments, ritualistic in form, corresponding to the priestly, anti-Baal revolution at Jerusalem, which
took place in the same epoch as the prophetic anti-Baal upheaval at
Samaria.

Aversion to Baal was implicit in the social and economic history
of the Josephite enclave—that is, the Ephraimite hill country. But
a concrete occasion was necessary to bring the earliest, or Ephraimite, commandments into formal existence. Such an occasion,
which corresponds accurately and significantly with one-half the
salient features in the code, is found in the Ephraimite tragedy of
Naboth. The atmosphere of the case was thoroughly saturated with
Baalism as typified by Jezebel, the Phoenician wife of King Ahab.
Her actions were consistent with the regime of Baalism in contact
with the more primitive cult of Yahweh as followed by the farmers
and shepherds of Ephraim; while the Naboth case itself involved (1)
desire for another's property, (2) false witness, in the trumped-up
trial of the unfortunate Ephraimite, (3) murder, and (4) actual
theft of the land from Naboth's family. Thus we find realistic starting points for the first commandment (against other gods), the sixth
(against murder), the eighth (against theft), the ninth (against false
witness), and the tenth (against coveting the property of another).

These five injunctions may have been the original Ephraimite commandments; since there were not necessarily ten at first, and the present order is not necessarily the original one.

Slavery and the commandments

Modern translations obscure the fact that the commandments were formulated in a society which was based upon human slavery as a fundamental premise. "Thou shalt not covet thy neighbor's *ebed* (male slave), nor his *amah* (female slave)" is wrongly translated "manservant" and "maidservant." There would be no point in a commandment against coveting such workers if they were not held as property, like sheep and oxen; because if they were merely "servants" in the modern sense, no moral wrong could attach to a desire for their services if coupled with an offer of higher wages. The passage of wage and salary earners from one employer to another is an essential condition of a "free" labor market. Such transfers were precluded by the property system on which the tenth commandment was based; consequently there was no free labor market in ancient Israel.

The injunction against coveting slaves is part of a schedule including another item which raises the subject in another way—the modern version being, "Thou shalt not covet thy neighbor's wife." But in the Hebrew text the term is merely the word for woman; and it must be interpreted in the light of domestic practices according to which the man, or "husband," could legally have as many women, or "wives," as he could purchase in the matrimonial market or capture in war. Thus we find the father of Samuel the prophet in possession of two women (I Sam. 1:2). The modern translations read, "And he had two wives," but the Hebrew text merely says women. Another example is David, who had more "wives" than Samuel's father (I Sam. 18:20; cf. 25:42, 43, and II Sam. 5:13). The term inaccurately translated "wife" does not, therefore, mean what the word "wife" signifies in modern Jewish and Christian communities. The woman, in fact, was in the category of property; she was bought from her father for money, and could be returned to him with a private bill of divorce, written by the "husband" without even the formality of appeal to a court.

In view of these facts we must evaluate the seventh commandment, "Thou shalt not commit adultery," looking at it first from the standpoint of man, and then from that of the woman. When this rule of the code is broken by a man having (for example) six wives, just what is the force of the injunction? Does it regard the holding of six purchased women as being "moral," whereas relationship with a seventh unpurchased woman is "immoral"? Manifestly, this commandment, as it stands in the Hebrew text, has nothing to do with what is regarded as "morals," or "ethics," among modern Jews and Christians. Because under the social conditions prevailing when the commandments were first formulated if a man had relationship with a woman whom he had not regularly purchased, he was interfering with the property rights of some other man who had already bought her, or who (as in the case of a father) was holding her for sale.

Morality and rights of property

The fact thus becomes clear that under Hebrew law not only adultery but also other sex offenses are in the nature of damage to the rights of private property. Thus, if a man seduces a virgin, he shall buy her as his wife; but if her father will not sell her, the man shall pay the regular price nevertheless (Exod. 22:16, 17). A male offender could thus usually be assessed or fined. But a guilty woman fared worse; because, being the property of some man, she therefore had no property or money of her own with which to compensate her father for the impairment of his rights or her husband for the invasion of his domestic prerogative. The idea of ethical significance had, in the first instance, nothing to do with the case; the sense of abstract moral values grew up very slowly and obscurely within the terms of economic and social relationships.

In view of the foregoing facts it is instructive to consider the injunction "Thou shalt not steal." Here, apparently, is a clear, unambiguous command whose meaning cannot possibly be obscure.

You must not appropriate anything which belongs to your neighbor. He plants a crop of corn in his field, cares for it while growing, and finally reaps it. Everybody admits that the corn is his and that if someone else appropriates the corn, he steals it.

But according to Hebrew law, if a man's bond-servants or slaves (*abadim*) plant, tend, and reap a field of corn, the owner of the slaves takes the crop as his own. Thus, while one may not "steal" the crop raised by his neighbor, he may "take" the crop raised by his slaves. In other words, the injunction "thou shalt not steal" refers to one's neighbor, not to one's slaves. In the view of the commandments, therefore, the slave is not a "neighbor," because (according to the tenth commandment) the slave himself is in the category of "property" which ought not to be "coveted."

Murder and rights of property

Likewise, the command "thou shalt not kill" is to be interpreted in relation to other legislation specifying differences of degree in the taking of human life. Thus, "he that smiteth a man, so that he die, shall be surely put to death" (Exod. 21:12). But on the other hand, "if a man smite his slave [*ebed*] with a rod, and he die under his hand, he shall surely be punished. Notwithstanding, if he [the slave] continue a day or two, he shall not be punished, because he is his money" (Exod. 21:20, 21). In any case, the master is not to be put to death for killing a slave, but only "punished"; and if the slave, when beaten, does not actually die "under his master's hand," but "continues a day or two" and then dies, the master is not even to be "punished."

A scientific study of Bible history must interpret the commandments in terms of evolution. Approached from this point of view, history reveals that the original significance of the various injunctions is lost when they are used in the modern rituals of Jewish and Christian religious assemblies; as they are at present repeated, the meaning differs from that which was formerly attached to them. When thus used, the ten commandments are lifted out of, or abstracted from, their historical context, whereupon they are transformed into symbols of an ongoing moral process which imparts to them a higher meaning; their ethical impulse becomes a creative spiritual force.

AMALEKITES IN BIBLE HISTORY

EXTREME AND UNUSUAL hatred against "Amalek" is registered in the Old Testament sources. Denunciation of this tribe, or people, rises to a pitch of intensity unequaled elsewhere in the Hebrew Bible. Amalekites figure in attacks upon Israel after the settlement west of Jordan during the Judges period. It is not merely Moab which oppresses the Benjaminites in the time of Ehud; but coöperating with Moab are Amalekites (Judg. 3:12, 13). Also, it is not simply the Midianites who invade the land in the days of Gideon; along with them are Amalekites (Judg. 6:3, 33; 7:12). Complete destruction of Amalek is decreed by Samuel the seer, in the name of Yahweh; and King Saul is commissioned to carry out the sentence. An Amalekite, with news of Saul's death, hastens to David at the Philistine city of Ziklag, asserting that he himself slew the Ephraimite king and assuming that David shares the Amalekite hatred of Ephraim (II Sam. 1:1–16). David's unfriendly reception of the news and his treatment of the messenger did not necessarily express his own, personal feelings, but were essential, rather, to his policy in currying favor with Ephraim.

Ephraim identified with problem

For it is Ephraim, once more, that comes to the front as the Amalekite problem is investigated. The tribe, or people, called Amalek is first brought into view by the E source, which records the demand of Yahweh to blot their name from under heaven; this curse being retribution for an alleged onslaught upon Israel after leaving Egypt (Exod. 17:8, 14, E). And likewise, it was the Ephraimite seer, Samuel, who pronounced the other sentence of utter destruction upon the same people (I Sam. 15:18). The invasions by Moab-Amalek and by Midian-Amalek were both aimed at the territory of the "Josephite enclave," that is, the hill country of Ephraim. Still more definite is a reference to the burial place of a certain Ephraimite chief at Pirathon "in the land of Ephraim—in the hill country of the Amalekites" (Judg. 12:15). The E source contains the statement "the Amalekites and the Canaanites are there before you" (Numb. 14:43); "then the Amalekites came down, and the Canaanites . . ." (Numb. 14:45). Likewise, in the E document Balaam, standing upon mount Pisgah, looks toward Canaan, where he sees Amalek, which he calls "the first of the nations" (Numb. 24:20).

Following these various hints that Amalek possessed a portion of the country west of Jordan prior to the settlement of Israel in that country, the latest document, P, makes Amalek a grandson of Esau, sharing thus the fate of his ancestor, who was banished from Canaan by the wiles of Jacob-Israel, through whom Esau was deprived of his birthright (Gen. 36:12; cf. chap. 27). This brings up the uncertain passage in the Ephraimitic "Song of Deborah," usually translated "out of Ephraim came they whose root is in Amalek" (Judg. 5:14). This passage is so obscure in the Hebrew text that the "American Translation," issued by the University of Chicago, makes it read "Ephraim surged into the valley (*emek*)." But the other version of this passage is worth considering in view of all the evidence.

"Joseph," or "Ephraim," replaces Amalekite aristrocracy

Even if this particular passage reveals no connection with Amalek, the total evidence already brought forward suggests that the occupation of the "Josephite enclave" by "Israel" was founded upon a frightful conquest which replaced a dominant Amalekite aristocracy by a new upper class which eventually organized itself under the name Ephraim; that the subsequent incursions of Moab and Midian were promoted by Amalek, which was trying to recover its territory; and that in the time of King Saul, when Samuel, transported by fanatic rage, took Agag, the king of Amalek, and "hewed him in pieces before Yahweh," the Amalekite problem had reached a crisis which finally assured central Canaan to Israel.

If this view is correct, it is obvious that the obscurity of the general situation has been caused by the inclusion of Ephraim in the kingdom of David and the crystallizing of a tradition according to which all pre-Hebrew possessors of the land as a whole were generalized under the familiar alternative terms "Canaanite" and "Amorite." A total historical situation always tends to dominate and obscure any part of it, because economy of attention in subsequent ages tyrannizes over details.

If Amalekites, not Amorites, were the immediate predecessors of Ephraim, or Joseph, in central Canaan, this fact would not be revolutionary for the interpretation of Hebrew history; but it might help to explain some features of the history with more clearness. If the "enclave" were previously held by an Amalekite landed aristocracy controlling a mass of alien slaves, this element would have been distinct from the Amorite, or Canaanite, aristocracy outside the enclave, and would thus have intruded into the highlands more recently. How else, in fact, would the expression "hill country of the Amalekites" be equated, as above, with "the land of Ephraim" (Judg. 12:15); and how else can we explain the source which declares that the Amalekites and the Canaanites were in the land before Israel (Numb. 14:43), or the statement that "the Amalekites came down" (Numb. 14:45), or the source which makes Balaam, standing upon Pisgah, refer to them as "the first of the nations" (Numb. 24:20)?

If the original conquest of Canaan were in fact the ousting of an Amalekite aristocracy from the "enclave" area, the contest would have been waged between opponents more nearly equal in savage quality than if the Josephites merely attacked the older and more effete Amorite ruling class, which, according to the Tell el Amarna letters prior to the Israelite attack, had already become degenerate. Such a conquest, by clans fresh from the desert, coping with clans more vigorous than the Amorites, would account for the ferocity of the traditional conquest which would then confuse the Amorites with Amalek, as having been completely destroyed, instead of the latter. In other words, the legend about "utter extermination" (*herem*) of the previous inhabitants would have this local basis in fact, and would explain certain anomalies in the sources.

DODD'S *HISTORY AND THE GOSPEL*

THE RESURGENCE of orthodox attitudes toward history finds a useful and striking illustration in the recent volume *History and the Gospel* (New York, 1938), by C. H. Dodd, Professor of Divinity in the University of Cambridge, England. The existence of the Church, he says, has become one of the crucial problems of European civilization; and he is unable to tell what is going to happen (*ibid.*, p. 179).

The author solves the problem of religion and the Church as cavalierly as King Charles I solved the governmental problem. "Government and a subject," said Charles, "are two clean different things." Professor Dodd solves the religious problem by saying, in effect, that history and the gospel are utterly different facts, although coexisting throughout a part of the time-order. Secular history, he declares, is a series of empirical events, linked together by efficient causes and by succession in time. This time-succession of events, he says, constitutes a process which is not proceeding from any recognizable starting point or going toward any recognizable end; it is just sheer process, of which we cannot predicate any meaning or value (*ibid.*, 166–67). What an estimate he puts upon the total experience of mankind!

Speaking in symbolic terms, Professor Dodd looks upon the process of secular history as a kind of river, flowing onward horizontally, as rivers do; while, on the other hand, the gospel is an external deposit from beyond history, which is impressed supernaturally upon history by a vertical revelation from above (*ibid.*, p. 181). His idea of Hebrew history is that it consisted of a prophetic warfare against Baal worship considered as a nature-religion, essentially a fertility cult (*ibid.*, p. 31). Reducing Old Testament history to this crude and simple antithesis, he merely repeats a worn-out

formula of Wellhausen criticism and puts on exhibit the incompe-
tence of his own historical scholarship.

This notice of the volume in question is not intended to imply that
Dr. Dodd gives no worth-while testimony in behalf of God and
religion. But the positive inference is that he operates with an out-
moded methodology which is not in step with today's academic
thought forms and has no valid bearing on the moral and spiritual
issues of our epoch. His book is a genteel, refined "fundamentalism"
which has no affinity with modern scientific scholarship.

PIPER'S *GOD IN HISTORY*

THIS BOOK by Professor Otto Piper (New York, 1939) takes much the same ground as that of Dodd. Human history is a secular process; but when God interferes with the process in a special, "supernatural" way, for a special purpose, then it becomes "holy history" (*Heilsgeschichte*) as long as the divine interference is effectual in changing the course of natural, secular history. But secular events themselves have the character of being what they are simply because they represent a departure of man from a primeval "holy history." The "original structure" of human life is distorted so completely, declares Dr. Piper, that only by divine interference can history be rendered "meaningful" (*ibid.*, p. 42).

God "supernaturally" interfered with pre-Christian history, according to Piper, for the purpose of establishing the Jewish religion as preparatory to the Christian religion; which, in turn, was based upon a further supernatural interference effected through the virgin birth of Jesus. And in this way Jesus became directly operative in history without being subject to its "basic forces" (*ibid.*, p. 18).

But at the same time, in spite of supernatural interference as manifested in the Jewish and Christian religions, Professor Piper assures us that God is at work "everywhere" in history (*ibid.*, p. 67), and that God used World War I and its results as a means of awakening self-complacent churches and individual Christians to a recognition of the true nature of the world (*ibid.*, p. 161). And yet, according to Dr. Piper secular history does not have the appropriateness of "holy history" as a field for God's work, because in secular affairs the operation of Divine guidance is less obvious than "Satanic interference" (*ibid.*, p. 67). The historic omniscience of this writer may well be envied by investigators and scholars who do not share his outlook. If God is able (as Piper declares) to be the power behind "secular" history, the question might then be in order why God has to use the extraordinary, supernatural methods allegedly employed in "holy" history. But the same authority would no doubt reply to this inquiry by saying that the field of secular history has been effectively preëmpted by Satan, and that God is therefore compelled to resort to the miraculous in order to overcome the wiles of the Devil.

The real nature of the author's training in historical study and investigation, however, is betrayed by his reference to the higher criticism of the Bible. He assumes that Biblical criticism as it stood, say, about the beginning of the present century, was a finished intellectual process which had then issued in a consistent structure of historico-Biblical doctrine. And in this assumption he is supported by the Scottish Wellhausenian critic, W. R. Smith, who praised Wellhausen and Kuenen as investigators whose acumen and research had left nothing of importance to be done for the historical study of the Old Testament! *Religion of the Semites* (1894), Preface. As a matter of fact, the higher criticism represented by Smith and Wellhausen was only a new theory of the Biblical sources, which is itself open to criticism; and Dr. Piper, in turn, commits the error of assuming that the criticism in question constituted a finished body of Biblical interpretation instead of having the incomplete character of a literary hypothesis. Hence, he deals with the subject cavalierly by saying that the higher criticism, which tried to refute supernatural revelation by facts of experience, was itself refuted by archaeological excavations in Palestine (*ibid.*, p. 153). According to Professors Piper and Dodd, therefore, Jewish history, considered as a secular process, is an "insoluble riddle" (*ibid.*, p. 73).

BIBLICAL SCHOLARSHIP IN GERMANY AND GREAT BRITAIN

IN PARTIAL EXPLANATION of the trends toward aristocracy and democracy, respectively, in Germany and Great Britain, the paper here reprinted was first published in 1918, in the *Biblical World*, under the heading: "The Paradox of Modern Biblical Criticism," by Louis Wallis. It is republished here because of its bearing on the general situation leading up to Naziism.

Although German scholars have done a great deal to promote scientific investigation of Scripture, these scholars live under a government whose autocratic heresy laws make it impossible to popularize modern biblical knowledge in Germany. All German clergymen must base their preaching on strict orthodoxy. All German youths are given orthodox religious instructions by authorized teachers who represent the junker system of church and state. All German professors of biblical criticism are virtually put into a genteel quarantine. The so-called "academic freedom" enjoyed by these professors is merely freedom to disseminate their ideas to scholars. Germany has a false reputation for intellectual liberty, and this reputation should be quickly killed by the simple recital of plain facts. These facts ought to be mastered at once by all thoughtful persons in the allied countries and then advertised everywhere as part of the drive against Kaiserism.

Most of us are aware that the English-speaking nations encourage a greater intellectual and religious liberty than does the German Empire. But not many of us have had the time or opportunity to examine this remarkable difference with care. The status of Bible-study in the Anglo-Saxon world contrasts very sharply with the narrow, hidebound paternalism which rules the subjects of the Kaiser. We have become quite familiar with the fact that Germany is politically subject to her master-class, but we have yet to realize the depth to which the virus of autocracy has penetrated the religious life of the German people.

Of course it will be asked at once, Have not the biblical scholars of Germany led the world? Have not American and British theological students by thousands gone across the water to sit at the feet of German professors? And are not the libraries of British and American divinity schools crammed with volumes of German critical scholarship? So simple and easy do the facts appear that the reactionaries and the millennial dawnists eagerly come forward proclaiming that they have a clear case against all divinity schools in which criticism is recognized. They assure us that Germany invented criticism in order to make the Bible a scrap of paper and find an excuse for the war. Consequently all theological professors who have adopted critical methods and conclusions and who would now prove their patriotism should forthwith "hit the saw dust trail"!

This is the paradox of modern biblical scholarship. First, Prussianism puts German higher critics in quarantine. Then Germany gets a camouflaged reputation for intellectual liberty. Then British and American theological schools import the books of German Professors whose teachings the Kaiser will not allow in German churches. Then popular evangelists brand these theological seminaries as proGerman because they teach doctrines which no German pastor can recognize without losing his position.

The answer to the charges now being laid at the door of AngloSaxon biblical scholars is threefold: (1) Biblical criticism was not invented by Germans, but was imported into Germany from other countries. (2) After critical methods were adopted by German investigators the governmental authorities of that country took up a hostile attitude, putting restrictions on liberal professors of theology, forbidding popular propaganda of their views, and making it illegal for the German pulpit to base its ministry on the results of modern scholarship. (3) Biblical criticism is not an instrument of autocracy, as orthodox theorists now endeavor to make out, but on the contrary its tendency is to make plain the essential democracy of the Bible, helping us to trace the channels through which God has entered the heart and mind of humanity, lifting the children of men gradually upward from barbarism into an ever more intelligent faith that the world is founded on divine laws of justice and righteousness. Those who raise an outcry against theological seminaries where scientific methods are followed, and seek to stampede the public mind with millennialism are holding back the progress of democracy and are doing exactly what the Kaiser wants them to do. Their attitude is Prussian.

Let us consider these points seriatim: First as to the claim that biblical criticism is an invention of the German intellect. The introductory proposition of modern biblical scholarship is that the Law of Moses, in its present form, originated at the *end* of Hebrew national history instead of at the beginning; and that the Law took its present form after the Babylonian exile, as a compilation from earlier documents, traditions, and primitive legal codes. But this view is not original to Germany. It was distinctly foreshadowed by a Spanish Jew, Ibn Ezra, the most eminent biblical scholar of the Middle Ages, far back in the twelfth century A. D. The idea was taken up by the English scholar Hobbes, in his book *Leviathan*, published in 1651; by the Frenchman La Peyrere, in his book *Pre-Adamites*, issued in 1655; and by the Jewish philosopher Spinoza, of Amsterdam, Holland, in *Tractatus-Theologico-Politicus*, which came out in 1670. In the meanwhile the Frenchman Louis Cappellus in 1650 published his *Critica Sacra*, demonstrating the imperfect and fallible condition of the Hebrew vowel points. In 1678, Richard Simon, another Frenchman, put forth a volume entitled *Critical History of the Old Testament*, showing that the Mosaic Law was compiled and edited centuries after the time of Moses. In 1753 appeared a work by Astruc, a French writer, identifying the so-called Jehovist and Elohist documents in Genesis. In 1800 was published the *Critical Remarks* of Alexander Geddes, a Scotchman, who denied the Mosaic authorship of the Pentateuch. And although German scholars in the nineteenth century did more for biblical interpretation than did the scholars of other countries, they were matched in critical acumen during that period by Renan of France, Colenso of England, and Kuenen of Holland.[1]

Having seen that biblical criticism did not originate in Germany, let us inquire more closely into its fortunes after being adopted in that country. The policy of the junker government was foreshadowed in the case of Professor Kant, of the Prussian University of Konigsberg, in the latter part of the eighteenth century. Kant's *Critique of Pure Reason* and his *Religion within the Limits of Mere Reason* excited the alarm of the junkers and pietists. Kant was an admirer of the new American Republic; and when the French Revolution broke out the philosopher exclaimed, "Lord, now lettest thou thy servant depart in peace, for mine eyes have seen thy salvation!" With these facts in mind it is highly instructive to read the letter of warning sent to the Konigsberg professor by the reigning Hohenzollern:

1st Oct., 1794

"Our gracious greeting first. Worthy and high-learned, dear liegeman, our highest Person has already since considerable time observed with much dissatisfaction how ye misuse your philosophy to disfigure and depreciate many head and foundation doctrines of the Holy Scripture and Christianity; which thing ye have especially done in your book *Religion within the Limits of Mere Reason* and likewise in other shorter treatises. We had expected better things of you; for ye must see yourself how little your action herein answers to your duty as teacher of youth, and to our paternal interests in the land, whereof ye are well aware. We desire at the earliest your most conscientious conformity, and expect of you, if ye would avoid our highest disfavor, that ye henceforth be found guilty of no

---

[1] For Ibn Ezra see Professor G. F. Moore's introduction to Bacon's *Genesis of Genesis* (Hartford, 1891). On the general subject, S. I. Curtiss, *Sketches of Pentateuch Criticism* ("Bibliotheca Sacra," Oberlin, 1884); Addis, *Documents of the Hexateuch* (London, 1892), Preface; Cheyne, *Founders of Old Testament Criticism* (London, 1893); Carpenter-Hartford, *The Composition of the Hexateuch* (London, 1902), chap. iii; Duff, *History of Old Testament Criticism* (New York, 1910).

such acts, but rather, as your duty bids, apply your influence and talents so that our paternal intention may be more and more attained: contrariwise, with continued obstinacy, ye have infalliby to expect unpleasant measures."

This letter, written in the name of the Prussian king, by the Prussian minister of education, is a monument of that German theological censorship which has continued until now, and which has developed along a line contrasting greatly with Anglo-Saxon policy. In Kant's reply he promised to say nothing more in public about religion or the Bible. Another example is found in the case of Professor Martin Lebrecht de Wette, of the Prussian University of Berlin, in the first part of the nineteenth century. As Wellhausen says, De Wette was the first German "clearly to perceive and point how disconnected are the alleged starting-point of Israel's history and that history itself." The able and brilliant De Wette was ejected from his biblical chair on a mere pretext, over the objection of the entire theological faculty at the University of Berlin, led by the celebrated Schleiermacher, who was himself in great danger of the same treatment.[2]

Biblical scholarship in Germany today is an intellectual curiosity to which no German pastor can give public attention. The higher criticism in Germany is bottled up in professorial sanctums and lecture halls. The professors write books about it. They quarrel with each other over the details of it. And before the war they condescendingly delivered lectures to hopeful youths from England, Canada, Australia, the United States, and other countries who labored under the delusion that there was more intellectual liberty in Germany than in other lands.[3]

The legal partnership of orthodoxy with junkerism has been es-

---

[2] On Kant, see Überweg, *History of Philosophy* (New York, 1898, trans.), II, 140–42. The Hohenzollern letter is given in the book on Kant by Professor Wallace, of Oxford, published by Lippincott, Philadelphia. On De Wette, see Wellhausen, *History of Israel* (Edinburgh, 1885, trans.), pp. 4–5. Also Cheyne, *op. cit.*, chap. iii.

[3] See "The New Prussian Heresy Law and Its Workings," in *American Journal of Theology*, XVI (Apr., 1912), and "Another Case of Discipline in the Prussian Church," *ibid.*, Vol. XVII (January, 1913).

pecially hateful to German workingmen in the great industrial centers of the Empire. German proletarians behold the [junker] aristocracy enthroned in the midst of a social system propped up for ages on church orthodoxy. The German ecclesiastical machine is prostituted to the will of the imperial government. The German socialist hates both God and the church because German religion is identified with aristocratic rule. Religion and the church, in the eyes of the German socialist, are a cloak for the robbery of the common people by the economic and political masters of Germany. The socialistic workingman therefore believes that he has a *moral* reason for hating the only God of whom he has ever heard. Is it any wonder then that the extreme forms of atheistic socialism, spreading over the world like some foul poison, should have originated in the industrial centers of the nation with which we are at war? Cause and effect along a number of lines now begin to stand out distinctly.

German orthodoxy draws a peremptory line of demarcation between the "holy" and the "worldly." God sits on high above the people, as an autocrat in the fashion of the Kaiser, passing down the divine law from heaven in the same way that the Kaiser passes down his decrees. Religion comes "from above." Hence the masses are bidden to "look up." Orthodoxy proclaims the duty of *submission*. Be obedient to the authorities, look for your reward in the "other world," and in the meanwhile leave the affairs of *this* world to the government. The clergymen of modern Germany must live in the realm of traditional theology, repeating obsolete shibboleths and wornout formulas, because orthodoxy fits the state of mind which the junkers desire to maintain among the masses.

But on the other hand the liberal professors of theology stand for an intellectual movement which, if given free rein by the authorities, would threaten the docility of the German people. Critical scholarship, in the eyes of the junker, would undermine the existing order of church and state. It is contrary to conventionality, and its advocates are therefore potential transgressors. But since Germany cannot afford to suppress its intellectuals entirely, the government has learned to handle the problem by putting its potential criminals on a pension and isolating them in an academic quarantine where they are out of real and vital connection with life. And to crown it all the Kaiser tickles the vanity of liberal professors by inviting them to visit him and talk about higher criticism! Great progress has been made since the days of De Wette and Kant. German autocracy has reduced bribery to a fine art. The Herr Professor belongs to a class which associates with royalty, and he is too dignified to impart his esoteric heresies to the common people. The trick is quite simple. Instead of shooting a heretic, you invite him to lunch!

Having seen how German biblical scholarship fares at the hands of German imperialism, we now inquire what becomes of the democracy which we have attributed to higher criticism. Here we enter upon a new and still more fascinating aspect of our theme. The democracy of higher criticism thus far has been implicit rather than explicit. German scholars, expressing themselves in the respectable obscurity of polysyllabic jargon, declare that the orthodox idea of the Bible is wrong. They say that the biblical doctrine of God was not thrust autocratically into human life from an outside realm. But they are destructive rather than constructive. They fail to supply in the place of orthodoxy a clear-cut, well-rounded view of the Bible which can function spiritually in the life of the German people. And the reason why German scholarship has this limited, unvital character is because German autocracy limits these professors themselves in their contact with life. Placed in a cramped, artificial position, breathing the arid, poisoned atmosphere of imperialism, standing out of real and vital connection with the community, it is inevitable that they should misunderstand life. And hence they fail to interpret the Book of Life in a living way.

Although successful in vindicating certain concrete methods and results, German biblical scholarship has failed in the practical, reconstructive task that faces modern theologians. This is tragically evident in the almost cynical confession made by Professor Wellhausen a few years before the war. He declares that we cannot tell why the religious experience of the Hebrew nation has functional value and significance for the world at large, rather than the religious experience of any other ancient people. His words are: "We cannot tell why Jehovah, of Israel, rather than Chemosh, the god of Moab, became the patron of righteousness and the Creator of the Universe." [4]

More than thirty years prior to this declaration Wellhausen himself wrote the epoch-marking book, *Geschichte Israels,* which gathered up the results of previous Old Testament criticism into a statement so clear and cogent that Bible-study everywhere took a new start. Wellhausen indeed has been the leading figure in biblical research during the last generation. His *Geschichte* was published in 1878, seven years after the founding of the present German Empire, and in the midst of the upheaval attending Bismarck's promulgation of the "May Laws" against socialism. Wellhausen reverses the orthodox formula "The Law and the Prophets" so as to read, "The Prophets and the Law." In the critical restatement of Hebrew history the force which leads up to the adoption of the true religion is found in the work of Jehovah's prophets, who stand opposed to the kings, and who champion the cause of justice for the common people. Here surely is material for democracy! But what avails it for the German churches and the German people?

The prodigious effort needed to establish this view in the face of intrenched orthodoxy, the intellectual and spiritual revolution required for the vindication of critical methods and the official disfavor of a government hostile to every manifestation of liberalism and progressivism—all these considerations have resulted in slowing down the complex process of scriptural interpretation in Germany, making it of no effect as a positive influence in the life of the Empire. German divinity professors themselves have taken the social standpoint of the aristocracy, have been satisfied to be let alone in the enjoyment of their stipends, and have been permitted to develop the minute analysis of biblical documents in cloistered isolation.

Turning away from the depressing spectacle of autocratic Germany, we are now prepared to glance at the Anglo-Saxon world.

[4] "Israelitisch-jüdische Religion," in *Kultur der Gegenwart* (Berlin, 1909), Teil 1, p. 15.

British churchmen have a legal and social status unknown to subjects of the Kaiser. Although there are legally established churches in Britain, as there are in Germany, the religion of Britain stands on a vastly freer basis than the religion of the Hohenzollerns. The constitution of the United States goes a step farther still, providing that the national government shall make no "establishment" of religion —similar measures being in effect in the state constitutions. The religious life of English-speaking communities marks a tremendous advance over the spiritual tyranny of the Kaiser. Thus in Britain it is legal for the clergy to speak in terms of modern biblical scholarship. A number of court decisions bearing on religious freedom were delivered by the English courts in the nineteenth century. The first and most remarkable of these decisions was given more than fifty years ago by the highest tribunal of the British Empire.

A number of Episcopal clergymen contributed separate articles to a volume which appeared in 1860 under the title *Essays and Reviews,* and which gave utterance to ideas at variance with orthodoxy. The book is very moderate according to present standards of liberalism; but at the time of its appearance it seemed very dangerous in the eyes of many good people. One of the writers, a professor in Oxford University, said, "Interpret the Scripture like any other book. . . . This can only be done in the same careful and impartial way that we ascertain the meaning of Sophocles or of Plato. . . . Excessive system tends to create an impression that the meaning of Scripture is out of our reach, or is to be attained in some other way than by the exercise of manly sense and industry. . . . Let us not set out on our journey so heavily equipped that there is little chance of arriving at the end of it."

In a panic of wild alarm proceedings were instituted in the Arches Court of Canterbury by the high-church party, acting through the Bishop of Salisbury. One of the authors of the book was charged with denying the plenary inspiration of the Bible, and another was indicted for denying the doctrine of everlasting punishment. The court found these charges proved, and thereupon suspended the accused from the exercise of their official functions. But the defendants appealed to the Supreme Court, the "Crown in Council," which, in the year 1864, reversed the lower court. The overruling decision was written by Richard Baron Westbury, Lord High Chancellor. A facetious observer characterized this weighty judgment as "dismissing hell with costs, and taking away from the orthodox members of the Church of England their last hope of eternal damnation." [5]

Another landmark of spiritual freedom is furnished by the case of Bishop Colenso, who was sent to Africa as a missionary. In trying to convert a Zulu chief to Christianity, Colenso was greatly embarrassed by critical questions which the black man raised with regard to the stories in Genesis. The bishop had not paid much attention to the Scriptures up to that time, but stimulated by Zulu criticism, he now proceeded to investigate the Bible with a new interest, and in 1862 published a book entitled *The Pentateuch and Joshua Critically Examined*. (When mentioning biblical critics outside of Germany in the earlier part of this article we overlooked the Zulus.) Colenso's originality was acknowledged by continental scholars. In England his book produced results identical in character with those in the Essays and Reviews case. An attempt was made to convict the bishop, but he was triumphantly vindicated by the British courts. [6]

Religious liberalism was now seen to be inevitable. The publication of Wellhausen's book in 1878 accelerated the spread of the new views; and thenceforward the growth of critical opinion was very marked in Britain and the United States. The democracy of these nations, as compared with Germany, is shown in a very significant way by the outcome of several heresy trials during the eighties and nineties on both sides of the Atlantic, which established in still greater degree the rights of intellectual and spiritual freedom. The foremost theological seminaries of the English-speaking world are now manned by faculties which, contrary to the German divinity schools, are preparing young men to base their ministry on the

---

[5] Nash, *Life of Richard Baron Westbury* (London, 1888), Vol. II, chap. iii. See also the *Quarterly Review*, April, 1864.

[6] See Cox, *Life of Colenso* (London, 1888); Kuenen, *The Hexateuch* (London, 1886), pp. xiv–xvii; Cheyne, *op. cit.*, chap. ix.

newer interpretation of the Bible. At the same time large numbers of mature clergymen who graduated under the old regime, are quietly adjusting themselves to the changing environment. As our church life, with irresistible momentum, swings away from the older orthodoxy to which the Kaiser's ecclesiastical machine remains anchored, the contrast between Germany and the Anglo-Saxon world is more and more sharp. The transformation which is now going forward represents a democratic triumph whose possibilities have not yet been fully realized. The educational process immediately ahead of us will be abridged by the shock of war.

During the time in which our churches have been permeated by modern biblical criticism they have also been stirred by the new social awakening. Here again Germany can show nothing like this movement which is now sweeping over the religious life of Britain and America. The "Forum" meetings, held in the United States under church auspices and giving a novel emphasis to the claims of democracy and justice, would be impossible under Prussianism. At first glance the social awakening seems to bear no relation to biblical scholarship. But as we study the deeper forces of history we begin to see that this movement is preparing us to understand the fundamental meaning of biblical criticism. Various forces indeed are combining to make the new epoch.

It should now be clear that, while German scholars did more for Bible-study during the nineteenth century than did the scholars of other lands, the Anglo-Saxon people are today in a far better position than the people of Germany to grasp the meaning of the Bible as revealed by modern science, and to take the next great step in church progress. German religion is bound hand and foot in the toils of autocracy. But our churches move onward in the atmosphere of spiritual freedom.

For democracy is the ultimate meaning of the new biblical interpretation. The paradox of criticism arises from the conflict between aristocratic and democratic forces in the church life of modern civilization. The shock of the great war is preparing us to realize the logic of Christianity and the Bible. The whole drift of

Hohenzollernism—and indeed of orthodoxy everywhere—is to obscure the tremendous fact that the Jewish and Christian churches were developed out of ancient heathenism through the powerful force of social movements based on justice and brotherhood. Amidst the terrible agony of a struggle for human rights, in a time when arrogant wealth bestrode the masses and mighty empires crushed out the liberties of small nations, the biblical faith in the one true and righteous God was born. Every church spire is a symbol of democracy and a threat against autocratic power. The church has grown up out of the struggle to make the world safe for government by the people.

It is this wonderful religious evolution, with God at the center of it, that modern biblical scholars are investigating. Hebrew history assumes ever growing reality as we discard the orthodox formula "The Law and the Prophets," and replace it by the critical formula "The Prophets and the Law." Opposing the kings and upholding the cause of justice for the common people, the prophets of Jehovah led forward to the final victory of monotheism over the heathen gods. The democracy of the Bible cannot be really understood by German critics who live in the poisoned atmosphere of tyranny. If they comprehended Scripture they would have to teach that the religion of Jesus and the prophets is against the system of junkerism; and their failure to do so proves that the usefulness of German biblical scholarship has come to an end.[7]

What the awakening church needs is not orthodoxy but a conservatism which maintains all the religious values enshrined in the Scriptures. Orthodoxy is a human theory about the origin and nature of a religion which was established among men long before orthodoxy itself was ever heard of. Our Bible and our faith are calling for interpretation today in terms of the awful crisis through which the world is now passing. We must gird ourselves for a task

[7] The democracy of criticism will be more apparent when it is generally realized that the struggle of the prophets against injustice was identical with the warfare against false gods, growing out of the development of Hebrew nationality at the point of assimilation between Israelite worshipers of Jehovah and Amorite worshipers of Baal. See article by the present writer in *Biblical World*, XLV (April, 1915), entitled "Amorite Influence in the Religion of the Bible."

which widens beyond anything hitherto attempted by the church. We must explain the Bible in clear, honest words that can be understood by the people; and if the crasser supernaturalism of our fathers must go, it will be replaced by a deeper supernaturalism which finds God in the commonplace events of history, and in which the evolution of the world gives expression to the personality of the Most High. And while the church cannot formulate the political and economic program of democracy, it must become as a city set on a hill, the inspiration of social justice and the dynamic center of public righteousness.

The religious emotion and idealism of the people constitute a great fund of social strength which must and will be put behind the drive against Kaiserism and back of the movement to make the world a fit abode for mankind. These emotions were operative in the times of the prophets and Jesus Christ, the early church, the Reformation, the Puritan revolution, and the American Civil War. The time has now come when they must inevitably give direction and purpose to the currents of civic energy now being unloosed in such astounding measure. The Kaiser cannot afford to have the German people understand the Bible. But the world will move onward through the flames of war into the splendid franchise of the gospel.

BIBLIOGRAPHICAL NOTE
REGARDING SECULAR
BIBLE HISTORY

THE CONCEPTION of Hebrew history as a purely secular process
has been slow in emerging, as compared with other fields of ancient
history, which have been more promptly emancipated from the
dominion of myth and miracle. The tardiness attending inclusion
of Israel within the scope of modern scientific methodology is not
a result of mere obstinacy or contumaciousness in the prevailing
culture. It is because the subject of Hebrew history is bound up
in a special way with the idea of God as an outstanding fact in the
religious life of Israel and of the nations whose history stands connected with Israel. If it were not for this peculiar theological quality in the experience of the ancient Hebrews, their history would
have but little interest in the eyes of the modern world.

Also, the problem at the very center of the history is, how did
the God-idea become a distinctive peculiarity of Israel's life? All
nations are theologically as conservative about the "how" as they
are about the actual content of the God-idea itself. This tenacity
about the actual way in which the religion of Israel came to be a
matter of human experience is one of the forces which have tended
to slow up the march of science in the field of Hebrew history.
The orthodox view that the religion was imparted miraculously,
at a single stroke, accords with ancient theology in general and has
prevailed for many centuries.

But mere theological conservatism does not account for the
whole situation. Delay in the scientific explanation of Hebrew
history has been due also to the deliberateness which attends all
scientific enterprise. Christian and Jewish orthodoxy itself began to
fade out of many scholarly minds before the real problem of Bibli-

cal religion was understood even in a tentative way. Several generations passed before the literary analysis of the Old Testament had reached a preliminary conclusion. And while the minute investigation of the writings went forward, a sense of the history behind the literature emerged very slowly. The question which then became uppermost was not, "How did the religion evolve?" but, "How are the sources related in the order of time?"

In the wake of the new literary analysis, therefore, several histories of Israel were published; and it is instructive to observe the developing sense of "*Geschichte*" and "*histoire*" among German and French scholars in relation to the problem of the Bible. The first considerable treatise was that of Ewald, *Geschichte des Volkes Israel* (Leipzig, 1843), based on a mistaken source-theory which makes the "Priestly" writings in the Old Testament earlier than the other documents. Of about the same value in French is the work of Renan, *Histoire du peuple d'Israël* (Paris, 1887), of great literary merit, but deficient in critical analysis. Renan, seeking to account for the Hebrew idea of God, postulated a "Semitic tendency toward monotheism." Neither Ewald nor Renan envisaged the historical problem of the Bible; but such works as theirs were necessary and useful as beginnings.

In 1878, gathering up in brilliant style the results of analysis by a number of investigators more penetrating than Renan or Ewald, an epochal work was issued by Professor Julius Wellhausen under the title *Geschichte Israels*. This book, placing the Priestly element at the end of the Pentateuchal evolution instead of at the beginning, brought into view a more intelligible historic perspective. The J, or Yahwist, element was placed first; the Elohist, or Ephraimite, source was viewed as coming after J; while the Deuteronomic strata were located between the Ephraimite and the Priestly documents. The resulting critical formula was therefore JEDP. Wellhausen, however, was candid enough to retract the title "*Geschichte*"; and in later editions of his book he substituted the more accurate *Prolegomena zur Geschichte Israels* (Berlin, 1883). Accordingly, a short time before his death (1909) he admitted his inability to show how or why Yahweh of Israel rather than Chemosh, the god of Moab, for example, should have evolved into the righteous God of the universe. He thus conceded that the central problem of Hebrew history (the only question which makes that history significant) was still unsolved. Likewise, Professor Francis Brown, of Union Theological Seminary, New York, declared that the differentiation of the later Yahweh from the earlier Yahweh had not been solved (*Old Testament and Semitic Studies in Honor of William Rainey Harper*, Chicago, 1908, p. xxx).

After the appearance of Wellhausen's *Prolegomena* a number of attempts at historical construction were made without recognizing definitely the nature of the issue around which the critical investigation was revolving. Outstanding in this category are: B. Stade, *Geschichte des Volkes Israel* (Leipzig, 1881); R. Kittel, *Geschichte der Hebräer* (Leipzig, 1888); H. Guthe, *Geschichte des Volkes Israel* (Leipzig, 1899); E. Sellin, *Geschichte des israelitisch-jüdischen Volkes* (Leipzig, 1932). Decided improvement upon Renan is registered by C. Piepenbring, *Histoire du peuple d'Israël* (Paris, 1898), and by A. Lods, *Israël, des origines au milieu du viiie siècle* (Paris, 1930). Similar works in English are: C. F. Kent, *History of the Hebrew People* (New York, 1896); G. Wade, *Old Testament History* (London, 1901); R. Ottley, *Short History of the Hebrews* (London, 1901); H. P. Smith, *Old Testament History* (New York, 1903); W. Oesterley and T. H. Robinson, *History of Israel* (Oxford, 1932). All these writers abandoned the orthodox version of Hebrew history and sought to reconstruct the drama of Israel without interpreting the chief character (Yahweh) in a cause-and-effect relation to the story. But their books are based upon sound scholarship and have been of great value as aids to the growing historical sense of Israel.

At the same time, there was also a new sense of Hebrew religion and Hebrew prophecy as problems within the larger framework of the history; and in this interest works of a more special nature appeared, some of which were: A. Kuenen, *The Religion of Israel* (New York, 1874); W. R. Smith, *The Prophets of Israel*

(London, 1882); C. Cornill, *The Prophets of Israel* (Chicago, 1897); K. Budde, *Religion of Israel to the Exile* (New York, 1899); A. Loisy, *La Religion d'Israël* (Paris, 1902–4); Addis, *Hebrew Religion* (New York, 1906); K. Marti, *Religion of the Old Testament* (New York, 1907); H. P. Smith, *Religion of Israel* (New York, 1914); G. Hölscher, *Die Profeten* (Leipzig, 1914), and *Geschichte der israelitischen und jüdischen Religion* (Geissen, 1922); E. Kautzsch, *Die Heilige Schrift des Alten Testaments* (Leipzig, 1923); W. Oesterley and T. H. Robinson, *Hebrew Religion* (New York, 1934); M. Toussaint, *Les Origines de la religion d'Israel* (Paris, 1931); M. J. Lagrange, *Le Judaisme avant Jesus-Christ* (Paris, 1931); O. Eissfeldt, *Einleitung in das Alte Testament* (Tübingen, 1934); A. Lods, *Les Prophets d'Israël* (Paris, 1935); and *La Religion d'Israël* (Paris, 1939); E. Leslie, *Old Testament Religion* (New York, 1936).

At the same time, in search of origins and evolutionary forces, investigators broadened their explorations to cover the oriental field at large. Some titles relating to this point of view follow: W. R. Smith, *Kinship and Marriage in Early Arabia* (London, 1885); *Religion of the Semites* (London, 1889); Wellhausen, *Reste arabischen Heidenthums* (Berlin, 1887); M. J. Lagrange, *Etudes sur religions sémitiques* (Paris, 1905); C. Steuernagel, *Die Einwanderung der israelitischen Stämme in Kanaan* (Berlin, 1901); E. Meyer, *Die Israeliten und ihre Nachbarstämme* (Halle, 1906); René Dussaud, *Les Origines cananéennes du sacrifice israélite* (Paris, 1921); P. Volz, *Das Dämonische in Jahwe* (Tübingen, 1924).

The deficiency of Biblical criticism in terms of institutional sociology was emphasized as early as 1890 by Joseph Jacobs (Cheyne, *Founders of Old Testament Criticism*, London, 1893, p. 330). Shortly thereafter Professor C. H. Toy, of Harvard, said, "Religion may be regarded as a branch of sociology, subject to all the laws that control general human progress" (*Judaism and Christianity*, New York, 1892, p. 1). In 1898 Professor Graham Taylor, of Chicago, spoke of "the demand for a distinct department of research and scientific formulation dealing with the social data of the Scriptures which ultimately is sure to create a biblical sociology" (*American Journal of Theology*, II, 891). In 1899 Professor F. Buhl, of Leipzig, published *Die socialen Verhältnisse der Israeliten*. In 1901 Professor Cheyne, of Oxford, spoke of Biblical criticism as entering a new period influenced by comparative study of social customs (*Encyclopedia Biblica*, col. 2057).

In 1903 the writer issued a volume entitled *An Examination of Society*, one third of which was devoted to Hebrew history as a continuation of pre-Hebrew Canaanite history and as a factor in Semitic evolution. In 1907 an article, "Sociological Significance of the Bible," was published in *The American Journal of Sociology*, followed the same year by another, "Sociology and Theism." In 1908 an article entitled "Professor Orr and Higher Criticism," was published in *The American Journal of Theology*. During the years 1908–11 seven papers entitled "Biblical Sociology" were published in *The American Journal of Sociology*.

The foregoing matter was preparatory to the writer's volume *Sociological Study of the Bible* (1912), which takes up the evolution of the Hebrew people from two main points of view: (1) the rise of the national State as a political organism, at the point of assimilation between a resident Canaanite, or Amorite, element and certain primitive clan elements which intruded into the country from the desert of Arabia, and (2) the eventual outbreak of a clash within this organism between two ideologies which had been carried along in social solution while the political State was in process of taking form—one being identified with "Baal" cults derived from the Canaanite side of the nation's ancestry and representing (among other ideas and practices) commercialized monopoly of natural resources in the hands of a small proprietary class; the other symbolized by the term "Yahweh," in reaction against commercialism and calling for wider distribution of the soil among primitive clanships in the open country outside the walled cities. The ideological clash revolved around the term *mishpat*, which the two sides of the controversy wanted to define officially by gaining possession of governmental power and fixing the standards of economic and moral sanction. In other words, the term *mishpat*, as we find it in the Hebrew text, is a problem, not a solution.

When a scholar had the necessary sociological presuppositions (e. g., Professor C. H. Toy, of Harvard), the argument of this book was accepted at once. But some critics raised the point that the terms "Yahweh" and "Baal" stood for "more than a mere fight over landed property." The answer to this was, and is, that while both cultic terms represent a wider field of concept, the Yahweh-Baal antithesis contains at least the opposite ideas that land is inalienable and that it is commercial—this fundamental variance being all that the argument demands.

Meanwhile the general subject began to be disclosed in unexpected ways through further investigation of the Hebrew text and through the stimulus of an extended visit to Palestine. Using the country itself as a "source" of history, several facts emerged into clear view: Jerusalem was always out of center as a focal point for the political organism called "Israel"; while the real center of the Israelite clans and State, throughout most of the time covered by the books of Judges, Samuel, and Kings, was Ephraim, or "the house of Joseph," which represented the original and continuous core of the Hebrew nation, the dominance of the house of David at Jerusalem being therefore only an interlude in the history of Israel proper.

Along with purely objective, historical considerations of this kind, certain facts of a more subjective, psychological nature began to clamor for attention. The myths and legends of Genesis were found to be in adjustment with objective history to such an extent that the Ephraimite, or Josephite, core of the nation evidently exercised the legend-building power. In other words, the legends of Israel are Josephite; and in the few cases where Judaic interests are favored, the legendary material has been manipulated so as to depart from the Ephraimite original. This being the case, the J or Yahwistic, or Judaic, source could not be earlier than the E, or Ephraimite, source, as contemplated by the criticism which came to a focus in Wellhausen's *Prolegomena*. The arguments for the priority of J, which have become conventional since Wellhausen, are literary and without reference to the objective history. These arguments, in fact, are so tenuous that responsible scholars such as Oesterley and Robinson have recently declared that there is some uncertainty as to whether J or E is the earlier and that the point is not of serious importance (W. Oesterley and T. H. Robinson, *Introduction to the Books of the Old Testament*, New York, 1934, p. 65).

The inappositeness of these remarks, however, becomes clear in view of a hitherto unperceived contrast between J and E, which goes down into the sociological and economic problem of Hebrew history: Common to both documents is the designation of the master class in Israel by the primitive, rustic term *adon;* but in the Ephraimite, or E source, a powerful tendency is at work to supersede *adon* by the pre-Hebrew, Canaanite term *baal*—the J document, at the same time, continuing to use the earlier designation common to both sources. That E is far earlier than J becomes clear when the *adon-baal* distinction is considered with reference to (1) the centrality of Ephraim as the Hebrew core, (2) the Ephraimite control of Hebrew legend-building, and (3) the fact that Israel's conquest of Canaan was primarily in the hill country of Ephraim. That part of Canaan included the majority of baalized walled cities and fell under the *baal* influence to such an extent that the anti-*baal* reaction began in Ephraim with Elijah, Elisha, and Micaiah ben Imlah, continued throughout the revolution of Jehu, and received its first literary expression in the Ephraimite book of Hosea.

These further studies in the general subject gave rise to the volume entitled *God and the Social Process* (1935), which endeavors to show more clearly the correspondence between the subjective religious evolution of Israel and the external development of the national organism, or group. It also seeks to pave the way for consideration of Hebrew history as a wholly natural process of cause and effect in the same category as the histories of other nations. The present book, *The Bible Is Human*, based on the sociological and economic foundations of its predecessors, undertakes, without being exhaustive, to mark out the main lines on which Biblical history will be interpreted and studied in future.

Even yet, little has been done by German and French scholars toward explaining the Bible and Hebrew history in terms of the problem here outlined. Professor E. Troeltsch, of Berlin University, writing in *Theologische Literaturzeitung* (July 19, 1913), reproduced and endorsed the argument of *Sociological Study of the Bible*. His book, *Die Soziallehren der christlichen Kirchen und Gruppen* (Berlin, 1912), represents the "religious history" standpoint, which is consistent with modern sociology. The disastrous course of German affairs has undoubtedly prevented the growth of a hopeful movement in the Biblical scholarship of that country. The journal *Archives sociologiques* (1914, pp. 871ff.) contains a paper by Richard Kreglinger entitled "Les Facteurs sociaux de l'évolution du culte de Jahveh," "suggere par un livre recent de Louis Wallis." Professor A. Causse has issued a book, *Du groupe ethnique a la communaute religieuse: le problem sociologique de la religion d'Israël* (1937). While oriented constructively, the book is only an averaging of German, French, and English investigations, and presents nothing new. It approaches the religion of Israel from the standpoint of social customs and institutions, but not of social functions and processes, thus overlooking the technical problem. Professor M. Loehr, of the University of Koenigsberg, has issued a volume, *History of Religion in the Old Testament* (1936), which, although scholarly, does not come to terms with the fundamental economic and sociological problem of the religion as a dynamic process. Professor Leslie's book (*supra*) is more advanced in this respect than the other works listed in the same connection.

INDEX

INDEX

Aaron, given priestly monopoly, 258, 263

Abel, pre-Hebrew patriarch, 182

Abel-meholah, Ephraimite village, 169

Abiathar, David's priest, 109, 114; rebellion against David, 129, 130

Abiezer clan, warfare with Midianites, 59

Abigail, David's sister, 125

Abijah, (Abijam), king of Judah, 150 f.

Abimelech, son of Gideon, 61; becomes king of Shechem, 62; death, 122

Abinadab, Yahweh's ark in house of, 96

Abishai, David's nephew, 125

Abraham (Abram), pre-Hebrew patriarch, 146; Genesis legends, 32, 87, 88, 181, 182, 233, 234, 248, 253; term *adon* applied to, 185 f.; idea of "Abraham's Bosom," 236

Absalom, David's son, 111, 124, 126, 159; rebellion of, 127 f.

Academic freedom in Germany, 240, 283, 287

Acco, pre-Hebrew fortified city, 78

Achish, King, alliance with David against Saul, 99

Addis, *Hebrew Religion*, 299

Adonijah, David's son, revolt against father, 128 f.; murdered, 130

Adonim, 113, Ephraimite aristocratic ideal, 87; *baal-adon* distinction, 88, 121 f., 128, 182-89, 191, 214, 220*n*, 223, 245, 302; allegiance to Yahweh, 106, 193, 232; David's exactions upon, 120; attitude toward land, 124; Samaria's rule, 157 f.; under Ahab, 160; wealthier transformed into *baalim*, 187-89; status in Judah, 208, 209, 211, 213, 217; enslavement of poorer group, 211; "right-wing" element, 213; restoration of enslaved to old status, 217; Deuteronomy's attitude, 220; *adon* replaces name Yahweh, 232

Adoniram (Adoram), heads David's fiscal department, 119; retains office under Sh'lomoh, 130; death, 141

Adullam, Canaanite walled city, 30, 104; David takes refuge in, 103, 107

Adultery, commandment against, 273

Agag, king of Amalek, 277

Ahab, king of Ephraim, 55, 116, 177, 186*n*, 198; Naboth's refusal to sell land to, 32, 80, 156, 162-64, 165, 167, 169, 191, 267, 268, 271; marriage, 157; enthroned, 160 f.; coalition against Assyrian empire, 161, 164; Syrians attack kingdom, 168; death, 170; end of dynasty, 173 f., 189, 199, 205, 242

Ahaz, king of Judah, pays tribute to Assyria, 208

Ahaziah, king of Judah, 205

Ahijah, prophet of Shiloh, 139, 147, 165, 245

Ahitophel, David's counselor, 125; seeks to depose David, 127

Aholiab, in charge of Israel's workmen, 259

Amalekites in Bible history, 276-78

Amasa, supersedes Joab as leader of David's army, 125

Amaziah, king of Judah, 175, 206

Amaziah, priest, drives Amos away, 178, 193

America, see United States

American Journal of Sociology, The, 300

American Journal of Theology, The, 300

American Revised Bible, 277; Isaiah passage, 13; Judah legend, 31; Moses as ancestor of Danite priests, 70

American School of Oriental Research, archaelogical expedition into Edom, 135-38

Am ha'arets, poor and needy *adonim*, 205, 216, 232

Ammonites, war against Gilead, 67, 89, 91, 93, 95, 99; origin of, 116, 248; threatened by Assyrian empire, 161

Amon, king of Judah, same name as Egyptian god, 215, 216

Amorites, conquered by Jacob, 35, 36;

161; coalition against Assyrians, 201, 208

Taanach, ancient city of Canaan, 27, 28, 46, 78, 130, 152, 194
Tabor, Mount, Josephite outpost, 59
Talmai, king of Geshur, 111; daughter marries David, 100
Taxation, under David, 119, 130; under Sh'lomoh, 130, 131; in Ephraim, 200, 204; in Judah, 204, 208 f., 213
Taylor, Graham, Biblical criticism, 299
Tell el Amarna letters, 278
Ten commandments, 219, 271-75; three different editions, 271; slavery and, 272 f., 274; morality and property rights, 273 f.; murder and property rights, 274; evolutionary aspect, 274
Terach, abandons city for rural life, 234
Thatcher, on identity of Gilead, 50; on Samson story, 67n
Theological seminaries, scientific method, 285
Theologische Literaturzeitung, 303
Theology, arises out of experience, 58; *see also* Religion
Tibni ben Ginath, fights for throne of Israel, 155
Tiglath-pileser, Assyrian ruler, 201
Tirzah, capital of Ephraim, 155, 157
Torah, *see* Pentateuch
Toussaint, M., *Les Origines de la religion d'Israël*, 299
Toy, C. H., Biblical criticism, 299, 301
Transjordan Department of Antiquities, archaeological expedition into Edom, 135-38
Troeltsch, E., 240; review of *Sociological Study of the Bible*, ix; *Die Soziallehren der christlichen Kirchen und Gruppen*, 303
Tsadokee priesthood, *see* Sadducee priesthood
Tyre, ancient city of Canaan, 28; king of, 120; alliance with Israel, 132, 167, 205; attitude toward sale of land, 163; Baal worship, 173 f., 189, 205

United States, Biblical scholarship, 240, 283, 291, 292, 293; religious evolution in churches, 241
Ur, Chaldean city, 234
Uriah the Hittite, 29, 183; David seduces wife of, 120 ff.; legally murdered, 121, 122
Uzziah, king of Judah, 207

Virgin Birth, dogma of, x
Volz, P., *Das Dämonische in Jahwe*, 299

Wade, G., *Old Testament History*, 298
Wallis, Louis, *Sociological Study of the Bible*, viii, ix, 300, 303; *God and the Social Process*, ix, 263, 302; "The Paradox of Modern Biblical Criticism," 283-95
Warfare, passes from extermination to domination, 26 f.
Weber, German Bible scholar, 240
Wellhausen, Julius, 241, 282; *Geschichte Israels*, viii, 226, 290, 292, 297, 298, 302; on Yahweh as nature-fertility god, 194; treatment of Hosea's anti-Baalism, 195; Yahweh-Chemosh struggle for rule of the universe, 241, 265, 289, 298; *Reste arabischen Heidenthums*, 299
Westbury, Richard Baron, decision establishes landmark of spiritual freedom, 292
Westphalia, Peace of, 240
Wette, Martin Lebrecht de, 289; persecuted by Prussian authorities, 287
Wife, use of term in the commandments, 272 f.
Willett, Herbert L., on Hebrew traditions, x
Witchcraft, penalty for, 191
Women, Baalism exploits, 225; treatment of, in commandments, 272 f.
World War I, act of God, 281

Yahweh, "The Book of the Wars of Yahweh," vii; tendency toward monotheism, viii, 6 f., 15, 29, 34, 147, 151, 166, 167, 188, 205, 231 f., 237 f., 239, 294; Yahweh-Baal struggle, 5, 6, 7, 8-10, 15, 28 ff., 78, 83, 84, 94 f., 102, 107, 112, 113, 119, 155, 157, 166, 172-74, 178, 187, 191, 195-99, 205, 213, 214 f., 217, 218 f., 222-24, 225, 231, 232, 237, 239, 251, 265 f., 270, 271, 294n, 300, 301; expanding conception of, after battle of Esdraelon, 57, 58; power to cause rain, 57, 86, 110n; sword of, and of Gideon, 58-60, 66; and Israel growing in power,